Beyond the Pale

Sir Oswald Mosley and family

1933–1980

NICHOLAS MOSLEY

Secker & Warburg
London

First published in England 1983 by
Martin Secker & Warburg Limited
54 Poland Street, London W1V 3DF

British Library Cataloguing in Publication Data
Mosley, Nicholas
    Beyond the pale : Sir Oswald Mosley, 1933–1980.
    1. Mosley, Sir Oswald   2. Politicians——
    Great Britain——Biography
    I. Title
    941.082′092′4   DA574.M6

ISBN 0-436-28852-4

Filmset by Northumberland Press Ltd, Gateshead
Printed and bound in Great Britain by
Richard Clay (The Chaucer Press) Ltd, Bungay, Suffolk

This book is to be returned on or before
the last date stamped below.

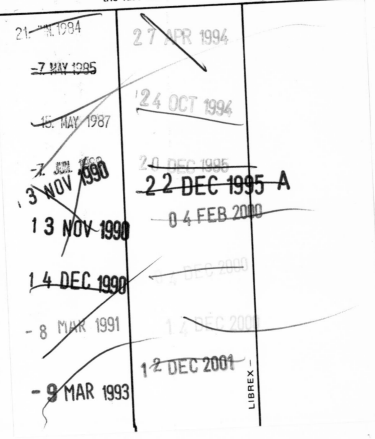

21. JUN 1984   2 7 APR 1994

−7 MAY 1985   '2 4 OCT 1994

15. MAY 1987

−7. JUN 1990   2 0 DEC 1995
3 NOV 1990   2 2 DEC 1995 A
1 3 NOV 1990   0 4 FEB 2000

1 4 DEC 1990

− 8 MAR 1991

1 2 DEC 2001
− 9 MAR 1993

LIBREX −

Beyond the Pale

Also by Nicholas Mosley

African Switchback
The Life of Raymond Raynes
Experience and Religion
The Assassination of Trotsky
Julian Grenfell
Rules of the Game

Novels

Spaces of the Dark
The Rainbearers
Corruption
Meeting Place
Accident
Assassins
Impossible Object
Natalie Natalia
Catastrophe Practice
Imago Bird
Serpent

Contents

vi   *Contents*

List of Illustrations

Foreword

At the beginning of *Rules of the Game*, the first volume of these memoirs, I wrote –

> On May 11th 1979 a remark was reported in the *New Statesman* that my father, Oswald Mosley, 'must be the only Englishman today who is beyond the pale'. This statement was made about a man of eighty-two who had not been in active politics for thirteen years: who when he had been active – a period of world-wide violence and crime – had been convicted of no offence (he had been acquitted of one charge of assault and one of riotous assembly) and whose policies had for the most part been ignored and had come to nothing. The remark seemed ridiculous but in one sense apt – as being representative of what undoubtedly were many people's feelings about him.

This second volume deals with the period of the 1930s and the 1940s during which societies prepared for, or let themselves be caught up by, the second world war. At such a time there were virtues, as well as outrages, in being beyond the pale.

N.M.

Prologue

In the autumn of 1932, when my father, Oswald Mosley, was approaching his thirty-sixth birthday, an article was published in the *Evening Standard* which summarised his career up to that date. It referred to him as both an 'astonishing man' and an 'astonishing failure': it suggested that he had 'thrown away a succession of wonderful opportunities' and was now destined for 'an ultimate and tragic retirement into obscurity'. The occasion for this article was the founding by my father of the British Union of Fascists, and thus the ending of his involvement with conventional politics.

My father wrote a long reply to this article: in it he echoed and mocked the way in which the *Evening Standard* had summarised his career. By this style – which was typical of a certain side of him – he seemed both to be trying to justify himself and to show his contempt for the conventional attitudes of those against him. The *Evening Standard* had described, he said, how he had begun as 'an obscure member of the disappearing and politically impotent landowning class' yet by the age of twenty-two he had become a Conservative member of Parliament; then, at the age of twenty-four, he had taken 'some crankish exception to the Versailles Treaty which pushed Europe back into the cauldron of war which had already swallowed up the great majority of his friends in an old man's holocaust' and had also manifested 'some squeamish feelings about the shooting of women and children in Ireland'. It was true that these 'callow sentiments' had resulted in his having to face 'some social ostracism'; and it was this sort of thing that the *Evening Standard* must be referring to as the throwing away of 'wonderful opportunities'. My father commented – still as if it were the *Evening Standard's* comment on himself – 'What an impossible fellow! He never knew which side his bread was buttered!' After he

had left the Conservative Party, and after 'a long and painful period
of transition', he had 'adhered to the Labour Party which, with all its
faults, was the only party presenting any hope of any action of any
kind'. It was indeed the case – this was now my father talking more
passionately and directly about himself – 'that he had a curious predilection for dynamic things; he cherished the strange belief that after
the war something had to be done by someone to clear up the mess'.
He wrote:

> For two winters running he spoke every night for three months
> without a break and often two or three times a night at large meet-
> ings. He was employed by Labour Headquarters to wind up their
> campaign on the eve of the poll at almost every by-election. At all
> these great meetings, in which he addressed hundreds and thousands
> of his fellow countrymen, he persuaded men and women to vote
> Labour on the plea that they would 'tackle unemployment'.
>
> The election came, and Labour won. He was given the job of
> tackling unemployment in the company of Mr J. H. Thomas. The
> dreary farce of those efforts has become one of the stale jokes of
> politics. Every proposal he made to implement the Labour pledges
> by a policy of action was rejected. No alternative was forthcoming
> from those who rejected these proposals, although they were equally
> pledged to keep faith with the unemployed: he decided to keep faith
> with those whom he had asked to vote Labour, and whom Labour
> had betrayed. This time he had a really serious seizure: he actually
> resigned from the government and gave up a safe job. Notwith-
> standing this fresh aberration or 'tactical blunder', the *Evening
> Standard* says that at this stage 'massed behind him was the whole
> rank and file of Labour'. This was largely true, as at the Party Con-
> ference at which I challenged the government the overwhelming
> majority of constituency representatives voted with me.....
>
> So then followed another strange aberration. Our curious case had
> worked within the Old Parties for a period of twelve years in a
> great variety of attempts to secure some policy of action in post-war
> Britain. In a fit of petulant impatience at his inability to remedy
> at all conditions which left him very comfortable but which left
> the majority of his fellow countrymen very uncomfortable, he
> decided to fight for a policy of action outside the Old Parties. This
> time the seizure was fatal. He 'turned again' and for the second time
> left an established Party. He waded through all the classic and
> inevitable failure which in every country in post-war Europe has

preceded the arrival in power of a new and modern movement, until he had laid the foundations of a Fascist organisation.

My father continued in this vein. The *Evening Standard* was 'generous enough to admit' that he changed each time his party rather than his principles: it admonished him with Disraeli's words: 'Damn your principles; stick to your party!' This was 'certainly the way to get on in England in 1932: yet even the young among us remember days in England – and not the least days in her history – when principles were not "scraps of paper". But those days were when England had muscle instead of fat around the heart'.

He summarised the conventional attitudes towards him:

He could not have done these things because he believed in them! Away with that absurd idea! Are we really being driven to the conclusion that a public man actually did something because he thought it was right?

In the first volume of these memoirs I told the story of my father up to the time of the *Evening Standard* article and just beyond. During this period he demonstrated something common to both the *Evening Standard's* view of him and the view that he had of himself. During the twenties and the first two years of the thirties it had indeed been possible to see him as someone who, for all his passion for politics, had never found a style by which he could appear wholly committed: his open contempt for the two political parties with which he had hitherto had to work must have given him at least a temporary impatience with himself. Everything depended on the future. He was only thirty-five. Either he would be able to create for himself a political movement which would have a chance of putting into effect his passionately held principles, or he would not.

In his reply to the *Evening Standard* it is as if his sarcastic view of the conventional attitudes towards him and his serious view of himself suddenly coincided:

The fellow is clearly a great gambler, who prefers backing a horse at 5 to 1 with a prospect of winning great stakes, to backing an even-money favourite with the prospect of winning stakes too small to attract him. He is not interested to play for the small stakes of normal politics; he is only interested to play for the great stakes of abnormal politics. To his peculiar mind, the blue and gold prizes of democratic statesmanship – the pomp and decoration without power of achievement – are not worth the having or the buying. He prefers a great gamble on abnormal events; on the winning of a position which might enable him to re-write the pages of history in terms of achievement for the British Race.

At the end of my first volume the founding of the British Union of Fascists was followed shortly by my mother's death. This was an end, for my father, of a time not only of political confusion but of disruption and confusion in his private life. Now he announced that his total commitment to his fascist movement would be a fitting memorial to his late wife: he told his followers at their headquarters – 'From now on this will be my home.' He did in fact give up nearly all the social life that he had once shared with his wife Cimmie – that had run parallel to the life he had with her in politics and which indeed, colouring both areas, had given him something of the reputation of a playboy. Now his dedication to politics was to be manifest. But this meant also that he was to meet fewer people who might give him criticism – even the nagging sort of criticism that had, from time to time, come from my mother.

All this was happening at a time when throughout Europe men of my father's age were feeling that there was a compulsion to commit themselves personally to some extreme in politics: old forms of civilisation were seen to be cracking up: systems of balances, and a feeling for transcendency upon which these systems depended, appeared to have collapsed. It was felt that some rebuilding process had to be undertaken in which old moderating influences should be sacrificed for the sake of the task in hand. In 1930 my mother had travelled in communist Russia and had observed, as well as the obvious inefficiency and the signs of oppression, an atmosphere of what she had felt was hope: my father had been to Italy in 1931 and had been excited by what seemed to him to be the dedicated energy of fascist young men. Repressions and even certain brutalities might be taken, it seemed, as the growing pains of any youthful revolutionary movement: they might be dealt with, in time, with the movement's coming of age. It would have been impossible for my father to have become a communist: he came from a tradition in which there was no sense in the idea of an autocratic organisation pretending to be anything other than what it was.

The founder-members of the British Union of Fascists saw themselves as being on a crusade: their aim was to wipe out the sins of an older generation and to lay the foundations for a new society in which there would be no more prevarication and no more war. Mussolini's fascism was pragmatic: it had been to him in the first place a way of obtaining and wielding power. The way in which such power might be used in 1932 still seemed open to choice. It was not then part of even conventional thinking to dwell on theories about the corruptions inherent in all power. Hitler was not in power in 1932.

When Hitler became Chancellor of Germany in January 1933 he brought with him a whole paraphernalia of theories about racialism and the necessity for conquest which were accepted by his nation of national socialists: fascists soon seemed to feel they had little choice except to follow him. The question of whether fascism could have moved in a different direction without Hitler is hypothetical; no fascist leader ever felt strong or secure enough to stand out clearly against Hitler.

My father was unique amongst fascist leaders in that with regard to his own country he was dedicatedly against war: he was even, at least with the formal side of him that gave orders, against his followers being responsible for violence. But his attitude was permissive of Hitler's attitudes to war; and he seemed content to allow himself and his followers to put themselves in situations conducive to violence and thus to become identified with it in the public mind. When Mussolini had struggled for power in 1919–1922, between one and two thousand people had been killed in street fighting; during Hitler's years on either side of gaining power his men killed hundreds, not only of his opponents, but of his potentially troublesome friends. Throughout all my father's fascist years in England no one, whether friend or enemy, was killed in a street fight; and at the time of the height of his reputation for violence – that surrounding the Olympia meeting in 1934 – there were, according to the records, only three victims kept in hospital overnight. This evidence is not a condonation of such violence as there was; but it is evidence that there was something quite different happening in England from that which was happening on the Continent. Nevertheless, my father allowed himself to be seen as representative of things going on on the Continent.

When Hitler, with Mussolini as his camp follower, went to war and conquered most of Europe, my father, protesting against war, went to jail. The course on which Hitler and Mussolini set themselves resulted in their self-destruction: my father used to say that in jail he had had a chance to learn. How much he did learn, and what, are questions opened, if not precisely answered, by this book. The book begins with a slight overlap with the previous volume: there was both an end and a beginning with the founding of the British Union of Fascists. At the end of this second volume my father seems to set out again in 1948 to repeat many of the political mistakes that he had made in the 1930s – but on an even less realistic level, as if he felt constrained to follow some echo. But on another level there was perhaps something he had learned. The questions at stake were: are politics best seen as belonging to an area in which precise plans can be made and ruthlessly fought for, or are they more to do with plainly demonstrating one's attitudes and then not caring too much about whether people follow one or not? My father, towards the end of his long life, seemed able to embrace both attitudes. He still thought that he had the answers to most questions about politics; yet how genial he remained when so few people listened! Perhaps it was because of this (it is unnerving for others if a failed revolutionary seems to be happy) as well as because of his reputation, that people continued to see him as somehow beyond the pale.

CHAPTER 1

British Fascism

Fascism had emerged on to the British political scene in 1923 when Miss Lintorn Orman – the granddaughter of a Field Marshal as was often pointed out – was working in her kitchen garden and the idea came to her that Britain was being invaded by alien influences just as her vegetables were being overrun by weeds; she advertised for volunteers to join a movement which would be called the British Fascisti, and which would fight the forces of disruption.

By the summer of 1924 her organisation claimed (the figure was exaggerated) a membership of 100,000 which was distributed, on paper at least, in military-style units throughout the country. The movement had no policy; it saw itself simply as a force to defend King and Parliament. It had come into existence specifically in reaction to what was felt as an enemy threat: the enemy was an amalgam of communists, socialists, anarchists, freemasons and Jews. The British Fascisti were not particularly anti-semitic: Jews were seen as no more than likely members, because uprooted, of a much wider alien conspiracy.

The British Fascisti had no uniform: they wore a badge with the words 'For King and Country' encircling the initials B.F. As more public-school and military-type men entered the movement, they persuaded Miss Lintorn Orman to change these initials to simply F. After a time Miss Lintorn Orman increasingly withdrew to her Somerset background and the headquarters in London were taken over by Brigadier Blakeney, who had until recently been head of the Egyptian State Railways; he changed the wording of the title from 'Fascisti' to 'Fascists' and found other ex-service officers to take over local leadership: there was a General Tyndal-Biscoe in Bournemouth and an Admiral Tupper at Liss. The chief activity of the British Fascists was to act as stewards at right-wing meetings when these were in danger of being broken up.

When the editor of the movement's newspaper *The British Fascist Bulletin* had to print some sort of policy in order to fill up space, he suggested that, as a means of reducing unemployment, income tax should be lowered so that rich people could employ more servants.

During 1924 when there was a Labour Government, and during 1925 and 1926 when there was the threat of strikes paralysing a Conservative Government, the British Fascists to a certain extent flourished; there was talk of, and some training in, motor-cycle squads which could be rushed to the aid of government forces in an emergency. But even during these years there was the tendency for individuals dedicated to discipline to choose, somewhat anarchically, their own style of commitment: during 1925 there broke away from the British Fascists groups calling themselves the British Empire Fascists, the Fascist League, the Fascist Movement, the National Fascisti and the British National Fascists. The latter's speciality was the attempt to break up Labour Party meetings: one of their victims in 1927 was the young up-and-coming Labour MP Oswald Mosley, addressing a meeting at Cambridge.

During the general strike of 1926 the British Fascists offered their services to the Home Secretary but were told that these would be acceptable only if they dropped the word 'Fascist'. They achieved their first martyr when one of their members, acting unofficially as a fireman on a train, leaned too far out of his cab window and hit his head on a bridge.

British Fascists were mostly middle-class men who had no experience of, nor indeed taste for, serious revolutionary nor counter-revolutionary violence: they never went in for the intimidation of civilians by street fighting as their counterparts on the Continent did. The violence of the British middle class had for years and for the most part been absorbed somewhat formally in the business of controlling outlandish parts of the Empire. At home, such violence as existed was mostly of the student-ragging, de-bagging type which might be perpetrated after a rugger match or on Boat Race night. It was to these sort of people that, in 1932, Oswald Mosley sent Robert Forgan, his henchman from Labour and New Party days, to take soundings about whether the members of the various fascist groups would come together under his leadership. He felt it sensible, before he launched a wider appeal, to try to get control of such forces as seemed readily available.

There was by this time one slightly more strident fascist group in Britain – the Imperial Fascist League, a late (1929) breakaway group from the British Fascists and run by Arnold Leese, a retired veterinary surgeon. Arnold Leese was specifically and strongly anti-semitic: it was said that his feelings had arisen from his objections to kosher methods of slaughtering animals. When in 1932 Robert Forgan approached him with a proposal that he should accept Oswald Mosley's leadership he replied that he considered that Oswald Mosley himself was in the pay of Jews. Miss Lintorn Orman refused on the grounds that, from his record, Mosley must be a near-communist. Many other fascists however agreed to the proposal.

My father launched the British Union of Fascists on 1st October 1932 at a flag-unfurling ceremony in the old New Party offices in Great George Street. There were thirty-two founder members present – new recruits from the fascist splinter-groups and remnants from the New Party. The New Party had been my father's trial run, as it were, for fascism. Started in March 1931, some eight months after his resignation from the Labour Government, it had been an attempt to enfold all the people who were attracted to him and his ideas at that time – maverick Labour intellectuals, impatient Tory radicals, aesthetes yearning for political commitment, young toughs looking for a cause on behalf of which to exercise their energy. The New Party had lasted for no more than a year: it had failed spectacularly at the general election in the autumn of 1931. It had contained too many disparate elements for even such a magnetic figure as Oswald Mosley to hold together. In particular, there had been a conflict between those who did not wish to be responsible for organised force even when it was used in defence against left-wing militants who were trying to break up New Party meetings, and those who did. The intellectuals and the aesthetes had for the most part gone; those who lingered on in the New Party through the summer of 1932 were mainly those who had been involved with the NUPA (jargon for New Party) Youth Movement and who were trained to defend meetings: it was men of this kind who were present at the launching ceremony of the BUF. Oswald Mosley told them that he had 'finished with those who think: henceforth I shall go to those who feel'. He perorated – 'We ask those who join us to march with us in a great and hazardous adventure. We ask them to be prepared to sacrifice all, but to do so for no small and unworthy ends. We can only offer them the deep belief that they are fighting that a great land may live'.

Thus at the beginning the nucleus of the British Union of Fascists was composed of people who were concerned not so much with the elaboration of a message as with the business of allowing to be heard whatever message might be felt to suit the occasion: the NUPA Youth Movement was transformed without difficulty into the Fascist Defence Force. Fascism is a mechanism by which an individual can commit himself dramatically to the service of a society: it does not presuppose

what a society shall necessarily be committed to. My father was, again,
unusual as a fascist leader in that he did in fact promulgate a message
at the same time as he unfurled the banners which were the symbols
of commitment: the message was contained in his book *The Greater
Britain*, published on the same day as the ceremony in Great George
Street. In *The Greater Britain* he reiterated much of the economic policies
of his New Party and indeed of his Labour Party days: there was to
be created and organised a self-contained home-market-plus-empire
economic area within which prices, wages, investment and the bulk-
buying of raw materials would all be centrally controlled and balanced
by government executive committees. In *The Greater Britain* however
there is a new emphasis on how this, rather than what, should be done.
There was the specific call to service and to dedication to a leader:
'the Leader must be prepared to shoulder absolute responsibility'. There
was the impression that once this handing over of responsibility had
been done, there need be few doubts about the availability of solutions.
Looking back in 1935 my father wrote of this time* –

> The origin of the British Union of Fascists was the formation of
> an emergency group of men and women to advocate a practical
> policy capable of being put into immediate operation in order to
> meet a specific plan for the crisis in Britain. There was no dogma,
> no theory, no principle.

In the conditions of 1932, this attitude was not naive. There was indeed
a crisis in Britain: it seemed likely to get worse. Financiers had panicked;
unemployment was at nearly three million; there had recently been
the mutiny of the fleet at Invergordon. Mussolini had come to power
in Italy by leaving himself free to make multifarious changes of policy
according to whatever crisis presented itself. Hitler was now playing
down the explicit dogmas of *Mein Kampf* in order to appeal to different
sorts of people in different ways. What fascists offered to people in
the early nineteen thirties was order: it seemed that for them to gain
support what was required was not so much doctrine, as evidence of
strength. It was still reasonable to think that the crisis in England over
the moribund body of democratic politics would resolve itself into a
battle between communists and fascists; and it seemed incumbent on
fascists to make it seem likely that they would win.
  The first public meeting of the BUF was in Trafalgar Square on
15th October 1932; there were some interruptions and a few scuffles;

* *The Fascist Quarterly.*

on the whole the scene was peaceful. Then on 24th October at an indoor meeting at the Memorial Hall in Farringdon Street three hecklers, after due warning, were thrown out by members of the Fascist Defence Force with what was seen, according to the predilections of the viewer, as either unavoidable or undue violence. This set the tone for many fascist meetings in the future. After the Farringdon Street meeting the columns of fascists and left-wing militants marched through the streets singing *The Red Flag* and *Rule Britannia* in counterpoint; they hurled abuse and slogans to and fro; not yet bricks and stones. But then, by December, Mosley was complaining to the press that he was being followed from meeting to meeting 'by an organised band of communists whose object was to interrupt all my speeches' and at Battersea Town Hall there was a fight in which bottles and chairs were used by a group of fifty hecklers during which time nothing of Mosley's speech could be heard. The Fascist Defence Force quietened the hall in five minutes. After this the speech continued. But what the audience remembered, of course, was the violence.

All this made sense if what was being demonstrated was the ability of fascists to keep order when threatened by disruption – if the paramount fear in the country was the likelihood of anarchy. But the danger to fascists here was that it could be suggested by their opponents (who had their own techniques for fighting battles) that it was the fascists who were themselves provoking the crisis which they claimed they would be so good at dealing with when it came: was it not indeed reasonable to suppose that people who claimed to be so dynamic would not wait for their expected crisis to materialise in its own time, but would help it on its way?

In February 1933 there was a public debate between Oswald Mosley and his old friend from Independent Labour Party days James Maxton; many of the Mosleys' old social friends were present – fascism was still potentially fashionable. In the course of the debate Maxton challenged Mosley about what exactly his Fascist Defence Force would do in the face of what he might judge to be a threatened left-wing take-over. Mosley replied that when the Labour Party had 'led us more rapidly to the situation which comes anyhow but which they precipitate, behind them will emerge the real man, the organised communist, the man who knows what he wants; and if and when he ever comes out we will be there in the streets with Fascist machine guns to meet him'. The next day the evening newspaper the *Star* reported that 'Sir Oswald Mosley warned Mr Maxton that he and his Fascists would be ready to take over the government with the aid of machine

guns when the moment arrived'. Mosley brought a case for libel against
the *Star* which eventually came to court a year later. Then the fear
of a communist take-over – and the distinction between combatting
this and instigating a take-over oneself – were still sufficiently clear
in people's minds for a jury to award Mosley £5,000 damages. But
from the beginning it was difficult for him to walk the tightrope
between impressing people with the resoluteness of his followers in
their ability to maintain order, and exposing himself to the charge of
being responsible for violence.

At Stoke there was a meeting at which a heckler advanced to the
platform and challenged Mosley personally to a fight; Mosley jumped
down from the platform to face him and a general fracas ensued. Then
in March 1933 – perhaps as a result of the sort of reputation the fascists
were getting – there was a meeting at the Free Trade Hall in Manchester
at which Mosley tried to restrain his stewards from being obviously
rough to a heckler; the police intervened to restore order and told the
Defence Force to leave the building. Mosley instructed his followers
to obey, and 'stood with folded arms' (according to press reports) while
the police tried, and failed, to produce conditions in which his speech
could be heard. Afterwards he pointed out that his Defence Force, if
left to itself, could always restore order; it was only the police who
could not ensure free speech. But anxieties concerning the cost of the
successes of his Defence Force remained. At the Manchester meeting
the press reported – 'Lady Cynthia [my mother Cimmie] sat in a box
in the hall watching'.

This was one of the last meetings of my father's at which my mother
was an observer. In April they went together on an official visit to
Rome; she was a spectator again while my father took the salute at
a march past of Italian fascists. The next month she became ill with
appendicitis; she got peritonitis; tragically, she died. This came at the
end of the previous volume. My mother seems to have become reconciled to the theory of fascism before she died: it cannot be known
what she would have been able to become reconciled to in practice.

There was a bizarre epilogue to the involvement of my mother with
fascism. One of my father's most bitter opponents continued to be
Arnold Leese, the head of the Imperial Fascist League, who called my
father a 'Kosher Fascist'. (There was indeed some support for this idea
from the *Jewish Chronicle*, which reported that 'our greatest supporters
in our fight against the Imperial Fascists are the Mosley Fascists themselves.') After Cimmie's death the Imperial Fascists began printing stories
that she herself was half Jewish on the grounds that her maternal grand-

father had been called Levi Zebidee Leiter: it was even suggested that Jewish rites had been used at her funeral. In retaliation for this (the Leiter family, in fact appear not to have been in origin Jewish but members of a Dutch Protestant sect called the Mennonites) members of the BUF set out one day to break up a meeting of the Imperial Fascist League; they used more violence, it seemed, than they were accustomed to use even against communist opponents; Arnold Leese was debagged and thrown into the street and General Blakeney, in temporary alliance with Leese, was injured in the eye. My father later wrote that this was the one occasion of which he knew at which his followers had deliberately provoked a fight: he had had to deal with them 'very severely' to prevent such an incident happening again.

In the more public arena it was disputed by neither side at the time that it was the communists who set out to break up fascist meetings: fascists did not break up communist meetings possibly because communists did not possess speakers of sufficient quality to attract large audiences, but also, and mainly, because it was fascists' policy to demonstrate orderliness. Oswald Mosley wanted to run a movement that could use to advantage the disruptive tendency that fascists said they would show themselves ready to combat; but at the same time he wished to appear sensible, rational, humane. These were qualities that no other fascist or national socialist leaders bothered even to claim to make much use of. But then, what was Mosley doing so unequivocally putting himself forward as a fascist? This was a question that his old friends continued to ask perhaps more often than his enemies – who assumed for the most part that his appeal to decency and rationality was hypocritical. To those who had once been close to him it must have seemed that there was something wildly foolhardy about this gamble of his with history: either the crisis in the Western world would occur exactly in the style he said it would, or what hope had he of straightforward political power when he was the purveyor of so many opposites? He was the leader of an embryonic private army dedicated to preventing war; he was a revolutionary leader issuing orders to obey the police; he was appealing to men of feeling but was ruling out – at least with the conscious part of him – the sort of hatred and fears by which men's urges towards power have traditionally been canalised. His experiment, certainly, seemed likely to be one of the oddest in political history. He never made any secret of the fact that to him it was the gamble of winning everything – power and decency and orderliness – that drove him on: of secondary consideration was the knowledge, or at least the suspicion, that the odds were quite high that he would fail.

CHAPTER 2

Family Life

So long as my mother had been alive my father's tendency to gamble on the chances of winning everything had extended over his private as well as his political life: he had tried to be adoring husband, sexual conqueror, searcher after truth; someone both ruthlessly manipulative and yet known for humanitarian concerns; at home equally in Independent Labour Party Summer Schools and in the palazzos and villas of Venice and Antibes. For a time he seemed to succeed. It was his achievements in so many diverse fields that perhaps caused people who felt envious of him to call him a dilettante beyond normal pales.

My mother Cimmie had tried to keep up with him; she had encouraged him in his going for high stakes; her letters expressed the determination that jointly they not only should succeed in work but should have 'fun'. She used to tell him how sad she was when he went his own way; but she did not put up a serious case against him, nor did she manage to find much of a life on her own. After a time it was as if his complexities became too much for her. It was coincidentally that she became ill and died.

There is a sense in which my mother's death affected my father in the way that Gretchen's death affected Faust (I do not know if my father had yet read Goethe's *Faust*; in later years both the play and the character became something of a paradigm for him). Faust, too, had wanted to have a taste of everything: he had made a bargain with Mephistopheles that he should be shown all manner of interests and delights: if ever he should find a vision for the sake of which he would cry Stop! – then Mephistopheles might claim Faust's soul for his own. The death of Gretchen – a girl whom he had loved and seduced – made Faust suffer; but it did not seem an occasion at which he should cry Stop! It was rather one from which he felt he might drive himself more fiercely on. In the second part of the tragedy Faust gives up such simple pleasures as revelry and seduction, and throws himself into efforts at understanding and re-ordering the world.

After Cimmie's death my father gave up almost all his old social pleasures in London and on the Mediterranean and occupied himself with work at his headquarters and in speaking tours round the country. He maintained some formal complexity in personal affairs: but this was nothing like the restless drive which had previously characterised his relationships with women. One way in which it did not seem, however, that he made much of an effort to emulate Faust at this time was that in which Faust struggled to understand and perhaps to transform himself by means symbolised by alchemy.

Diana Guinness, aged twenty-two, had left her husband and had set up house with her two small children in Eaton Square; her intention was, she said, to be available for my father whenever he had time to give to her after the demands of his work and his family. While Cimmie had been alive there had been no question of his leaving Cimmie; the matter had been, for my father, simply that he had wanted to have as it were two wives. It was this that, even in the somewhat raffish society in which he lived, had been considered the breaking of some taboo. So when Cimmie unexpectedly died people could say – We told you so! Diana remembers the day of Cimmie's death as one of the worst days of her life.

My father was left with three children the eldest of whom was twelve and the youngest one year old. He had a house in the country with a retinue of four or five servants and a house and a flat in London, the former of which he sold. He also found himself with a mother and two sisters-in-law – Baroness Ravensdale (Irene) and Lady Alexandra Metcalfe (Baba) – who seemd eager in their different ways to fill some of the spaces that Cimmie had left. They wished to be involved in looking after his work, his children and himself: above all, it seemed, they were intent on trying to discourage him from seeing Diana Guinness.

They would explain that it was their duty to do this in memory of Cimmie: my father would explain that he had certain responsibilities towards Diana. But he would come down to the family home at Denham and be (in our Nanny's words) 'wonderfully attentive to the children': he could also then be in the company of people trying to be attentive to him – especially his ex-sister-in-law Baba. On to her he seemed to have transferred (she used to say) something of his feelings for Cimmie. Then he would return to London and to Diana's house

in Eaton Square, walking from his flat in Ebury Street at night and
tapping on her ground floor window with his walking stick. He still
had to be careful about his meetings with Diana: she was in the process of divorce – her husband was acting (according to the customs
about decency at the time) as the so-called guilty party – and this was
the time when there had to be no suspicion of adultery on the part
of the so-called innocent party because if there were, and it were brought
to the attention of an official called the King's Proctor, the divorce
could be made invalid. There was once in fact a threat of blackmail
by a maid: my father countered this by a technique which he found
effective in politics – that of categorical denial, with a demand that
the accuser should produce cast-iron evidence. There were many people
of course in my father's and Diana's social world who knew of their
relationship and who were hostile to them; but to have caused trouble
in this area would have been outside the rules of their particular social
game.

Few people doubted the genuineness of my father's great grief after
Cimmie's death: people who knew him at all knew that he was a person
capable of containing truly different sorts of emotion at once. An
elaborate tomb was constructed for Cimmie at the family home of
Savehay Farm near Denham: it was of pink marble, somewhat like
Napoleon's tomb, and was designed by Sir Edwin Lutyens and his son
Robert. It was placed in a sunken garden in the two-acre wood by
the river which Cimmie had been clearing with her children just before
she died. Around the top of the marble were carved the words *A little
space was allowed her to show at least a heroic purpose and to attest a high
design.* At the side of the tomb was just a circle with the inscription –
Cynthia Mosley My Beloved.

Cimmie's body had lain for a time in the chapel of the Astors' house
at Cliveden a few miles away. When it was placed in its tomb we
children were at last (we had been taken neither to the funeral nor
to the chapel) allowed to come near it. I remember a wooden bridge
across a ditch and then the gate into the wood and the stillness and
the insects buzzing; and then – what do you do with a tomb, what
is it that is happening, you walk round and round it: it seems to be
a landfall blocking enormous events elsewhere.

For the summer holidays of 1933 – three months after my mother's
death – my grandmother 'Ma' Mosley went with Nanny and my
brother Micky, aged one, to a seaside resort in the Isle of Wight; my
Aunt Irene took myself, aged ten, and my sister Vivien, aged twelve,
with my mother's ex-lady's-maid Andrée on a cruise to the Canary

Isles; my Aunt Baba went off with my father on a motoring trip through France. Diana Guinness went with her sister Unity Mitford to the first big Nazi rally at Nuremberg. This was where the first volume ended.

During the next year there were repetitions and variations on these themes. Ma Mosley became the leader of the Women's Section of the British Union of Fascists; Irene, who was unmarried (she had been engaged at the time of Cimmie's death but the engagement was broken off) continued with her supervisory role of the children; Baba played her part in the restoring of my father's confidence and affections. Andrée became housekeeper at Savehay Farm; Nanny, as usual, performed all the mundane tasks for the children.

There was not much noticeable change in our finances. Of my mother's money, under the terms of her grandfather Levi Leiter's will, the capital had to remain within the Leiter trust in America; the income (some £8,000 or £9,000 a year) was divided between her three children. So long as we were under age this money was under the surveillance of the Chancery Court and the Official Solicitor, but my father, in theory at least, could call on it to pay for schools and the upkeep of the family house at Denham. Later there was difficulty about this money; a judge withheld some of it on the grounds that its distribution would enable my father to spend more of his own money on fascism.

In the winter of 1933–34 my father and Diana Guinness went on a holiday together to the South of France: my father had been ill with a recurrence of phlebitis, and his doctor ordered him to rest. Diana wrote of this time that they were very happy: 'We sat out in the sun by day and dined in front of a wood fire: I went for long walks in the hills, coming upon washer-women beating their linen on oaken boards in the bright streams and chatting together as they worked, like Joyce's washer-women in *Anna Livia Plurabel*.'*

The watchfulness that his mother and ex-sisters-in-law had kept upon my father in his dealings with Diana seemed to have abated; there is no mention in my Aunt Irene's diaries for instance of this holiday, whereas only a few months earlier she had been recording with 'horror' any likelihood of his meeting Diana in London. Irene seems in fact to have transferred her interest to encouraging my father's growing relationship with her sister Baba; she recorded with approval an afternoon at Savehay Farm when 'Tom [my father was always known to his friends as Tom] and Baba walked the lawn, Tom's arm round her

* *A Life of Contrasts.*

waist, speaking his speech to her'. Irene even told Baba's husband
'Fruity' Metcalfe that he must learn to put up with this sort of thing,
and enrolled Fruity's sister to give him 'a good stern talking to about
his jealousy'. Irene's idea apparently was that not only was Baba giving
comfort to Tom after Cimmie's death, but also he was being good
for Baba; Baba had been 'intellectually starved' (so Irene wrote in her
diary) for years and it was 'no wonder she blossomed with Tom'. At
the same time and on the same grounds Irene seems to have encouraged
another relationship of Baba's; this was with Count Dino Grandi,
Mussolini's Ambassador in London, whom Irene described as being in
love with Baba. There was a weekend at Cliveden at which Nancy
Astor wished to interrupt a tête-à-tête between Grandi and Baba but
Irene said (according to her diary) 'Leave them alone, it is the first
time she has talked to a good brain for years.' Irene also recorded –
'Fruity's retaliation took the form of reading aloud to Mrs Packenham.'

In May 1934 there was a big 'Blackshirt Dinner' at the Savoy with
everyone in full evening dress and my father and grandmother, aunt
Irene and Fruity Metcalfe photographed for the *Tatler*. Then in the
summer of 1934 it was Baba who was planning to have a look at the
Nazi rally at Nuremberg; and she sent to my father a picture postcard
of Hitler's house at Obersalzberg with the question – is Mrs G still
at Denham? I do not remember anything directly of Diana Guinness
at Denham during these years just after my mother's death; what
I remember is Nanny's strange persistence in refusing to talk to
her.

Granny Mosley wrote to my father after a weekend at Savehay Farm
– 'Those children really adore you: I think you mean more to them
than you can possibly believe.'

Irene recorded in her diary how my father's attentiveness to his
children included what seemed to her unnecessary badinage with
thirteen-year-old Viv: she called this 'his insensate silly slapping chaffing
"boppy" chaff that makes Viv rude and on the defensive'. My father
had this way of teasing children: it was a means of making contact
with them: they defended themselves as best they could. References
to myself in Irene's diaries at this time are to do with my stammer;
it was becoming so bad that I 'could not answer questions in lessons';
yet there was something in my temperament that would apparently
'permit no teaching'. Irene recorded that I said to her – ' "I wish Daddy
would tell me about fascism, I know nothing about it." ' Also – ' "I
would like to see Daddy a dictator." '

Vivien wrote for her school a report on one of her father's speeches:

I think Daddy wants to make the Modern World better
than the old one.
He said Stability and Progress were the main things.
He said Progress had been confused with talk.
In Chemistry, if you put two colours together they make
another colour.
You have to have belief in change.

My memories of life at Savehay Farm during these years are
awakened chiefly by mentions in my Aunt Irene's diaries. I would
wander alone with my .410 shot-gun round woods and streams uselessly
slaughtering water-rats and moorhens; I fashioned from the garden a
golf-course on which I played with my father's walking-sticks and
tennis balls. There were games of cricket on the lawn into which friends,
servants, sisters and aunts were dragged. Irene recorded how she was
once 'severely bruised' by the 'fearfully fast bowling of Nicky's boy-
friend Stubbs'. A few days later however she 'made 31 and got Viv
and Nick and Florence [the nurserymaid] all out in 9 balls'.
Occasionally my father brought down friends from London for only
slightly more formal sport. Irene recorded a Boxing Day shoot on
Savehay Farm's hundred somewhat suburban acres –

An incredible Italian Swordsman from the London Sporting Club
arrived with a wild demented galloping setter at 10.30. At last Daddy,
Bill Allen, the Swordsman, Nick and Paula [ex-Casa Maury, now
married to Bill Allen] made the guns. Granny, Viv, Cox and James
[butler and footman] and I beat every field, river, copse and bog
till our backs broke. Coveys of partridges flew in every direction
and not one was shot; and only Nick got a poor moorhen.

What I remember about these shoots was the mixture of formality
and sudden irreverence; once one of the visiting guns – I think some
Italian Contessa – was going for a high pheasant and managed to hit
the signal-box on the embankment of the main London-to-Oxford
line; my father had difficulty in placating the signalman for laughter.
As the summer holidays of 1934 approached there were the jockeyings as there had been the previous year about who should do what
for the sake of which grown-ups and which children. Baba and Irene
and grandmother 'Ma' all had a hand in renting a house in France
near Toulon in order that my father should re-establish the tradition
observed by him and Cimmie of spending the summer holidays by

the Mediterranean with the children. It had been decided that Baba
should spend at least half the holidays with us, but it had been made
evident that Irene was not invited ('Ma and I are left looking like waiting
housemaids') – she was to go to some English resort with Nanny and
my brother Micky. In the event Baba came to Toulon for the last
two weeks of the holidays, and for the first two there was Diana
Guinness. My memory begins to come back about this holiday: I
remember a white house with a huge terrace above a rocky sea: my
father would stride up and down – 'communing with the muses', as
he would say jokingly, or 'contemplating the eternal verities'. There
was a gardener's son with whom I played until he introduced me to
his sport of snipping off the eyes of snails with a pair of scissors. My
father would throw empty wine-bottles into the sea and practise shooting at them with an automatic pistol. He let me fire this pistol once
or twice; I remember the way it jumped up in my hand. I did not
want to hide away and sulk on this holiday as I had done on previous
ones: I suppose that to have done this as some sort of challenge to
my father would have seemed absurd.

It must have been about this time that something began to sink in
about what people felt about my father and Mrs Guinness. There was
Nanny who would not speak – who, when Mrs Guinness was
mentioned, looked like Medusa. There was the scene in the night
nursery when I had pursued Nanny to try to make her tell me her
reasons for this (I was a crafty little boy: I would say – I know why
you won't talk to me, it's because of my stammer); and eventually
Nanny had said – Well, if it hadn't been for Mrs Guinness, I think
perhaps your mother – and so on. And I thought (such are the compensations perhaps of being a crafty little boy) – But life isn't like that,
is it? It's not because of that sort of thing that people die?

It was after this summer holiday of 1934 that I was first taken to
one of my father's huge political meetings: for the most part, he kept
his public life separate from his life with his children. We read about
him in the papers of course: there seemed to be something grand as
well as embarrassing about his one-man drive to alter the world. The
impression we got of his politics from overhearing aunts and other
grown-ups talk was that he had what was often referred to as one of
the most brilliant 'brains' in England; that this brain was for some reason
not being properly used; that this was both his fault, but also in some
way England's. When I was taken for the first time to this big political
meeting in Hyde Park I had no idea what I would see. My sister and
my Aunt Irene were with friends in the country. I went with other

members of my father's family to the roof of the Cumberland Hotel.

It was a Sunday afternoon, about tea-time, and there was an enormous crowd in the Park: people were eddying like particles of sand in gentle waves. There was what seemed to be a rather small formation of Blackshirts on the stretch of grass to the south of Marble Arch: this was separated from the crowd by a narrow line of police. Then after a time – our party on the roof of the Cumberland Hotel were like onlookers at some tournament – there was the sound of a drum-and-fife band from the direction of Bayswater Road; a rather straggling procession came in through a gate; this was not the fascists, it was explained to me on the roof, but the anti-fascists coming to make their counter-demonstration. The crowd flowed towards the anti-fascists; they were held back by police; the anti-fascists assembled round a nucleus of what looked like a cart. It was all rather like the sort of thing that went on underneath microscopes at school – forms of life jostled and re-jostled for shape and identity. Then from the other direction, from Park Lane, there was another line of people marching briskly and firmly in a column of threes: these were the fascists; they were rather frail-looking men with stern faces and close-cut hair; they were wearing their black shirts and black or grey trousers. At the head of them was my father, thin and upright and somehow vulnerable; he was striding along so purposefully; but as if to – what? – some platform, scaffold, on which courage could be displayed? By the side of the column were hundreds of police; they wandered along sometimes smiling at the crowd. As they all entered the Park – there had been discussion on the roof about how well my father's leg would stand the march; had he not been warned by doctors about his phlebitis? – the fascists already in the Park formed up in two lines as if making a tube; my father marched up inside them at the head of his men; the fascists on either side of him had their arms up, reaching. The column arrived at an area within which there were four or five vans with ladders up to the roof. The anti-fascists were in a further part of the Park and there was a man speaking from the top of the cart with the crowd held back; fascist speakers climbed to the tops of their vans and began to speak with the crowd held back; we on the roof of the Cumberland Hotel could not hear what anyone was saying. It did not seem possible that anyone in the Park could hear what anyone was saying: it was explained to me that the police had forbidden the use of loud-speakers. A police helicopter, or autogyro, went slowly overhead; it made a great noise; it was a novelty. In the Park the speakers on the tops of vans were waving their arms and opening and shutting their mouths; my father had his hands on his hips and was striking some attitude at the sky; a few people in the crowd were shaking their fists and making faces. It appeared from the papers the next day that the most popular anti-fascist slogans were – 'Where's the old school tie?', and 'You look like kippers sideways'. The discussion on the roof of the Cumberland Hotel had turned to the question of what had happened to Ma Mosley: had she or had she not been marching at the head of her Women's Section? She was fifty-nine now, or was it sixty? There was a big white tent at the edge of the crowd like the buffet at a race meeting: ambulance men stood around with their stretchers like furled flags. Someone spotted Ma Mosley: there she was on the bonnet of a van, at the feet of my father who was above her orating. It was getting cold now; bits of paper blew about like confetti. On the roof of the Cumberland Hotel someone pulled out a hip-flask; was it six o'clock yet? or wasn't it Sunday anyway? After a time my father and the other speakers climbed down from their vans and formed up in their columns to go home. The tournament was over. But what had happened? Or had nothing happened – was it not this that the police had been there for? Everything had been kept separate: cells had just formed, broken up; there had been no connections. In the papers the next day it was said that there had been six thousand police; there had been five thousand fascists; no one seemed to have tried to enumerate the anti-fascists separately from the crowd which was esti-mated at anything from fifty thousand to a hundred and fifty thousand. In the Cumberland Hotel there was a discussion as we descended – had the demonstration been a success or a failure? But what might be meant by this – was it a success that the demonstration had just taken place and no violence had occurred, or was it a failure for almost the same reason that nothing much had happened? No one seemed to know. No one seemed able to formulate quite the right question. What was it that my father had been trying to do? It had been important, yes, that his meeting should be peaceable; but still, what was the point of a meeting if nothing had been heard? My father had been involved with his movement now for nearly two years: he was giving up his life to it. What was it that was happening?

CHAPTER 3

Italian Connections

During the first ten months of its existence the British Union of Fascists had expanded so rapidly that it had had to move to larger headquarters – first to 12 Grosvenor Place and then, in August 1933, to a building in the King's Road which had previously been Whitelands Teacher Training College. This was a large, barrack-like structure (now pulled down) in which, the BUF claimed, there could, if required, be housed 5,000 London members. It was known by its inmates as the 'Black House' and by their opponents as the 'Fascist Fort'. In 1933 (in the words of one of its inmates) 'it was filled with students eager to learn everything about this new, exciting crusade; its club rooms rang with the laughter and song of men who felt that the advent of Fascism had made life again worth living'.

There was at this time enough money coming in for the organisation to be able to pay its regular workers. The first Director of Organisation – a post second only to that of the 'Leader' as Oswald Mosley was always called – was Dr Robert Forgan, who had been a Labour MP in 1929–30 and then had left the Labour Party with the Mosleys and John Strachey to form the New Party. Robert Forgan was a kindly, painstaking man whose task in the BUF was mainly to deal with outside contacts; within the movement he was known as someone who could usually be influenced by a hard-luck story. His Chief of Staff was Ian Dundas, the son of an Admiral, who at the age of twenty-four had just relinquished a commission in the navy: he was in charge of headquarters personnel and would go about his duties at the Black House accompanied by a bugler. The Commander of the Fascist Defence Force was Eric Piercy, a former insurance agent and still an inspector in the Special Constabulary of the police: his passion was for physical fitness and for drill. His adjutant, responsible for detailed planning of the

defence of fascist meetings, was Neil Francis-Hawkins, a recruit from
the British Fascists. He had been a salesman of surgical instruments,
and was renowned for his insistence on things being neat and tidy.

When recruits joined the BUF they undertook to pay a monthly
subscription of a shilling if employed and fourpence if unemployed;
they were expected to buy their own black shirts from headquarters
for seven shillings and sixpence – quite a large sum for an unemployed
man drawing the dole which in those days was eighteen shillings
a week. In the conditions of 1932 and 1933 it was inevitable that many
of the recruits were from the unemployed; when they were given jobs
at the Black House they had free accommodation and a pound or two
a week pocket money. Membership of the BUF was open to all British
subjects irrespective of race or colour: a candidate had to state just that
he or she was loyal to King and Empire, and would obey the rules
imposed by the leadership. Recruits were given a badge which was
a representation of the fasces – a bundle of sticks bound together round
a central axe – symbolising that a single stick might be broken but a
bunch could not be: this had been the symbol of the lictors (magis-
trates' officers) in ancient Rome, and was now the emblem of
Mussolini's fascist Italy. It was obligatory for members of the BUF
when on duty to wear their black shirts: this was a means not only
of making them feel separate from the crowd, but of encouraging a
lack of class distinction amongst themselves. On the back of the
membership card that was given to each newly enrolled member were
printed the aims and objects of the BUF. These were –

> To win power for Fascism and thereby establish in Great Britain
> the Corporate State which shall ensure that –
>
> All shall serve the State and none the Faction;
> All shall work and thus enrich their country and themselves;
> Opportunity shall be open to all but privilege to none;
> Great position shall be conceded only to those of great talent;
> Reward shall be accorded only to service;
> Poverty shall be abolished by the power of modern science released
> within the organised state;
> The barriers of class shall be destroyed and the energies of every
> citizen devoted to the service of the British Nation which, by the
> efforts and sacrifices of our fathers, has existed gloriously for centuries
> before this transient generation, and which by our exertions shall
> be raised to its higher destiny – the Greater Britain of Fascism.

Those who worked at Headquarters, apart from the Defence Force, were secretaries, typists, printers, messengers, drivers, paper-sellers and so on: they led a semi-military life with meal-times and reveille and lights-out regulated by the calls of Ian Dundas's bugle. In the evenings the inmates would box and fence and play billiards; or they could attend lectures on current politics and economic theory. In the provinces – it was planned that there should be a BUF organisation for each parliamentary division – there was at each headquarters an unpaid District Officer appointed by National Headquarters; he had under him a staff of volunteer officers responsible for propaganda, finance and transport. There were County and District Inspectors moving between the provinces and London. At all levels there were Women's Sections headed by Women Officers: the BUF prided itself on its emphasis on the equality of the sexes. A District Inspector wrote of the Women's Section at National Headquarters –

Lady Mosley, Oswald Mosley's mother, had her office at NHQ: she entered fully into the life of the Movement and was popular with the girls; she kept a motherly eye on some of the less staid and prettier ones and warned them of the hungry looks being cast in their direction by appreciative blackshirts and by one high-ranking officer in particular who was both an experienced politician and an experienced womaniser.

But at the centre of life at the Black House in London was the Fascist Defence Force, or 'I' Squad – the self-professed élite for whose sake much of the rest of the organisation existed. The 'I' Squad were the people involved in action, and action was what the BUF was dedicated to. The Squad had the privilege of wearing breeches and leather boots in place of the ordinary trousers and shoes; they were trained in boxing and judo in order to deal with interrupters at meetings – to be able to handle without weapons opponents who might be armed with weapons themselves. Eric Piercy on one occasion equipped his force with sticks like rubber truncheons: this was at the Free Trade Hall at Manchester in March 1933, but this was the meeting at which the Defence Force had been ordered out of the hall by the police with the result that the speech could not be heard. After this, the instructions that the Defence Force should not carry weapons was made explicit: the printed description of the required behaviour of a member of the 'I' Squad was –

He stands, together with his fellow stewards, smartly to attention with hands down. When the hecklers start, the speaker at first tries to calm them; but if this fails, and potatoes studded with razor-blades come sailing over, it is the steward's duty to stop the disturbance.

Often he finds that these missiles are being thrown by women while their menfolk stand well out of harm's way singing. He is not allowed to harm any woman. If he is hit by a man he is entitled to hit back — not otherwise.

If the police come upon the scene, any disorder is at once left to them. Fascists immediately drop their hands, even if they are in the act of being struck, and leave retaliation to the police.

The pattern of the meeting that had gone so badly at Manchester was not repeated; in October 1933, when Mosley returned to Manchester, there was a quiet meeting controlled by an orderly Defence Force and it was only after the meeting, when the fascists were marching away, that they were 'ambushed by a band of young men who came suddenly down a side street and attacked with a volley of stones.... three fascists received head injuries.... the blackshirts broke their ranks and made a counter attack.... then the fascists were recalled by bugle and reached the railway station without further disturbance'. This was from a report in a local newspaper: the provincial press was often impressed at this time by the fascists' discipline in the face of provocation.

The speakers whom the 'I' Squad were there to protect were themselves subject to training and discipline by headquarters: but it was not always easy (as indeed it became difficult with the Defence Force) to ensure that instructions were complied with. In the early days of the BUF when recruits were joining in large numbers there were more than a few who liked the idea of being given a platform from which they could pour forth their favourite streams of words. Officials at headquarters tried to regulate these; but what are politicians without their favourite streams of words? Speakers were classified according to what sort of audience a particular speaker might be suited to: there was one called Ramsbottom (our ex-District Inspector remembers) who was apt to use phrases like 'the parturition of Palestine' but who was held to be a good rabble-rouser outside a dock gate; there was another called Dalgleish who was of 'such painful refinement' that he was earmarked for 'suburban cultural associations'. By far the most effective speaker after the Leader himself was a small passionate American of Irish extraction called William Joyce. Joyce had joined the BUF in 1933 and by 1934 was playing such a large part in the movement that he began to be talked about as a possible successor to the Leader – if the Leader became seriously ill with his phlebitis.

Joyce had been born in America and brought up in Ireland: as a young man he had an obsessive patriotism for Great Britain and the British Empire. In 1924 while he was still a student (he took a first class honours degree in English at London University) he had been acting as a steward for the British Fascists at a Conservative meeting at Lambeth and after the meeting he had been caught by left-wing militants and had been held down in the street while a razor had been put in his mouth and his cheek had been cut up towards his ear. This was unusually venomous violence for the time; it left Joyce with a long scar at the side of the mouth from which he would pour, as if in some further vindictiveness, long and bitter tirades against aliens and Jews. Joyce thought that his injury had been done to him by Jews. During his early months with the BUF he seemed to accept the restraints on his anti-semitism imposed by the leadership; later, he seemed to feel himself more free to indulge it and he did the movement much harm.

There were the strict orders from the Leader that nothing should be said in speeches that could be taken as anti-semitic: 'racial and religious persecution are alien to the British character'. However – 'We do not attack Jews because they are Jews, we only attack them if we find them pursuing an anti-British policy: any Jew who is not anti-British will always get a square deal with us'. This was said by Oswald Mosley in January 1933. But such a statement of course left open to individual interpretation what might or might not be taken to be 'anti-British policy'; and in the long run such ambiguity seemed a connivance in whatever tendencies there were for anti-semitic phrases or behaviour to emerge. Without doubt many of the people who enrolled in the BUF were instinctively anti-semitic because anti-semitism was the sort of emotion that drew such would-be patriots to band together; on the other hand, Jews themselves were among the early members of the BUF. At first the BUF's anti-semitism was in fact less overt than was the hostility of Jews towards the BUF: the strength of this latter tendency was in the first place, it seems, largely due to what was going on in Hitler's Germany.

Hitler had come to power in January 1933: he had never made any pretence about his anti-semitic convictions. The British Union of Fascists was seen to be similar to the Nazis in certain obvious respects – they used the same salute, they sang their anthem to the same tune (that of the *Horst Wessel Lied*), they had the same style of dress and discipline. It would have been almost impossible for the Jews in the early 1930s not to have seen the BUF as setting itself up as anti-semitic (there is always a chance, of course, that Jews can defend themselves against any form of criticism by bringing charges of anti-semitism). During 1933 Oswald Mosley went out of his way to try to disassociate himself from Hitler's anti-semitism; he told the *Yorkshire Post* that he thought 'Hitler has made his greatest mistake in his attitude to the Jews': he even prophesied that their 'attacks on German Jews would very shortly cease'. (This was not wholly fanciful: in March 1933 Goering himself was reported as saying 'Germany does not intend to discriminate against Jews'.) But what had already been done to Jews in Germany (as soon as Hitler had come to power there had been outbreaks of anti-semitic brutality: it is a fact that for a time these abated) was sufficient to make many British Jews feel themselves justified in launching protests or even attacks on members of the British Union of Fascists; these were in retaliation for what was happening in Germany, and were aimed at preventing the same things happening here.

During 1933 there were several cases of individual and small groups of fascist paper-sellers being set upon by Jews: the *Daily Telegraph* reported that 'about eleven' fascists were giving away pamphlets in Coventry Street one evening when there was a shout of 'Come on Jews' and 'a mob swept round them and punched them and kicked'; a week later two Jews out of a mob of 'about a hundred' were sent to prison for five weeks for assaulting a Blackshirt in Shaftesbury Avenue. According to the police there was no evidence that Blackshirts at this time were indulging in such attacks. Jews, in their defence, claimed that in the current political circumstances just by wearing a black shirt the fascists were causing provocation. But the *Jewish World* gave its opinion at this time that attacks on Blackshirts were 'wicked and stupid, and condemned outright by all decent men of our faith'.

The songs that the Blackshirts sang and which, together with their dress and their salute and their badge and so on, seemed to many members of the public to justify their seeing the BUF as in alliance with German Nazis and Italian Fascists were, chiefly, their 'Marching Song' which was sung to the tune of the *Horst Wessel Lied* and the words of which went –

Comrades: the voices of the dead battalions
Of those who fell that Britain might be great
Join in our song, for they still march in spirit with us
And urge us on to win the People's State!

We're of their blood, and spirit of their spirit,
Sprung from the soil for whose dear sake they bled;
'Gainst vested powers, Red Front, and massed ranks of Reaction
We lead the fight for freedom and for bread!

The streets are still: the final struggle's ended;
Flushed with the fight we proudly hail the dawn!
See, over all the streets the Mosley banners waving –
Triumphant standards of a race reborn!

– and the song 'Onward Blackshirts', which was sung to the tune of
the Italian anthem *Giovinezza* –

> Hark! the sound of many voices
> Echoes through the vale of ages.
> Britain listens and rejoices
> Gazing on tradition's pages.
> Patriots: your cry is heeded!
> Heroes: your death was not in vain!
> We to your place have succeeded!
> Britain shall be great again!
>
> *Chorus*
> Onward Blackshirts! form your legions,
> Keep the flag for ever high.
> For a free and greater Britain
> Stand we fast to fight or die!

The *Horst Wessel Lied* was sung to one of the best and saddest tunes
that a revolutionary movement has ever produced: *Giovinezza* was a
fine rousing marching song. What is striking is that the words of each
are concerned with the image of the revolutionary spirit arising only
over the martyred bodies of the dead.

With its connections with Continental fascism being paraded so
openly it was inevitable that there would be speculation about where
the BUF was getting its money from. The money provided by Sir
William Morris (later Lord Nuffield) for the New Party had run out;
during 1933 there were few signs of large-scale backing from other
industrialists or financiers; yet by the autumn the BUF had moved
into its huge new headquarters in the Kings Road. It was true that
a lot of new recruits were coming in (the *News Chronicle* reported in
February 1934 that it 'understood from an official fascist source that

the membership of the Union up to last Wednesday was 17,707') and it was evident that Oswald Mosley was putting in his own money. He insisted that his movement was financed through the subscriptions and donations of British sympathisers. But there were persistent rumours that the BUF was being financed by Mussolini. These rumours continued, as did my father's denials of them, until the day of his death.

There is evidence now that the BUF was in fact being financed by Mussolini from the middle of 1933 to, probably, the summer of 1935. During the war all the BUF papers were in the hands of the authorities and although they found (according to a Home Office memorandum of 14 April 1943) that the 'income in the two years from February 1934 to February 1936 was £160,500' and the largest part of this was 'moneys which were paid into a secret account by two of its members' in the form of bundles of foreign currency and remittances 'which were further concealed by being passed from a Swiss bank into the account of an individual in this country before they reached the secret account' – in spite of all this, because of 'the elaborate steps taken to shroud the financial arrangements of British Union in mystery', there was still no definite evidence, the authorities reported, that the movement had been subsidised from abroad. Then after the war, on 6th June 1946, the then Home Secretary, Chuter Ede, announced in the House of Commons that there had come to light letters which had passed between Rome and Count Grandi, the Italian Ambassador in London, which showed that between 1933 and 1935 the BUF had received 'about £60,000 a year' from the Italian Government in monthly instalments of £5,000. This statement was 'categorically denied' by my father at the time: he wrote that 'evidence on any subject could now be available at a penny a packet in alleged Italian archives if any ill-disposed person sought to damage me or deceive authority'; and he challenged the government to produce any concrete evidence about the payments in the form of bank statements. But of course, care had been taken that there would be no evidence in bank statements; and in my father's denial he was careful to use the phrase – 'I have before me a Chartered Accountant's certificate concerning the origin of our funds for a considerable period before the war which shows each subscriber to be British'. Critics however could point to the phrase 'for a considerable period before the war' and ask – was it not significant that he had not used a phrase such as 'from the beginning'?

However letters to and from Count Grandi have now been found in Italian archives by the historian David Irving and details of these have been published in David Irving's broadsheet *Focal Point* of October 1981. (See the appendix to this chapter.) It seems unlikely that a forger fabricated these letters – what would have been the point? – and in any case those who were closest to my father at the time no longer deny the existence of the payments. There had been enough evidence for it to have been possible to guess the identity of the 'individual' at the British end of the transactions into whose bank account remittances were passed from the Swiss bank: this was W.E.D. (Bill) Allen, the old friend of my father's who had been a Conservative MP until he had joined the New Party in 1931 and was at the time (1933) married to my father's old friend Paula Casa Maury. Bill Allen was the managing director of a Northern Ireland printing and advertising firm which had financial contacts abroad; it would not have been difficult for him to have received payments and passed them on to the BUF in such ways as would not have aroused comment – though ex-BUF members did in fact remember bundles of foreign banknotes being carried here and there. My Aunt Baba, who was in the extraordinary position of being a confidante of both my father and Count Grandi, also felt she had reason to suspect that payments were coming from Italy; though she never discussed this with Grandi. It has been suggested by Diana that when in 1935 the payments were said to have stopped (it was stated by the Home Secretary in 1946 that a letter from Grandi to Mussolini had been found which said – 'with a tenth of what you give Mosley ... I feel that I could produce a result ten times better') one reason for this now apparently hostile attitude of Grandi's might have been some personal feeling of rivalry with my father.

In any event there seems little reason now to doubt the authenticity of the communications which appear to have passed between Grandi and Rome. The earliest document found is dated 25th August 1933 and is from the Italian Foreign Office to the Embassy in London: it is headed 'most secret and personal' and tells of a 'second payment' of £5,000 for Oswald Mosley made up of bundles of small denominations of Swiss and French francs, Reichsmarks, dollars and pounds; these will be in packets 'without any identification and secured by seals of no significance'; they will be sent by a special courier who has been instructed 'to carry out the consignment with the greatest caution'. The third and fourth payments, in October and December 1933, were also of £5,000 each in bundles of small currency; there were instructions to Grandi that he was to get them 'into Mosley's hands in whatever form Your Excellency considers best and in such a way that the consignment is made secretly'. Then on 24th January 1934 there was notification

of a payment of £20,000: this was a result of a personal meeting between
Oswald Mosley and Mussolini in Rome on January 9th during which
the considerably larger sum had been agreed. Grandi reported that on
January 30th this payment was handed personally to Mosley 'closed
and sealed exactly as it arrived at the Embassy from the Ministry –
the Embassy not having wished to open it'. On the same day Grandi
wrote a personal letter to Mussolini –

Dear President,
Mosley has entrusted me with expressing his gratitude to you for
sending the large sum which I have today arranged to have paid
to him. As soon as he got back from Rome he came to see me.
I have never seen him so sure of himself and so confident. He told
me that the talk he had with you 'recharged' and enlightened him,
and that he left Palazzo Venezia more determined than ever to fight
on. He also spoke gratefully to me of the simple generosity with
which you treated his requests for material help in the future, and
spoke at length, quoting figures, on how much this help should come
to, thinking I had already been told about arrangements he had made
in Rome.

No record of any consignment later than this one of January 1934 has
come to light: those payments of which records survive amount to
£40,000. From the Home Secretary's statement about the March 1935
letter from Grandi to Mussolini it would seem that some payments were
being made until then; such a supposition would not be in conflict
(though there is no hard evidence beyond the £40,000) with the Home
Secretary's suggestion that aid from Italy amounted to some £60,000
a year for two years. The fact that the expensive Black House had
to be given up and other economies made in the summer of 1935 would
also suggest that it was then that the payments stopped. What seems
certain is that during this period large sums passed; and my father felt
it vital to conceal this.

One of my father's techniques with his denials was to say, as lawyers
do, that of course this or that was not true, but then to ask – what did
it matter if it was? When denying the charge of having received money
from Mussolini he used at the same time to say – But the *Daily
Herald*, the semi-official organ of the Labour Party, received £75,000
from Russian funds during the nineteen twenties; and what is illegal
or wrong in a political movement receiving money from a friendly
foreign country? All this is a traditional legal style of argument to win

a case; but nevertheless it sets up doubts about truth, and even at the time it must have created an atmosphere at variance with the open, straightforward image that the British Union of Fascists was trying to create. There was another peculiarity about my father's lines of defence at this time: he said that he thought it proper to wash his hands of any control or indeed of any knowledge of his movement's finances on the grounds that he wished to be aloof from any suspicion of being influenced by anyone's money; but then, how could he reconcile this with his claim to be absolute and authoritative leader? He was fairly obviously, in fact, playing the game that nearly all politicians play – that of using words for self-protection or attack, since he believed these to be of more importance than truth. But the peculiarity of his position was that he had passionately to deny that this was what he was doing on account of the contempt that he had shown for the untruths of traditional political games. It would have been difficult for him of course in any circumstances to have admitted the payments from Mussolini: he would have known it would have exposed him damagingly to the charge of being in the pay of a foreign government – when so much of his appeal was to economic self-sufficiency, and so much of his attack was directed against interference in British politics by foreign finance.

But he needed the money; and in fact it was true that there was nothing illegal about the transactions; so what was there to stop him from behaving like an ordinary politician? – except, of course, that he was saying so vehemently that he was not. In August 1933 J. R. Clynes, who had been Home Secretary in the Labour Government at the time when my father had been Chancellor of the Duchy of Lancaster, wrote that Oswald Mosley was becoming 'the Greta Garbo of British politics': he was 'surrounding himself with a fog of mystery so dense that even his own followers must be finding it difficult to penetrate it'. This was a reference not only to the question of finances, but to the fact of so many foreign influences being evident in a movement which prided itself on being so patriotic. It also probably referred to my father's dramatic claims to straightforwardness which he defended with such skills in cunning rationalisation. But then – was not Greta Garbo the most adored actress in the Western world? And was not one reason why so many people adored her just her air of impenetrable mystery?

Appendix

The following is a facsimile of the communication of 25th August 1933
from the Italian Foreign Office in Rome to Count Grandi in London –

TELESPRESSO N. 6971

Ministero degli Affari Esteri

Gabinetto

SEGRETISSIMO-PERSONALE

Indirizzato a

A S.E. l'On. Dino GRANDI

R. Ambasciatore d'Italia

L O N D R A

Posizione .... *Roma, addì*   2 5 AGO. 1933 *Anno* XI   *Anno* ____

(Oggetto) Missione riservata

(Riferimento)

(Testo)   In relazione a precedente corrispondenza e da ultimo al te-
legramma ~~personalexxxSuxxxx~~ personale n.669 del 22 corrente, si ha il pregi
di far noto all'E.V. che con il corriere in partenza da Roma sabato 26
corrente, viene trasmessa la 2ª rata di sterline 5.000 per Sir Oswald
Mosley. Tale somma viene trasmessa nelle seguenti valute, al cambio del
7 agosto corr. :

Franchi francesi	169.850
sterline	1.000
dollari	7.000
marchi	1.900
franchi svizzeri	5.200

corrispondenti rispettivamente ai pacchi n.1, n.2, n.3 (composto di due
buste), n.4 e n.5. E' stato curato, nei limiti del possibile, di poter
ottenere biglietti di piccolo taglio, specialmente nelle sterline.

     Nella giornata di martedi' partirà da Roma il nipote del
Dott. Enderle, Signor Arturo Resio, persona del Dott. Enderle garantita
sotto ogni rispetto, che conosce già l'Inghilterra e la lingua inglese,
incaricato di mettersi a disposizione di cotesta R. Ambasciata per ef-
fettuare con la massima cautela la consegna della detta somma.

     Non è stato questa volta inviato a Londra il Dott. Enderle
perchè non è da escludere che egli possa più facilmente essere indivi-
duato, avendo in passato già adempiuto simile incarico. D'altra parte
il Signor Enderle è persona di cui questo Ministero pensa di potersi
servire anche in altre circostanze e pertanto conviene che egli
non offra occasione di poter essere segnalato o sospettato.

     Le buste contenenti le dette valute sono senza intesta-
zione, i sigilli che le chiudono contengono una sigla che non
ha nessun significato.

     L'E.V. disporrà nella forma che riterrà più opportuna
perchè la delicata operazione della consegna avvenga nel modo
più segreto. ·

     Accluso al presente dispaccio si trasmette una lettera
che il Dott. Enderle indirizza al Signor John Hope con preghiera
di farla pervenire a destinazione a mezzo posta.

CHAPTER 4

The Philosophy of Fascism

Shortly after his launching of the BUF my father gave a lecture to
the English Speaking Union entitled *The Philosophy of Fascism*.* This
was his attempt to give an account of his beliefs and aims that would
give them an intellectual background: that would be on a different
level of seriousness from Hitler's threatening rhetoric or indeed from
Mussolini's insistence that he had no philosophy at all.

Early in the lecture my father spoke of Oswald Spengler as 'the great
German philosopher' who had 'probably done more than any other
to paint in the broad background of Fascist thought'. My father did
not feel it necessary to go into detail about what this 'broad background' might be; Spengler's book *The Decline of the West* had recently
been published in English and he would have assumed that the gist
of it would have been sufficiently known to his audience for them
to understand to what he referred. Spengler's main thesis was that each
separate civilisation – Western, Classical, Indian and so on – had a
life-span analogous to that of any living organism – a spring and a
summer and an autumn and a winter – and that these patterns of growth
and decay were inexorable, making absurd the idea that one civilisation
could be said to be more 'advanced' than any other in the sense that
it was indefinitely developing and expanding. The fact that at a stage
in a civilisation's history such an illusion might be held was in fact
evidence of that civilisation being in decline: a naive faith in 'progress'
was a symptom of ossification. In the light of what became known
as Spengler's 'pessimism' it is one of the mysteries of fascism – a creed
dedicated ostensibly to the dynamic re-structuring of the world –
how fascists took Spengler as their intellectual hero.

* Published in *The Fascist Quarterly*.

In his speech to the English Speaking Union my father suggested
that Spengler's pessimism about Western civilisation was vitiated by
'his entire ignorance of modern scientific and mechanical development:
if you look through the Spenglerian spectacles you are bound to come
to a conclusion of extreme pessimism because they obscure the factor
which for the first time places in the hands of man the ability entirely
to eliminate the poverty problem'. In addition to modern science, what
my father suggested Spengler had failed to take into account was the
ability of Western man to learn from what indeed might be potentially
stultifying conflicts of ideas – and to make from these a synthesis which
could counteract the forces of decay. 'Where, in an age of culture,
of thought, of abstract speculation, you find two great cultures in sharp
antithesis, you usually find, in the following age of action, some synthesis in practice between those two sharp antitheses which leads to
a practical creed of action.' In this way Spengler's conclusions about
present civilisation might be refuted while his analysis of the patterns
of earlier civilisations could be accepted: all this might indeed provide
fascists with the sort of 'challenge' that they liked. But still – this could
be seen by an outsider either as a 'going-beyond' Spengler which was
my father's description of his own ideas, or as one more symptom
of the delusions of 'Caesarism' which was how Spengler described the
characteristics of a civilisation on the decline.

The antithetical forces which, in contemporary culture, my father
thought could be put into some practical synthesis were Christianity
and Nietzscheanism: 'I would suggest to you that in the last century
the major intellectual struggle arose from the tremendous impact of
Nietzschean thought on the Christian civilisation of two thousand years
ago.... its full implications are only today working themselves out'.

My father's interpretation of what Nietzsche had been saying about
Christianity was – 'This is the religion of the slaves and the weakling.
This is the faith of the people who are in flight from life, who will
not face reality, who look for salvation in some dreamy hereafter –
the salvation which they have not the vitality nor the manhood to
seize for themselves here on earth'. My father explained that this was
not his own view of Christianity because – 'I am going to show you
how I believe the Nietzschean and the Christian doctrines are capable
of synthesis'.

What he saw as the Nietzschean doctrine was his (my father's)
interpretation of Nietzsche's idea of the superman – 'the man who faces
difficulty, danger, goes forward through material things and through
the difficulties of environment to achieve, to win and create, here on

earth, a world of his own'. It was not the fascist doctrine directly to advocate the implementation of this interpretation of Nietzsche, but to combine it with Christianity to form a synthesis.

In the Fascist doctrine today you find a complete welding of the great characteristics of both creeds. On the one hand you find in Fascism, taken from Christianity, taken directly from the Christian conception, the immense vision of service, of self-abnegation, of self-sacrifice in the cause of others, in the cause of the world, in the cause of your country; not the elimination of the individual so much as the fusion of the individual in something far greater than himself . . . On the other hand you find taken from Nietzschean thought the virility, the challenge to all existing things which impede the march of mankind, the absolute abnegation of the doctrine of surrender: the firm ability to grapple with and to overcome all obstructions. You have, in fact, the creation of a doctrine of men of vigour and of a self-help which is the other outstanding characteristic of Fascism.

From the belief that such a synthesis might be possible – that by such an effort of will and by scientific understanding a going-against-the-grain of Spenglerian pessimism might take place – arose the beliefs about the possibilities of the practical workings of the fascist state. If men were rational and dynamic enough to be able to 'go beyond' Spengler and harmoniously to synthesise Nietzschean and Christian thought, then indeed they might be vigorous and self-sacrificing enough to choose and fashion a form of authoritative government that they could reasonably trust and obey – that might do its job without the safeguards traditionally imposed upon democratic governments just because of fears about the stupidities and corruptions of ordinary people wielding power. But such beliefs and hopes were still in the form of words: it was up to my father – as he himself would have admitted – to prove the worth of his words in action. In the meantime, as a result of fascists having taken Spengler and Nietzsche as their intellectual heroes, there was the odd impression that the challenge they had chosen to involve themselves with was one in which they must see that there was a strong chance of their defeat; either this, or they would have to have an ironic vision of the nature of success.

Spengler had specified that during the decay of a civilisation there would be times when the 'private and family policies of individual leaders' would hold sway; this would coincide with 'the inward decline of the nations into a formless population and constitution thereof as an Imperium of gradually-increasing crudity of despotism'. A symptom of this time would be the 'immense optical illusion' that 'everyone can demand something of the rest: we say "thou shalt" in the conviction that so-and-so in fact will, can and must be changed or fashioned or arranged conformably to the order; and our belief both in the efficacy of, and in our title to give, such orders is unshakeable'. Such a tendency to think that people can be ordered and arranged as if they were words was, Spengler continued to insist, a symptom of that which was self-defeating.

With regard to my father's interpretation of Nietzsche's idea of the superman there seemed also to be a confusion between facts and words. My father assumed that Nietzsche was using words as recommendations about how in practice things should be arranged: whereas Nietzsche for the most part himself seemed to say he was talking ironically: he was using words to describe people's hopes and illusions about how things should be arranged and just by this – the recognition of people's capacities for illusion – perhaps not to be trapped by them. Nietzsche's superman is someone who hopes by seeing people's struggles for power and their capacities to delude themselves about these, to have some power over himself; not, in any way except this, to have power over others.

There is in fact something of this ironic sort of optimism even in Spengler – though it is an optimism that neither his admirers nor his critics seemed to see. Spengler did not relent from his vision of the life-and-death cycle of all civilisations; what he did say might be unique about Western civilisation was its ability in some sense to be free of this not in practical terms but in terms of being aware of what the facts of its situation were: 'No culture is at liberty to choose the path and conduct of its thought; but here for the first time a culture can foresee the way that destiny has chosen for it'. It is by the use of this vision that we might yet 'set to work upon the formation of our own future' – not in the way of vainly willing to alter what is inexorable, but in the way of understanding what occurs and thus perhaps altering its style. There is some human freedom here – even power – but on a different level.

Both Spengler and especially Nietzsche were concerned with the fact that if words are used as orders or recommendations they often seem to bring about the opposite of what they set out to recommend; that if anything is positively to be altered it has to come about in its own way – influenced at the best by human efforts at understanding. Nietzsche dealt specifically with these ideas: he, and his superman, would laugh at themselves holding even such elusive hopes of power – or words might still run away with them. The way to deal with the 'inexorability of history' was to say to it – All right, go your own way. Then, because you were watching it, it might not.

When my father talked about Nietzsche he seemed both to see this and yet often not to see it: one of his favourite themes at the dinner table was to criticise what he saw as Nietzsche's idea of the 'Will to Power'. He took it that by this phrase Nietzsche was recommending as proper human behaviour something like the ordering of human beings as if they were monkeys in cages: but Nietzsche used the phrase (or so it seems to me) in the hope that by recognising such primitive tendencies a human might overcome them. My father would suggest that one could 'go beyond' what he saw as Nietzsche's 'Will to Power' by his, my father's, own recommendation of a 'Will to Achievement' – not the ordering of monkeys for the sake of exercising power, but the ordering of human beings for the sake of the enjoyment of a full and harmonious life – but still with the presupposition (seen as so disastrous by Spengler) that what was required of humans was the business of imposing order by will. But then – almost as part of the same oration at the dinner-table – my father's voice would move into a different key; his eyes would become distant, gentle; he would produce one of his favourite quotations from Nietzsche – the lines near the beginning of *Thus Spoke Zarathustra* which refer to the three stages in the development of humanity – that of the camel, of the lion, and of the child. My father would say – perhaps now even with something indeed of the quiet irony commended by Nietzsche – Ah the camel, we know the camel! that which only moves as a result of the carrot or the stick! and the lion, we know the lion do we not, that which wishes to impose order on monkeys in cages: but the child – what is the child? And then he would do his trick of flashing his eyes on and off as if they were a lighthouse. And those watching him and listening to him might think that they had a glimpse, somewhere in the mist, of what might be the child.

The word used by Spengler to describe modern Western civilisation was 'Faustian': this was the symbol of someone always searching, striving, looking towards the infinite and the unknown. What Faust was looking for, but never found, was some state that might be embraced with the simplicity perhaps of a child. My father came increasingly and almost self-consciously to see himself as Faustian. Some fifteen years after the beginning of his incursion into fascism he wrote an introduction to Goethe's *Faust* in which he saw clearly that the problem for Faust was one of the loss of the simplicity of innocence: Faust learned that evil could produce good; but he learned also that the knowledge did not absolve a man from the ethical distinction he had made between evil and good; so, with this paradoxical knowledge, how should he act then? It might be that there was nothing much to be 'acted' at this level; there was the need primarily for acceptance and understanding; this was the area of Nietzsche's 'beyond good and evil'. What might be required, indeed, was something of the spontaneity of a child. And was not this also a Christian concept; and so – a synthesis! My father would then smile, with his lighthouse eyes. However – and this was a problem too for Faust – my father was dedicated to action, was he not? How could he become like a child? The effort that might produce effortlessness – were not such paradoxes anathema to men of action? After a while my father would let the vision of the child go. It seemed a grace that he sometimes had it.

It was Mephistopheles in Goethe's *Faust* who saw that the spur of evil often engenders good; that without this spur life in the form we know it might not go on. In *Faust* this matter of good and evil is split: it is Mephistopheles who consciously works the evil and Faust who hopes for the outcome of good; the two are a decadence from the child, whose innocence is that he is one. If men allow this split, their evil inevitably becomes planned like that of Mephistopheles; then guilt entraps them like that of Faust. This is perhaps an inevitable result of the demand for dynamic 'action' – the belief that a person can manipulate ends and means as if they were words.

C. J. Jung, whom during the war my father came to admire, wrote:*

In Faust we see the 'hungering for the infinite' born of inner contradiction and dichotomy, the eschatological expectation of the Great Fulfilment. In him we experience the loftiest flight of the mind, and the descent into the depths of guilt and darkness; and still worse, a fall so low that Faust sinks to the level of a mountebank and a wholesale murderer as a result of his pact with the devil. Faust is split, and sets up an 'evil' outside himself in the shape of Mephistopheles to serve as an alibi in case of need. He knows nothing of what has happened ... we never get the impression that he has real insight or suffers genuine remorse. His avowed and unavowed worship of success stands in the way of any moral reflection throughout, obscuring the ethical conflict so that Faust's moral personality remains misty.

Collected Works, Volume 10.

My father did not personally allow himself to end up like this: there was always something that constrained him like the vision of the child. He could see himself, that is, sometimes in the style of what Goethe called 'sweet self-irony'; he had little 'avowed worship of success'. But then often enough publicly, like some actor, he would be off careering down his slopes again – like some runaway tram, roaring – on his double rails of manipulator and, eventually, victim. Every actor, I suppose, likes to play the part of Mephistopheles; some like to play the striving but tormented Faust. No one – because it is to do with what acting is not – can quite act the child.

CHAPTER 5

Lord Rothermere

In January 1934 the British Union of Fascists was given a boost by Lord Rothermere who wrote an article in the *Daily Mail* headlined 'Hurrah for the Blackshirts!'. This announced that from now on the BUF would have the backing of his entire Rothermere Press – which as well as the *Daily Mail* included the *Evening News* and the *Sunday Dispatch*. Lord Rothermere declared – 'The Blackshirt movement is the organised effort of the younger generation to break this stranglehold which senile politicians have so long maintained on our public affairs'. As if in support of this attitude he admitted – 'Being myself in the middle sixties, I know how stealthily and steadily that seventh decade saps one's powers and stiffens one's prejudices.'

He praised Italy and Germany: 'These are beyond all doubt the best ruled nations in Europe today. From repeated visits to both under their present regimes I can vouch for it that in no other land does the over-whelming majority of the people feel such confidence and pride in its rulers'. He denied that the BUF was under foreign influence: 'the socialists who jeer at the principles and uniform of the Blackshirt being of foreign origin forget that the founder and High Priest of their own creed was the German Jew Karl Marx'. He insisted that the BUF was 'the only force in Britain' working for 'national discipline and organisation'.

However in the letter of January 30th 1934 from Count Grandi to Mussolini quoted in Chapter 3 Grandi wrote of Mussolini's influence over Rothermere: 'Mosley also told me, with what seemed like special gratitude, that he owed the definitive conversion of Lord Rothermere entirely to you ... a word from you was enough to put Rothermere quite suddenly beside Mosley'. Grandi went on to tell Mussolini of his, Grandi's, part in persuading Mosley to accept the backing of Rothermere –

In the May conversations I had with Mosley before Christmas I managed to overcome his doubts by pointing out the immediate and practical advantages that would accrue to his movement by suddenly gaining, without effort or expense, the group of newspapers which, because of its circulation and its influence on the masses in Great Britain (above all in the provinces) is by far the strongest of them all. The fact that Rothermere is only a second rate figure in politics (in spite of his claim to be the *deus ex machina* of English politics) is just another reason for not taking too seriously any harm that may later come out of being associated with him.

The 'harm' that might come from an association with Lord Rothermere, and my father's 'doubts', were, it seemed, due to the fact that Rothermere was known as a difficult and obstinate man to work with; also he saw the blackshirts not as a revolutionary force but rather as guardians of some extreme and imperialist right wing. Lord Rothermere was a shy, ponderous man who had pioneered modern tabloid newspaper techniques; he had been launched into politics by Lloyd George as Air Minister from 1916 to 1918; he had joined with Lord Beaverbrook in a crusade for Empire Free Trade in 1929. But it was a fact that the BUF agreed with him in advocating a closed home-and-empire free trade area; and Lord Rothermere was also attracted to the BUF's call for deeds rather than words. A *Daily Mail* leader-writer had the line, perhaps picked up dubiously from my father – 'As Goethe has said, action is the first and most important of worldly things.'

There were several people in the public eye taking the BUF seriously at this time. Lloyd George announced – 'Sir Oswald Mosley is a very able man and he is making considerable headway.' Bernard Shaw lectured to the Fabian Society – 'Sir Oswald Mosley is a very interesting man to read just now: one of the few people who is thinking and writing about real things and not about figments and phrases ... I know you dislike him, because he looks like a man who has some physical courage and is going to do something and that is a terrible thing ... you instinctively hate him because you do not know where he will land you, and he evidently means to uproot some of you.' The press reported that in the month following the announcement of Lord Rothermere's backing enrolments into the BUF at the London headquarters alone went up to over 1,000 in a week; and there were by now established over 300 branches throughout the country. However Aneurin Bevan was reported in the press as echoing the possibility that

Grandi had been at pains to dismiss – 'Nothing could do more damage to Sir Oswald Mosley's little movement than the sudden adherence of the Rothermere press.'

The part of Grandi's letter about Rothermere is of additional interest in that it shows how Grandi saw himself concerned in the BUF's affairs:

It is in the provinces they must begin and from where they must move to the siege and to the assault of the city: our own now proven revolutionary experience has taught us this. In fact, what happened in our own revolution will happen with Rothermere: the reactionaries believed they could use us to defeat socialism and democracy and then be in charge themselves; when they realised that the threat of socialism was a joke compared to the revolution that you [Mussolini] were preparing, they were alarmed and tried to withdraw, but it was too late.

Grandi at this time (January 1934) was of course showing considerable admiration for my father –

From the very first day I arrived here Mosley appeared to me to be the expression of something absolutely new and unexpected in England, where no one – I don't say 'dares' – even imagines he could fall short of the standards of traditional Victorian patriotism ... Mosley doesn't give a damn for Queen Victoria, he says this and prints it to the scandal of everyone, and says he wants to bring back Tudor England, the England of Henry VIII and Elizabeth, the England that wasn't 'natural' but sectarian, that ate oxen roasted on the spit, chopped off people's heads, tilled the soil and committed piracy on the high seas. I remember the historian Cesare Balbo's definition of strong peoples – 'peoples possessed by civilised barbarism'.

During the month of January 1934 there were further articles by Lord Rothermere in the *Daily Mail* on 'Give the Blackshirts a Helping Hand' and 'The Blackshirts Will Stop War'. There were articles by Oswald Mosley not so much on policy, as on his resolution to get things done. By February he was writing –

The Blackshirts have only been organised in Britain for the last 16 months: in these early days they have advanced far more rapidly than any fascist movement in the world. Not only in mere numbers, but in organisation, in spirit and in discipline we have reached a point which our predecessors had not reached until a relatively short space before they came to power.

The mood in the Black House was that the B U F would probably be in power within twelve months: people were called pessimists who forecast a time-lag of two or three years. The ex-District Inspector whose memoirs have been quoted before remembers –

Day and night it [the Black House] buzzed with activity. Typewriters rattled in administrative offices, printing presses clattered out the *Blackshirt* – the first B U F weekly paper. In one lecture room a lesson on election law would be in progress; in another aspiring speakers would be put through their hesitant paces; elsewhere the young tough men of 'I' Squad were being taught their boxing and judo. Cars roared in and out of the transport yard, and all the time there was a constant stream of callers and enquirers, some of whom were well known figures in the literary, professional, business and sporting worlds.

One of these figures from the literary world was Wyndham Lewis, who would come 'hurrying in with his hat pulled down and his coat collar up around his ears': another was Ezra Pound, who somewhat later wrote a pamphlet for the B U F entitled *What is Money for*. This is as difficult to understand, and as full of odd capital letters, as are some of his *Cantos*.

Amongst the cars that roared in and out of the transport yard were five large vans with protective plating at the sides and wire mesh over the windows which had been acquired early in 1934 and were used by the 'I' Squad to ferry them between headquarters and stormy meetings. They were described by the press variously as being 'bottle-proof, capable of holding thirty people and having a top speed of 55 mph'; and as being 'bullet proof, capable of holding twenty people and having a top speed of 65 mph'. In answer to questions about whether or not they resembled the cars used by American gangsters, a B U F spokesman explained – 'In principle they are the same, but the design is different'.

Lord Rothermere put money into the B U F: he also proposed to my father a scheme for manufacturing and marketing B U F cigarettes – he would produce the cigarettes and members of the movement would distribute them. He thought this would be enormously profitable both for himself and for the movement.

As enrolments into the BUF increased (at the height of its popularity in 1934 there were estimated to be between 30,000 and 40,000 members) there was an increasing problem of indiscipline. When Aneurin Bevan had said that nothing could do the BUF more damage than the backing of the Rothermere press he had probably meant that it was Lord Rothermere's personality that would cause confusion; but more important was the fact that the publicity was bringing in so many recruits of all kinds that it was difficult to sift and to control them – and this, in a movement whose *raison d'être* was that it should be able to demonstrate order, was serious. Our District Inspector remembers that as a result of the *Daily Mail* articles the BUF seemed to have 'drawn to itself almost every unstable person and adventurer of either sex ... genuine people who had been attracted by the programme and policy felt that they could not afford to be associated with the types congregated at the local district headquarters, and either refrained from enrolling or, having joined, soon faded out'. This was written by someone who remained a devoted follower of Mosley all his life. He added – 'In these spots nothing remained but a bad odour, still lingering three or four years later.'

It seems to have been one of the peculiarities of fascists and national socialists that for all their emphasis on discipline and obedience to a leader they depended for their *élan* very much on the freedom of lieutenants to go their own way. This was perhaps an inevitable outcome of the appeal to dynamism and heroism. In Italian Fascism and German National Socialism these tendencies were to a certain extent harnessed and unified because there was a common advocacy of warfare and a common view of enemies and scapegoats. But with the BUF's insistence that what it was striving for was peace and that enemies should only be fought in self-defence, there was the chance for every would-be gang-leader to impose his own interpretations. There was the continuing problem about the BUF speakers who disobeyed the orders to say nothing that could be taken as anti-semitic: this problem often now centred on William Joyce. In January 1934 in a speech at Chiswick he said in reply to a question about 'class war' – 'I don't regard Jews as a class, I regard them as a privileged misfortune'. He perorated, 'the flower or weed of Israel shall never grow in ground fertilised by British blood!'. The *Jewish World* called on Mosley to issue 'an uncompromising official repudiation' of Joyce in the light of his, Mosley's, own stated policy: it argued (in perhaps tellingly ambiguous phrasing) – 'either his or Mr Joyce's scurrilous claptrap is the authentic revelation'. But if the would-be toughs of the BUF were not going to be allowed to find enemies against whom to exercise even their verbal aggressions – in what spirit was their aggressive energy to be kept going?

With the indiscriminate flood of recruits there were more haphazard stresses at headquarters. A man called George Crellin, or Captain Thornton, joined the movement and announced that he was a 'Director of Finance'; on the strength of this he hired a large car, and a horse on which to ride in Hyde Park: when it was discovered that he was a notorious con-man he was thrown out of the BUF and joined the British Fascists under the name of Captain Latch. There was a man called Jones who on enrolment persuaded the senior BUF officer in Sussex to appoint him a District Officer; he then ran off with not only the senior officer's wife but her child's nanny; when Jones was apprehended the BUF officer told the police that he thought Jones was acting 'either for the Labour Party at Brighton or the Co-op or both'. There was a certain Richardson who had got into the Black House (on his own admission) to sell to newspapers inside stories of what went on there; when he was exposed and expelled he sold a story to the papers of how he had been beaten up by fascist officials and made to drink castor oil. The officials charged with these assaults were acquitted through lack of evidence; but of course what stayed in the public's mind were headlines in newspapers such as – 'Flogging alleged' or 'Castor oil punishment denied'. This was unfair: but the leadership of the BUF did seem in some respects to be hedging its bets. It protested its innocence in matters of violence, but it still was at pains to project the sort of image of ruthlessness that was the hallmark of Mussolini.

There was a balancing act required here that called for a fine degree of judgment: the Leader himself could spell out his instructions in words – no force to be used unless provoked, a revolution to be won by the example of men standing with their hands by their sides – and if every predicament could have been referred to him and his decision obeyed, then perhaps the spirit of a balancing act might have been maintained. But as the movement grew and the expected crisis of chaos did not materialise – then where was all the canalisation of energy to go? Except for the spasmodic violence used in defence or retaliation at meetings the energy had to be turned inwards: and as with most hierarchical organisations dedicated to discipline there were thus favouritisms, jealousies, jockeyings for position – above all concerning questions about who should have the ear of the Leader. Oswald Mosley would turn up in his office: in theory he would be available for anyone who had information to give to him; in practice, power depended on who was in a position to let their own information through and to get the information of other people blocked. A system designed to allow everyone dynamically to perform his own function became a matter of court intrigue.

In an increasingly powerful position at headquarters was Neil Francis-Hawkins, who moved from being Adjutant of the Defence Force to the Director General's office and was soon to become Director General himself – a position (after Robert Forgan had gone) second only to the Leader. In the words of our District Inspector, Francis-Hawkins was –

> entirely devoted to the movement. He spent between ten and twelve hours daily at his office while most weekends were given to participation in the outside activities. He expected his subordinates to give an almost equal amount of time to their duties; those who went home after a mere eight or nine hours at their desks were labelled 'clock-watchers' and denounced as unworthy of the cause they served. As many of them had wives or young families, domestic unhappiness too frequently arose. 'Wife-trouble' became one of the recognised occupational hazards of British Fascism.

Francis-Hawkins was a bachelor who lived in a flat in Hampstead with his sister; he was thought to be homosexual: in evidence for this was the hostility he showed to married men and the favouritism he seemed to grant to the unmarried men who formed a group around him known as his 'Mafia'. Francis-Hawkins' aim was to produce a loyal and obedient fascist force; it does not seem likely that he was struck by subtleties such as that solidarity can sometimes produce a deadening constellation of lies; that shows of strength are sometimes counter-productive since they awaken people's resentments and fears. But then these were the sort of subtleties which, when he was talking of politics rather than of literature, were apt to by-pass the Leader.

There was one area early in 1934 in which the BUF did try to be active in a more constructive way than that of the ejection of its opponents from its meetings: members became involved in what was known as the 'Tithe War'. There had been a spontaneous protest by East Anglian farmers against the payment of tithes – levies raised in mediaeval times in the form of produce for the upkeep of the church and which were now payable to the Church Commission in the form of a cash tax. In the impoverished circumstances of farming in England at this time farmers were objecting to the fact that only one section of the community should be called on for this tax; they were refusing to pay, and police and bailiffs were moving in to 'distrain' their property. It had been a particular aspect of BUF policy that British agriculture should be protected; local District Officers thus saw the chance of a form of action which would be constructive and charitable. They were given legal advice that if members of the Fascist Defence Force went to farms at the invitation of farmers and just 'by their passive presence' prevented bailiffs from doing their job, they would be within the law.

Members went to farms and dug ditches and built barricades to make it difficult for bailiffs to carry away equipment and livestock; then they waited, in tents, while bailiffs and onlookers leaned on fences and watched. All this was photographed by the local press; small crowds turned out; there was genuine interest in what might be the outcome of such a challenge to authority. Then government lawyers dug up an ancient statue under which fascists, just by their presence on the farm, could be charged with 'conspiring together to effect a public mischief': nineteen of them were arrested and carried away by police. They made no resistance. At the Old Bailey they pleaded guilty and were conditionally discharged by a Judge who said, 'I am told you are good fellows, and I hope you will remain good fellows, realising how badly advised you were in this matter.' The blackshirts had abided by their policy of doing nothing against the law; but as a result, a self-proclaimed dynamic movement had been made to look somewhat ridiculous.

The faith and hope of the fascists was always with their Leader. When he returned from his illness in the spring of 1934 he held his largest indoor meeting yet – on April 22nd in London at the Albert Hall. There was an audience of 10,000; both those within and those without the movement felt that if anything positive and effective was to be created, it would depend on the will and the talents of the Leader.

It is difficult nowadays to recall the style of a large blackshirt meeting: it had something of the atmosphere of a pop concert. There were the warm-up bands; the waiting; the dramatic entrance of the star. At the Albert Hall a blackshirt orchestra played the songs to the tunes of *Giovinezza* and the *Horst Wessel Lied*: also a new song that had been specially written for the occasion by members of the BUF – the words by E. D. Randall and the music by Selwyn Watson. This was entitled simply 'Mosley!' and began –

> Mosley: Leader of thousands!
> Hope of our manhood, we proudly hail thee!
> Raise we this song of allegiance
> For we are sworn and shall not fail thee.

Lead us! We fearlessly follow
To conquest and freedom – or else to death!
From coast to coast throughout the Motherland
Rings out the summons of the chosen band.

After the singing of this, the *Manchester Guardian* reported –

Just before eight the spotlights were turned on to the long gangway
leading through the arena to the platform and a procession of twelve
standard bearers marched in carrying alternately Union Jacks and
Fascist banners. The standard bearers grouped themselves round the
organ, the spotlights swung back to the main entrance, and there
stood the Man of Destiny.... Slowly he paced across the hall, chest
out, handsome head flung back, while his followers, every man on
his feet, cheered and cried 'Hail Mosley! Mosley! Mosley!'

From the platform beneath the organ he spoke, without notes, for
an hour and a half; there were no interruptions and no violent incidents;
for much of the time his voice was calm, quiet, almost intoning. He
spoke of his movement's being not racialist nor anti-semitic; of its commitment to seek only by constitutional means to come to power. When
it had achieved power, it would alter the present Parliamentary system
in that the government would give itself power to govern by order;
Parliament would only be summoned if there was public demand for
a vote to see whether or not the government should continue. With
such a safeguard (no details of its operation were given) a government
could not be called dictatorial. After a time, it was true, the present
Parliamentary structure would be abolished and a corporate state would
be set up on a basis of occupational franchise. This would –

place every industry in the country under the direct control of a
self-governing corporation on which will sit representatives of
employers, workers and consumers. These will fix by negotiation
the rates of wages, hours of work and prices and terms of competition which will be legally binding for an industry as a whole.
These corporations will send representatives to a national council
of corporations which will function as an industrial parliament. Here
matters of general financial policy will be settled, and the operations
of the various industries controlled and regulated in the interests of
the nation as a whole.

There was always a large part of a speech by my father that was calmly and rationally presented: sometimes his critics said that this was too large a part – that he overestimated his audience by assuming it could follow the technicalities of his arguments. But the flow of fact and argument gave an impression of great control and authority. And then there would be a change; he would stand back from the microphone as if he were a boxer sizing up an opponent before a knock-out attack: he was coming to his peroration. There is still in existence a gramophone record of the end of this Albert Hall speech; my father's voice comes out lashing like some great sea: it is pulverising: it is also, from a human being, like something carried far away beyond sense. It sends shivers up and down the spine – of both wonder and alarm – what is it all for, this yell for immolation? People at the end of such a speech of my father's were on their feet and cheering: it was as if they had been lifted high on a wave; what did it matter if they were hurled against, or over the top of, a cliff?

Let us take this vast Empire of ours, this heritage of our race won by our fathers and forefathers, and let us build up a civilisation far greater than the world has ever known.

Again and again in the long story of the human race, races have struggled up to nations and nations up to mighty empires; have scaled the heights of history and have thought they were safe: and now lit by the flame of such high inspiration this movement rises from the very soul of England to give all, to dare all, that England may live in greatness and in glory.

CHAPTER 6

Schoolboy Patterns 1

The private school I had been sent to shortly before my mother's death was Abinger Hill, near Dorking in Surrey. It was a pleasantly anarchic place run on progressive lines: boys were allowed to do much of their work in their own time; masters played an aloof and somewhat formal role like that of gods. This left mundane matters largely in the hands of boys: we ourselves were free to exercise, and observe, some of the strange patterns of impulses that are at the back of humans' dramatic and grandiose pretensions.

We formed groups, or gangs, for self-identification and self-protection: for this each needed a style, and apparently some mode of aggression. We roamed in the corridors and woods like mediaeval actors or bandits: I was a member of a small gang that affected sophistication. We hoped by this to boost ourselves and ward off enemies; we were like the lizards that puff up their throats to make themselves seem more formidable than they are. We saw ourselves as aesthetes: I think our idea of an aesthete was the sort of young man who might whizz between roadhouses in his sports car on the Dorking by-pass. In my gang was a boy called Plaister and a boy called Mellor and someone called Titus, with whom much of the school was in love. It seemed in keeping with sophistication to be in love. I have an image now of our small group wandering through the Surrey landscape like some illustration to *Don Quixote* or *Winnie the Pooh*. Plaister was tall and rather languid; Mellor was short like Sancho Panza. Titus was like the drawing of the boy going up to bed dragging his faithful animal behind him.

We had our private language; which was of the throw-away, self-deprecating type probably gleaned from P. G. Wodehouse. Gangs need some private language – to make them feel separate from the crowd, and amongst themselves to discourage class distinctions.

We did not pay much attention to games (the school magazine reported 'Plaister often bowled well in the nets but not otherwise': 'Mosley – another bowler who did not come up to scratch') and we pretended to pay no attention at all to work, though at least two of us showed we were quite clever. Our aim was to get as far away and as often as we could from the purlieus of the school; to establish our little kingdom, like that of characters in *As You Like It*, in the forest.

One of my memories of prep-school is of an almost perpetual hunger. The shop in the village was out of bounds: we were conspicuous in our brown corduroy shorts and brown-and-orange jerseys. We tried out various disguises: Plaister got hold of a pork-pie hat; we affected drawling Dorking-by-pass voices. But for the most part we relied on bringing back food from home; we would store it in tin boxes in the woods; here we would gather and munch, like badgers. I remember ham, and butter, and bits of bread that were called baps. One day when we were gnawing away under the trees we were come upon by Mr Tunnard Moore, the cricket master, who had followed us under the impression perhaps that we might be up to more nefarious practices. When he saw that what we were up to was food, he went on his way – informing us briefly of the dangers of ptomaine poisoning. We learned – it is a fact, is it not, that gods do not seem very interested in the needs of people for food?

With regard to sex, which gods as well as humans did seem interested in, we picked up and swapped bits of technical information as if they were conkers or sweets. The would-be sophistication of my own small gang meant that we were somewhat la-di-da about the dirty stories; but the limericks! I still remember the limericks: our sexual education was imbued with such legendary figures as the Plumber of Dee; the Young Girl of Pitlochry. We hoped to find out more details about their strange experiences: our practical interest in this respect became concentrated on Miss Hedge, the Art Mistress. It seemed to be sophisticated to have curiosity about Miss Hedge; but how on earth were we to satisfy this? There was a time I think in my third year when part of the school buildings burned down (it was rumoured that the fire had started after my future brother-in-law, aged ten, had been smoking in an attic; in later life, according to mood, he used either indignantly to deny this or to confirm it) and many of the staff had to be accommodated in pre-fabricated huts on the cricket field. This gave our gang the idea that a positive attitude might be adopted towards Miss Hedge – we would get up at dawn one day and try to get a glimpse of her through her bedroom window. Was not this the sort of thing, we imagined, that young men might be up to on the Dorking by-pass?

What was odd about this incident was that we made no effort at concealment: bravado seemed to be part of the required experience: perhaps this is why I have such a clear memory of it. We awoke with an alarm-clock; set off into the dawn; how wonderful to be so heroic and so alive! As we approached the cricket field we became overcome by fits of giggles. In the event I think we got the wrong window and looked in not upon Miss Hedge, the Art Mistress, but on Miss Someone-else the Under-Matron. And of course we were seen; but we wandered back to our dormitory happy. Had we not completed our mission? And was not this what life was about? Later, when the headmaster questioned us, we said we had gone birds' nesting. We were duly beaten.

The business of being beaten played not a large part in fact in the school routine: it loomed larger in our imaginations. It seemed to be to do with drama, with challenge, with the involvement in great events. To be beaten meant going up to the door of the headmaster's study and waiting outside; others went in first; through the closed door one heard an almost interminable rumbling; this turned out to be the furniture being moved. Then there were six fearsome cracks like pistol shots. Then someone would stagger out clutching himself like people do through saloon doors in western films. When one went into the headmaster's study he seemed as nervous as oneself: and so in the end, what a weird, scruffy shoot-out! But afterwards, there was the rallying round some boy who claimed to have sure legal knowledge that, if it could be shown that skin had been broken, the headmaster could be prosecuted for assault: in which case what an amazing turning of the tables! There was much happy and legalistic discussion and inspection about this – quite like politics.

An even more bizarre way in which impulses and fascinations expressed themselves was in a school craze known as womb-fighting. Two boys would come across each other in a passageway or changing room (how much of school life seemed to take place in changing rooms!) and one boy would crouch, placing a forearm across his stomach, and with the other would grope outwards as if it were the claw of a crab: this was a challenge for the other boy to do the same. The fight would be, symbolically, to see who could tear out the other's 'womb': in practice, I suppose, it was a means of giving and sustaining a massive tickling. (A later vulgarisation of this craze was ball-fighting, an altogether more hostile and destructive ritual). Perhaps in its origins all masculine brawling is a desire to get back to (to get one's own back on?) the lovely but terrible tweaks and tickles of the mother: it is the impossibility of this, that leads to virulence.

As time went on the formation of gangs and alliances which is the style of any society took on at school a more formally grown-up air. The fact that my father was Leader of the British Union of Fascists had, of course, been noted; I had for a while been called by one of the masters (fairly affectionately) 'Baby Blackshirt'. Boys were not instinctively interested in such things: what mattered to us about our parents was that their appearance should not be embarrassing, and what sort of car they turned up in at weekends. I scored quite well in this respect when my father's chauffeur Mr Perrett came to pick me up in the dashing Bentley: also my Aunt Irene's huge Packard, which was like a hearse, stood me in quite good stead. But then there came a time when grown-up politics did impinge on what was anyway boys' liking for rivalry; this was in 1935 when Italy invaded Abyssinia. The war of course was the subject of newspaper headlines: it caught the school's imagination, like any craze. I wrote to my father –

Darling Daddy,   Sunday 6th October
Two parties have sprung up here, one for the Abbysinians and the other for the Italians. I am the leader of the Italians, and this afternoon we are having a huge fight in the woods. The Abbysinians are the bigger, but we have some good people and are hoping to win. The Abbysinians started their party first, so I thought it would be fun to start an Italian one.

I had taken it for granted, of course, that I should be 'Italian': my loyalty to my father was unquestionable. But I was over-optimistic (as indeed my father often was) about the strength of the forces on my side: Abinger Hill School, being 'progressive', consisted of boys whose parents were predominantly left-wing. I think my 'some good people' consisted of scarcely more than my loyal friend Titus and our mutual friend Frank, who happened to be the son of the Government Chief Whip. Surrounding our small colonial outpost in the woods the Abyssinians were legion: they came down on us in the evening, I remember, as we sat in our small tent; I like to think we went down bravely, like Gordon at Khartoum.

This was the first time I remember having any opinion about politics. I had, I think, been sent weekly copies of my father's paper *Blackshirt*: now I would explain to the benighted left-wing natives in the school – Do you not see that Mussolini is bringing culture and civilisation to a backward Africa? Is it not this that the British have done for hundreds of years with their glorious Empire?

The sort of books I read at this time were those by Sapper and Leslie Charteris and (perhaps this was somewhat later) Dornford Yates. These told of cool, relentless men who made sardonic quips as they dealt with anti-imperialist villains; there were killings but no pain; the enemy were members of an evil world-wide conspiracy of 'aliens' who could be thwarted only by small bands of self-professed 'saints'. All this fitted in with what I had gleaned from the world – both from the arbitrariness of the school world in which one's sanity was preserved by one's gang; also from the grown-up world where there were, were there not, the dark forces of which my father spoke that were spreading and preventing the introduction of order. However, towards the end of my time at Abinger Hill I remember being introduced to and reading Aldous Huxley's *Antic Hay*: this was a revelation. It told of a world of people who were indeed humorous and detached; but whose virtues were concerned not with the thwarting of gigantic machinations but with ways in which pretensions of machinations might, with artistry, be seen as funny – and thus might even best be thwarted?

What I remember most about Abinger Hill is the laughter: there was the impression sometimes that one might take off with suppressed laughter: laughter of course often had to be suppressed, this was the style of the world one lived in. There was a boy called Fawcett who, in the middle of daily prayers, once farted; this was no ordinary fart, it was the most drawn-out, painstaking, trumpet-cry one had ever heard – Roland's call at Roncesvalles; Siegfried's horn in his wood. This burst in upon the Prayer of St Chrysostom or whatever; the headmaster told Fawcett quietly to leave the room. For the rest of us it was as if the pressures were too great; we were lifted like rockets to some beatific vision; several others had to leave the room. I think Abinger Hill was a good school in that it allowed us to see things as slightly ridiculous: that this was not incompatible with a beatific vision.

I remember almost nothing of the classroom work at Abinger Hill: such information seemed to be taken in like stores on to an ocean liner at night. Latin verbs and geometrical theorems appeared to have nothing to do with anything real outside: still, they were perhaps representative of what was fantastical in the interests of the grown-up world. These continued to break into school life from time to time. I remember once talking to my friend Titus about our parents and the parents of some of our friends: he said – But you and I, we're different, aren't we? I did not know what he meant. I wondered – We are more clever? In love? Then I realised – he was referring to something about what the grown-up world called 'class'. I was not able to make much of this – neither of the fact that the grown-up world seemed to think so often in terms of class, nor of my own blankness towards my friend's suggestion. Perhaps I liked to think that my family was unique, incomparable – nothing to do with anything so vulgar as being upper-class. Was not my father after all a rich, ex-socialist, would-be dictator fascist baronet?

One of the activities I remember enjoying at this time was the founding of a school film society which I ran in collaboration with my friend Julian Mond: we hired films from a library in London and showed them on my mother's old projector to audiences who paid a penny or two entrance fee. Then one summer the school put on an ambitious performance of *Twelfth Night* and press-men came down to take photographs of the scene; for a reason I did not at first understand they insisted on my friend Julian Mond and me being photographed together. Later I read the caption to the photograph in the *News Review* – 'Jewish peer Lord Melchett's son Julian assists his schoolfellow Nicholas son of the Fascist Leader Sir Oswald Mosley'.

Quite often at this time I had recurring nightmares. There was one in which I was drinking water from a tumbler and the tumbler suddenly fastened itself over my mouth thus making it impossible for me to breathe: this had, I suppose, something to do with my stammer. In another I was by an ornamental pond upon which brightly-painted toy boats were floating to and fro; looking down, I became filled with terror.

The most lasting image of myself that I remember from Abinger Hill is of me as a machine within which I lived and which I controlled by moving levers as if I were like men in white coats facing dials; I had to tread carefully, as if I was walking through minefields; what was important, was to ensure the efficient working of my machine. I was something inside myself keeping a solicitous eye on myself; what went on outside was another matter. Occasionally there were miraculous moments in the woods for instance with friends when my machinery and that of the whole world seemed suddenly to click into gear: oneself became oneself in relation to everything. But for the most part one was one's own search for some holy grail. There were nights when one walked up a dark lane from the school to an outside dormitory building; there were all these little bits and pieces whirling about inside; there were also the distant stars. And there were connections: was not the network still oneself? Of course, one could not talk much about this: one could laugh – make a joke or pun or something. What was it, this grid, this riddle, this holy grail?

CHAPTER 7

Olympia

The success of the Albert Hall meeting in April 1934 and the continued backing of the Rothermere Press with the resulting influx of recruits had made members of the BUF imagine they were being carried forwards on a wave that might bring them to power within a few years. This enthusiasm made their opponents also feel there might be cause to think this.

The Albert Hall meeting had been orderly: Mosley had got his message across to an audience of 10,000. It was still believed at this time that promulgation of the spoken word was the way to be effective in politics: there was evidence for this from the careers of Mussolini and Hitler. There was one auditorium in London bigger than the Albert Hall – that of Olympia. The BUF arranged to hold a meeting there on 7th June 1934, to which they hoped to attract members of the un-committed public and especially the establishment intelligentsia who might be ready in the contemporary political climate to take a serious look at fascism.

The communists saw that the fascists had scored heavily at the Albert Hall by their demonstration of good order and discipline: it mattered less what had been said than that the fascist claim had seemed to be justified that it was a movement which could act cleanly and efficiently. Both sides therefore saw the meeting at Olympia as crucial. For the fascists it was a chance to demonstrate their disciplined strength to an audience more than usually sophisticated: for communists it was vital to try to expose the fascists as desperadoes and thugs.

There is little dispute about what actually occurred at Olympia. Contention about interpretation has continued.

The fascists planned, as they always planned, for the sort of orderly meeting which was necessary if the Leader was to be heard: the Defence

Force was given the same instructions as it was always given – not to use force to get rid of hecklers until they had been given due warning; not to strike first, and even then not to use unnecessary violence. It might have been a fault that no special instructions were given in the light of the style of the communist propaganda about this particular meeting: it might have been seen that attitudes more subtle than usual might be required if the image of discipline was to be maintained.

The communists made no attempt to conceal their intention to break up the meeting. On 26th May an announcement appeared in the *Daily Worker*:

In connection with the great anti-Fascist counter-demonstration which is being organised by the London District Committee of the Communist Party on June 7th when Mosley's Blackshirts are holding a Fascist Rally at Olympia, the following are the arrangements:

Marches will be organised from five different parts of London in the late afternoon to arrive in Hammersmith Road in the vicinity of Olympia at 6.30 p.m. Workers who cannot participate in the marches are asked to rally to Hammersmith Road from 6.30 p.m. onwards after leaving work. Arrangements should be made in the localities for parties of workers to travel on the underground and to obtain cheap facilities for parties.

The District Committee of the Communist Party have sent letters to the London Labour Party, London Trades Union Council, the I.L.P., and District Committees of Trades Unions, inviting their cooperation in the counter-demonstration.

There were further notices in the *Daily Worker* during the coming days: on 7th June it published a map illustrating the routes to Olympia and announced –

Inside the large hall and outside the challenge of Mosley will be met by the determined workers ... The workers' counteraction will cause them to tremble. All roads lead to Olympia tonight!

After the event there were accusations by each side that the other had armed itself with weapons – truncheons, knuckledusters, iron bars, and so on. The fascists denied that they used weapons and there is no hard evidence to the contrary. Communists made no secret about their carrying of weapons. Philip Toynbee described in his book *Friends Apart* how before Olympia he and Esmond Romilly 'bought knuckledusters at a Drury Lane ironmonger and I well remember the exaltation of trying them on'. Toynbee and Romilly were teenage schoolboys: they took it for granted that communists thus armed themselves before such a confrontation. Claud Cockburn wrote of these days when he was a communist demonstrator: 'It is fashionable to allege that we were starry-eyed idealists, but we certainly knew where to put the razor-blades in the potato when it came to a fight.'

Outside the hall when members of the audience arrived they had to push their way through a crowd of two or three thousand anti-fascists who were held back by police. There were the usual chants of – 'One two three four, What are the Fascists for, lechery treachery hunger and war'; 'Two three four five, we want Mosley dead or alive.' Most of the audience managed to get through; individual Blackshirts who were caught on the edge of the crowd were punched and kicked.

Inside, there were 13,000 seats costing between a shilling and seven-and-sixpence: communists had bought or forged tickets (some, it was said, had been won in a *Daily Mail* competition) but it would have been impossible in any event to try to stop agitators getting in because there were 2,000 seats available free on the day. Communist demonstrators seated themselves round the hall strategically in groups; some were said to be wearing blackshirts to add to the planned confusion.

There were the usual warm-up procedures of fanfares and songs: the start of the meeting was delayed owing to the trouble people outside were having in getting through. Then, in Philip Toynbee's words –

> The Leader strode into the arc lights. He was flanked by four blond young men, and a platoon of flag-waving blackshirts followed in their wake. The procession moved very slowly down the aisle, amid shouts, screams, and bellows of admiration; amid two forests of phallic, upraised arms. Sir Oswald held one arm at his side, thumb in leather belt: the other flapped nonchalantly from time to time as he turned a high chin to inspect us.

As soon as Mosley started speaking the interruptions began: individuals or groups chanted 'Fascism means murder!' or just 'Down with Mosley!' It had been learned from previous meetings that even with a battery of loudspeakers a speech in such conditions could not be heard. The speaker gave the usual warning – If the interrupters did not stop, they would be thrown out. They did not stop. Blackshirt stewards moved towards them.

There is little dispute even in detail about the sort of thing that now

took place. It was obviously in the fascists' interests to eject the interrupters quickly and efficiently or, at the worst, after what could be
seen by the uncommitted part of the audience as a fair fight: it was
in the interests of the interrupters to make the fascist stewards appear
to be incompetent and brutal. It was in this contest concerning the
fascists' image – as opposed to that of who simply won the fight –
that the communists came out on top.

The interrupters were spaced out in the hall so that when one lot
was being dealt with by stewards another lot would start: what seemed
to be a single interrupter was suddenly backed by a large number when
one or two stewards moved in to deal with him. There was what seemed
to be the use of women interrupters to taunt the stewards, who were
then fought by men. The result was that after an initial attempt to
stick to discipline the stewards, under provocation, manifestly got out
of control. Eye-witnesses who professed to have begun as neutral reported – 'Again and again as five or six fascists carried out an interrupter
by arms and legs several other fascists were engaged in hitting and
kicking his helpless body' (Geoffrey Lloyd MP): 'In the corridor a
young man.... was being chased by a horde of Blackshirts: some
collared him by the legs, some by the arms, and held in this way he
was beaten on the head by any fascist who could get near him' (Rev.
Dick Sheppard). While this sort of thing was going on in the auditorium
Mosley had stopped even trying to speak; he waited, hands on his hips,
while spotlights from the roof played on the violence below. This made
it seem as if the whole point of the show might be violence. Mosley
explained later that the working of the spotlights had had nothing to
do with him; they had been under the control of the Newsreel camera-
men who had come to film the occasion. Also, he said he sometimes
could not see what was happening because the spotlights were in his
eyes. But the impression given was of some sort of Roman circus.
Two demonstrators got amongst the girders of the roof and were
pursued there by Neil Francis-Hawkins. It took a long time for the
speech to get going, and then too much had happened for many people
to be interested in listening. Members of the audience had begun to
walk out 'in a steady trickle' because of what they felt as 'boredom'
(Vera Brittain).

Before the end three Conservative MPs – W. J. Anstruther-Gray,
J. Scrymgeour-Wedderburn and T. J. O'Connor – had left and were
making a dash to Printing House Square to get a letter into *The Times*
of the next day. 'We were involuntary witnesses of wholly unnecessary
violence inflicted by uniformed Blackshirts on interrupters. Men and

women were knocked down and were still assaulted and kicked on
the floor. It will be a matter of surprise to us if there were no fatal
injuries.' There was, in fact, nothing like a fatal injury: after the meeting
a number of people from both sides were treated in nearby hospitals
for cuts, broken teeth, broken noses and kicks in the stomach; but from
the records only one anti-fascist – a student from Sheffield – was kept
in hospital for more than a day. He claimed that he had been bludgeoned
on the head till he was 'half dead'; he turned up three weeks later
however to make this allegation at a meeting addressed by Mosley.
Two fascist stewards were kept in hospital overnight. In all, it was
the sort of fight that nowadays (1983) would be taken as not all that
unusual at a crucial football match.

But the important battle was the one of propaganda: there were
other members of the audience hurrying to get their statements to the
press. On the side of the blackshirts were M. W. Beaumont MP, who
wrote to *The Times* – 'While the forces of law and order make no
effort to safeguard the rights of free speech in this country, the use
of some such methods [by the stewards] is the only way in which those
putting forward an unknown and controversial case can obtain a
hearing' and Patrick Donner MP, who wrote to the *National Review* –
'The fact is that many of the Communists were armed with razors,
stockings filled with broken glass, knuckledusters and iron bars; that
they marched from the East End, the police kindly escorting, with the
avowed purpose of wrecking the meeting.... Can it in equity be
argued that the stewards used their fists, when provoked in this manner,
with more vigour than perhaps the situation required?' And Lloyd
George, who had not been at the meeting, wrote in the *Sunday Pictorial*
– 'It is difficult to explain why the fury of the champions of free speech
should be concentrated so exclusively not on those who deliberately
and resolutely attempted to prevent the public expression of opinions
of which they disapproved, but against those who fought, however
roughly, for freedom of speech.' Participants on each side spoke of
the 'unenglishness' of the other: to one it was the fascists in their black
shirts who were the 'alien' force; to the other, it was those yelling with
their 'hebraic features'.

The fascists won physically the battle of Olympia: the hecklers were,
for the most part, thrown out. That the communists won the propaganda war was due partly to the fact that they had a preponderance
of influential and literary eye-witnesses who supported their version
of what happened – they published a pamphlet called *Fascists at Olympia*
in which accounts of the violence, in addition to those mentioned above,

were given by Aldous Huxley, Storm Jameson, Naomi Mitchison, Ritchie Calder – but above all (and this probably influenced the way in which the eye-witnesses interpreted what they saw) the communist propaganda victory was due to the fact that the image of fascists as thugs was being imprinted in people's minds anyway – and this was to a certain extent irrespective of particular instances of behaviour of the BUF. Oswald Mosley could, as usual, win some sort of war with words – he gave interviews after the meeting on the lines of: the communists started the trouble, so what did they expect? – but none of this outweighed the public vision of fascism that was growing as a result of the example of Hitler's Germany. Hitler's SA and SS were seen as almost self-admitted thugs. The British Union of Fascists, people reasoned, must know Hitler's men were thugs; since the fascists seemed to emulate them – or at least made no effort to dissuade people from thinking they were emulating them – thus they must want to take the responsibility of appearing to be like thugs.

Shortly before the Olympia meeting the United Front Committee which had been summoned to co-ordinate the various plans for the anti-fascist demonstrations had written to the management of Olympia to try to get the meeting cancelled. They had said:

Realising the torture undergone by the thousands of individuals of all classes and the thousands at present suffering in concentration camps and the persecution of the Jews at the instance of Hitler and his Fascist regime, we demand that the letting of Olympia be cancelled to the British Union of Fascists and that on no future occasions will they be allowed to hold a meeting in your building.

Shortly after the Olympia meeting, on 30th June 1934, Hitler murdered Roehm, the SA leader, and at least eighty of his colleagues (the figure has been put as high as a thousand) in the purge that came to be known as the Night of the Long Knives. Roehm had been one of Hitler's closest friends: the SA had been the gang of loyal toughs to a large extent responsible for bringing Hitler to power. But now Hitler wanted to appear respectable: above all, he needed to get the support of the army to whom the SA were a threat. So he had his old friends the SA leaders killed by his new friends the SS – there was a whiff here of a new sort of terror – were fascists then people liable to kill not only their enemies but their friends? Norman Angell wrote in the *Foreign Affairs Digest* – 'One cannot imagine that Oswald Mosley was altogether happy at the news from Berlin on Saturday night.' Images that were floating around in the public mind must have seemed to constellate – those of Olympia, of the black uniforms of both the BUF and the SS, of attacks on Jews and of nights with long knives. Almost without anyone knowing, a pattern of mind had been set up that would be almost impossible to break – that of fascists being identified with thugs.

One of the first casualties on the fascist side in the propaganda war was Lord Rothermere: in July he withdrew his support from the BUF. It had lasted for no more than six months: there had been some mystery about why, apart from the encouragement of Mussolini, he had ever given it. He had met and admired Hitler, but he had always said he would not be associated with anti-semitism. After Olympia the chairmen of certain Jewish firms let Lord Rothermere know that if he continued to support fascism they would not advertise in his papers. It seemed to them evident that if the blackshirts got power, British Jews would be persecuted in the way that German Jews were being persecuted under Hitler. Rothermere asked Mosley to come and see him: Mosley later told the story:*

> I went to see him in a hotel he frequented and found him in a relatively modest apartment, an imposing figure of monumental form lying flat on his back on a narrow brass bedstead.... Lord Rothermere explained that he was in trouble with certain advertisers who had not liked his support for the blackshirts.... The long struggle fluctuated, but I lost. He felt that I was asking him to risk too much, not only for himself but for others who depended on him.

The threat of Jewish advertisers however was probably not the decisive influence in the story. On 20th July a correspondence between Mosley and Rothermere was published in *Blackshirt* –

> Dear Lord Rothermere,
> .... At present some doubt has arisen in the public mind as to our relationship. That doubt arises from the basic fact that you are a Conservative and we Blackshirts are Fascists. We hold the new creed of the modern world which we are striving to bring to Britain by British methods and in accordance with the British character.... You, on the other hand, are a Conservative and would like to see a revived Conservative Party.... You have stated your doubts as

---

* *My Life.*

to certain aspects of our policy, and have expressed your desire that we should abandon or modify them.

There followed a list of the areas in which Mosley suggested Lord Rothermere wanted modifications – The Corporate State, Reform of Parliament, the use of the word 'Fascist'. Mosley wrote – 'You would like us to abandon the creed of Fascism and the word "Fascist": we cannot do this because it is the creed which means everything in the world to us'. Then there was the question of Jews. Mosley continued:

We have given our pledge that no racial or religious persecution will occur under Fascism in Britain; but we shall require the Jews, like everyone else, to put the interests of 'Britain First'. We no longer admit Jews to membership of our movement because (a) they have bitterly attacked us; (b) they have organised as an international movement setting their racial interests above the national interests and are, therefore, unacceptable as members of a national movement which aims at national organisation and revival. We certainly are not prepared to relax our attitude towards the Jews in view of the fact that in the last year 80% of the convictions for physical attacks on Fascists were pronounced on Jews while the Jewish community represents only .6% of the population....

To this Lord Rothermere replied:

My dear Mosley,
...... As you know, I have never thought that a movement calling itself 'Fascist' could be successful in this country, and I have also made it clear in my conversation with you that I never could support any movement with an anti-semitic bias, any movement that had dictatorship as one of its objectives, nor any movement which would substitute a 'corporate state' for Parliamentary institutions in this country ... The assistance which I have rendered you was given in the hope that you would be prepared to ally yourself with the Conservative forces to defeat Socialism at the next and succeeding elections.
..... I have never thought that the political situation here bears any relation to the political situation in Italy or Germany. In each of these countries parliamentary institutions were largely of exotic growth, whereas in England they have, since the time of Queen Elizabeth, exercised the real decisive influence.

Lord Rothermere's support had landed the BUF with a crisis to do with the influx of unsuitable personnel; his withdrawal landed it with a crisis about money – the scheme to market BUF cigarettes fell through, and he made no more personal payments. The money crisis could, with courage and hard work, be surmounted; the problem of the BUF Defence Force being linked with Hitlerism was much more serious. There was the continuing dilemma – if the BUF turned back now from its aim of establishing itself in the public mind as a force able to deal promptly with the sort of crisis that it had always said was to be expected – what would it have left? On the other hand – if both the BUF and Hitler continued as they were, how could they not be linked in the patriotic public mind to the grave detriment of British fascism?

There is a sense in which Hitler made impossible the success of other fascist or national socialist movements in Europe: there was nothing in the philosophy of fascism necessarily to do with racialism or the desire for conquest which were the drives which pushed Hitler to destruction and eventually to self-destruction. On the other hand some archetypal drives (even excesses?) seem to be necessary if groups are to be welded dynamically into a single force. But Mussolini was not anti-semitic until he came under the influence of Hitler; and Franco in Spain, after his success in the Civil War, showed great skill in keeping out of warfare. In July 1934 it might have been possible for my father to have repudiated Hitler: he had already called Hitler 'mistaken' in his persecution of Jews: the public reaction to the Roehm purge must have struck him forcibly. (The magazine *John Bull* threw in its comment – 'Hitler killed fascism in this country on that night!') But my father chose to make no strong moral comment on all this: he did not try to find a different form of impetus. He probably felt it was too late to turn back now: movements such as his wither and die if their impetus is changed. And besides – in fact, did not Hitler seem to be winning?

Coincidences occur both in the public and in the personal world through which – and through a person's responses to which – life seems to be fashioned. Such coincidences are not matters of cause and effect: they are yet perhaps instances whereby a person's character can be decisive. It was perhaps never in my father's character to be someone who could turn back: with his passionate belief about how the world had swiftly to be altered, how could he? But being the sort of person he was – who gambled on everything – coincidences now seemed to turn against him. Coincidences perhaps work for those who watch and listen. He was like a ship moving into an area of icebergs.

CHAPTER 8

Hitler

When in the summer holidays of 1933 myself and my sister Vivien and Aunt Irene had gone on our cruise to the Canary Isles and my father and my Aunt Baba had gone on a motoring trip through France, Diana Guinness and her sister Unity Mitford had set off on their motoring trip through Germany: in Munich they were taken up by Hitler's friend Putzi Hanfstaengl and went with him to the first huge Nazi Rally or Parteitag at Nuremberg. There they attended the parades and were present at Hitler's speeches: Diana wrote years later of how 'a feeling of excited triumph was in the air, and when Hitler appeared an almost electric shock went through the multitude'. Diana and Unity asked Hanfstaengl if they could meet Hitler, but he put them off with excuses that Hitler was too busy for personal matters – and anyway he did not like women who wore lipstick. Unity became obsessed by the idea of meeting Hitler: she said however that even for him she would not remove her lipstick.

The following summer, after the holiday in which Diana spent two weeks with my father and Vivien and myself in the house near Toulon, Diana and Unity went again to Nuremberg. Hanfstaengl was still not helpful about an introduction to Hitler, so Diana and Unity went to Munich and Unity stayed there at a finishing school to learn German (she was just twenty) and Diana, after having returned home briefly and consulted my father, went back to Munich and took a flat there with her maid. Unity had discovered that when Hitler was in Munich (where the headquarters of the Nazi Party still were) he sometimes went for lunch to a restaurant called the Osteria Bavaria: Diana and Unity took to going there to catch a glimpse of him. He would come in from time to time with one or two adjutants and friends – Hoffman, his photographer; Dietrich, his press chief; Wagner, the Gauleiter of

Bavaria. There would be a table in the corner reserved for him: the waitresses would flutter; there would be an atmosphere both glamorous and informal like that surrounding a pop star. Unity recorded that Hitler had come in one day in his 'sweet' mackintosh and asked a waitress who she and Diana were; then he had stared at them in silence for a long time so that 'one couldn't think or move or anything'.

Diana returned to England before Christmas: Unity stayed on in Munich going hopefully to the Osteria Bavaria. Then in February 1935 she wrote to Diana –

Yesterday was the most wonderful and beautiful day of my life. I will try and describe it to you, though I can yet hardly write.

I went alone to lunch at the Osteria and sat at the little table by the stove where we sat you know last time you were there. At about 3, when I had finished my lunch, the Fuhrer came in and sat down at his usual table with two other men. I read the *Vogue* you sent me. About ten minutes after he arrived he spoke to the Manager and the Manager came over to me and said 'The Fuhrer would like to speak to you'. I got up and went over to him and he stood up and saluted and shook hands and introduced me to the others and asked me to sit next to him.

I sat and talked to him for about half an hour, at least of course I don't really know how long, but I think it was about that. Mona (the fat waitress) came and whispered to me 'Shall I bring you a postcard?' so I said Yes, really to please her. She brought it and I was rather embarrassed to ask him to sign it but in the end I did, and I said I hoped he wouldn't think it very American of me.

He made me write my name on a piece of paper which I did as you may believe very shakily and then he wrote on the card – Frl Unity Mitford, Zur freundlichen Erinnerung an Deutschland und Adolf Hitler. Tom [Unity's and Diana's brother] will tell you what it means. I can't tell you all the things we talked about as it would take too long. I told him he ought to come to England and he said he would love to but he was afraid there would be a revolution if he did. He asked me if I had ever been to Bayreuth and I said No, but I should like to, and he said to one of the other men that they must remember that the next time there was a Festspiel there. He said he felt he knew London well from his architectural studies, and that from what he had heard and read about it he thought it to be the best town, as a town, in the world. He thinks 'Cavalcade' is the best film he ever saw.

He talked about the war. He said it was like the Niebelungskampf, and that international Jews must never again be allowed to make two Nordic races fight against one another.

He told me all about the great road and halls and stadium they are building in Nuremberg for the Parteitags which are costing 8,000,000 marks and will be ready in 8 years. He says that then the Parteitags will be really tremendous.

Well, I can't remember more of our conversation but we talked of a lot of things. In the end he had to go. He kept the bit of paper with my name on. Mona told me it was the first time he had ever invited someone he didn't know to sit at his table like that. He had also apparently made sure my lunch was put on his bill.

So after all that you can imagine what I feel like. I am so happy that I wouldn't mind a bit dying. I suppose I am the luckiest girl in the world. I certainly never did anything to deserve such an honour.

In March Diana drove to Munich in a Voisin car that my father had bought for her: she got stuck in a snow-drift in the Black Forest and had to be pulled out by a team of farm-horses. In Munich she and Unity went to the Osteria Bavaria and Unity introduced Diana to Hitler. Diana's description of Hitler at the time of this her first meeting with him was* –

Hitler, at this time aged forty five, was about 5 feet 9 inches in height and neither fat nor thin. His eyes were dark blue, his skin fair, and his brown hair exceptionally fine. It was neatly brushed: I never saw him with a lock of hair over his forehead. His hands were white and well shaped. He was extremely neat and clean looking, so much so that beside him almost everyone looked coarse. His teeth had been mended with gold, as one saw when he laughed. At the Osteria he was generally in civilian clothes; he wore a grey suit and a white shirt and a rather furry soft hat which he called 'mein Shako'. His most unusual feature was his forehead. He had a high forehead which almost jutted forward above the eyes. I have seen this on one or two other people: generally they have been musicians. At this little bistro he was in a relaxed mood; if he had not been so he would have lunched at his flat.

* *A Life of Contrasts.*

Diana described how he was extremely polite to women; he would bow, and kiss their hand, and would not sit down till they did. He invariably ate 'eggs and mayonnaise and vegetables and pasta': his guests could order what they liked – even to having food sent from a renowned restaurant next door. Hitler listened to what his guests had to say and did not indulge in monologues – except occasionally one on the subject of motor cars, which Diana and Unity 'rather dreaded'.

During the next four and a half years Diana saw Hitler 'fairly often, though not nearly as often as Unity did'. Very many years later she said to me, the author, that she thought her meeting with Hitler had ruined her life. She added – 'And I think it ruined your father's.'

My father went to see Hitler for the first time in April 1935; he was received in his flat in Munich and the two of them talked through an interpreter for an hour before lunch. My father described the scene:*

At first Hitler was almost inert in his chair, pale, seemingly exhausted. He came suddenly to life when I said that war between Britain and Germany would be a terrible disaster, and used the simile of two splendid young men fighting each other until they both fall exhausted and bleeding to the ground, when the jackals of the world would mount triumphant on their bodies. His face flushed and he launched with much vigour into some of his main themes, but in the normal manner of any politician moved by strong convictions. The hypnotic manner was entirely absent; perhaps I was an unsuitable subject; in any case he made no attempt whatever to produce any effect of that kind. He was simple, and treated me throughout the occasion with a gentle, almost feminine charm.

My father said that this first interview with Hitler was 'exactly the opposite of a first encounter with Mussolini: there was no element of posture'. My father had got on well with Mussolini: he felt they had had things in common. He used to say that my mother, for instance, had liked Mussolini: she had called him 'that big booming man'. My father never, it seemed, much liked Hitler: in old age he used to refer to him as a 'terrible little man'. One of the sayings he liked to bring out over the dinner table was that Italy, being a feminine country, had fallen in love with Mussolini, a man; whereas Germany, being a masculine country, had fallen in love with Hitler, a woman. At the other end of the table my stepmother Diana would smile patiently

* *My Life.*

with closed eyes. There is some evidence that Hitler and his Nazis never much liked my father: in 1935 a member of the B U F called Dr Pfister was in Germany and brought back information that 'a certain high Nazi official who visited this country some time ago had not been favourably impressed of a meeting he had had with the Leader'; also that there was some displeasure over 'Ma' Mosley having given an interview to the press in which she stated that 'Hitler was the greatest enemy to the B U F since people in this country would not join on account of the brutal methods in Germany'. Dr Pfister also reported that 'the Nazi Party were very disappointed that the leader had shown so little appreciation of their victory in the Saar'.

In later years I once asked my stepmother why it was that Hitler seemed to have such hypnotic power over so many different kinds of people – storm-troopers, financiers, fashionable women, generals, peasants – whereas my father, however much he impressed people when they met him, had not evoked the same obsessed loyalty by which people even when they had not wanted to might seem ready to give up their lives. I had thought this would be a difficult question, but my stepmother said – I will tell you exactly: when people met your father they thought: Here is this wonderful man who has an answer to everything himself so what is there for us to do? When people met Hitler they thought: Here is this wonderful but unfortunate man who seems to have all the cares of the world on his shoulders, so we must do all we can to help him.

Unity was only twenty-one when she met Hitler: Diana was twenty-four. Germany was a place which had been transformed in two years from a country of hopelessness, cynicism and mass unemployment into a nation in which a large majority of people were observably purposeful and cheerful, and almost everyone and everything worked.

There was something in Hitler that evoked adoration; something in the people around him that wished to give it. Hitler's power of attraction resided in paradoxes: he was enormously confident yet awkwardly alone; people were awe-struck by him, yet felt he was so fragile they had to treat him gently. They rushed to gather what they needed of his confidence; in order to maintain this, they gave their confidence to him. Goebbels wrote of Hitler – 'He is like a child; kind, good, merciful: like a cat; cunning, clever, agile: like a lion; roaring, great, gigantic'. Goering put this in more ponderous terms: having likened what he saw as Hitler's infallibility to that of the Pope:★

★ In *Germany Reborn*.

Wherein lies the secret of the enormous influence he has on followers? Does it lie in his goodness as a man, in his strength of character, or in his unique modesty? Does it lie in his political genius, his gift of seeing what direction things are going to take, in his great bravery, or in his unbending loyalty to his followers? I think that, whatever qualities one may have in mind, one must nevertheless come to the conclusion that it is not the sum of all these virtues: it is something mystical, inexpressible, almost incomprehensible, which this unique man possesses; and he who cannot feel it instinctively will not be able to grasp it at all. For we love Adolf Hitler because we believe deeply and unswervingly that God has sent him to us to save Germany.

The needs of people to have an unswerving belief arise from a desire for salvation and yet an inability to hope for it from oneself. Albert Speer, one of the closest to Hitler in his entourage, wrote, 'The whole structure of the [Nazi] system was aimed at preventing conflicts of conscience from even arising.' By referring all questions to Hitler, and by Hitler's accepting this transference, people had no doubts.

C. J. Jung wrote of Hitler and of the Germans:*

He represented the shadow, the inferior part of everybody's personality, in an overwhelming degree, and this was another reason why they fell for him. But what could they have done? In Hitler, every German should have seen his own shadow, his own worst danger. It is everybody's allotted fate to become conscious of and learn to deal with the shadow. But how could the Germans be expected to understand this, when no one in the world can understand such a simple truth?

In Munich, Unity Mitford wrote of her second meeting with Hitler – 'When one sits beside him it's like sitting beside the sun, he gives out rays or something.' Then in June 1935 – 'Today he was so kind and so divine I suddenly thought I would not only like to *kill* all who say and do things against him, but also *torture* them. It is wonderful to think that someone like him can ever have been thought of.'

There were projections, transpositions here, of a child who has grabbed at an imagined heaven and is in terror of its being taken away.

* *Collected Works*, Volume 10.

It is possible to understand the desire to protect an imaginary perfection: but then, how does one distinguish between what is imaginary and what is real?

Unity wrote a letter to Streicher's Jew-baiting magazine *Der Stürmer* –

The English have no notion of the Jewish danger ... Our worst Jews work only behind the scenes. They never come out into the open, and so we cannot show them to the British Public in their true dreadfulness... I want everyone to know that I am a Jew hater.

One of the themes of this book is that politicians use grandiose words without believing the reality of what they say: it is also possible for people to say squalid things without being much in contact with what they say. Words are often expressions of primitive forces; the reality that results from them can still take one form or another.

What Unity in fact did was to accept an invitation from Streicher to attend a pagan festival in the country on midsummer night at which young Nazis rolled burning wheels down a hill. Unity was asked to 'say a few words' into a microphone. She said to the assembled company that there should be lasting peace between England and Germany. The young men cheered and shouted 'Heil England!'

This was a time (mid-1935) when in Germany not much openly was being done against Jews: the original violence had died down: the Nuremberg laws and the public displaying of anti-semitic posters came at the end of the summer. There was at this time even the beginning of talks between Nazis and Zionists by which both sides hoped to stimulate the peaceable movement of German Jews to Palestine: Eichmann was in Cairo two years later talking to Zionists.

Albert Speer has described the atmosphere of life amongst Hitler's closest entourage at the time when Unity and Diana met him. Hitler's personal style is of interest here because it shows the vacuum into which people were sucked which was the German National Socialist way of operating power; my father's style was never dominated by this – but then, of course, he never wielded that sort of power.

Speer wrote:*

During these days in Munich Hitler paid little attention to government and party business, even less than at Obersalzberg. Usually

* *Inside the Third Reich.*

only an hour or two a day remained available for conferences. Most of his time he spent marching about building sites, relaxing in studios, cafés and restaurants; or hurling long monologues at his associates who were already amply familiar with the unchanging themes and painfully tried to conceal their boredom.

And about life at Obersalzberg:*

The day actually began with a prolonged afternoon dinner... questions of fashion, of raising dogs, of the theatre and movies, of operettas and their stars were discussed, along with endless trivialities about the family lives of others. Hitler hardly ever said anything about the Jews, about his domestic opponents, let alone about the necessity of setting up of concentration camps.... Shortly after dinner the walk to the teahouse began... Hitler was addicted to this particular walk, which took about half an hour...

The second part of the evening began with a movie, as was also the custom when Hitler was in Berlin... Hitler preferred light entertainment, love and society films: revues with lots of leg display were sure to please him... Afterwards the company gathered around the huge fireplace... Occasionally the movies were discussed – Hitler commenting mainly on the female actors and Eva Braun on the males. No one bothered to raise the conversation above the level of trivialities... In the early hours of the morning we went home dead tired, exhausted from doing nothing. After a few days of this I was seized by what I called at the time 'the mountain disease'. That is, I felt exhausted and vacant from the constant waste of time.

Speer wrote of Hitler's relationship to himself as being like that of Mephistopheles to Faust: the attraction of Mephistopheles is that he has positive and energetic opinions about everyone and everything; he can have these because he is always contemptuous; he believes in nothing and in nobody, and so he has free rein to show any certainty he likes. And if others choose to trust him, he can impart such certainty to them, they are liberated into dreams – just because of the nothingness in reality.

Diana's descriptions of life with Hitler are in style the opposite of those of Speer; she writes of Hitler's jokes, his frankness, his cleverness, his charm; but the substance of her memories is not so very different.

---

* *Inside the Third Reich.*

Speer was hypnotically charmed at the time by life around Hitler, it was only in looking back that he saw that there had been emptiness. Hitler's power over people seems to have been due less to his persuasiveness about politics than to his conviction that by will he could put into effect any idea that he chose; it was this that ran away with people, as it ran away with himself, as it if were some cancer. Trust in will overreaches itself to self-destruction because there is no recognition of the balancing requirements of reality; without these, there can be no maintenance of life.

Unity, and later Diana, seem to have been liked and respected by Hitler perhaps because they themselves were too exuberant to be swallowed in his vacuum; they would have posed no great threat to him, coming from a different world. Hitler's adjutant Schaub wrote of Unity – 'With all her admiration for Hitler the young Lady Mitford is quite clearly of the opinion that she is more or less his equal.' Speer himself wrote that the 'sole exception' to the tacit agreement amongst Hitler's personal entourage that politics should not be mentioned was 'Lady Mitford, who even in the later years of international tension persistently spoke up for her country and often actually pleaded with Hitler to make a deal with England'.★

Unity died when she felt her hopes had ended; Diana lived; and gave up her life to, and succeeded in creating a life around, my father. My father put up with some of the vacuums of political life – he sat on platforms, he charmed people, he talked – but then he would get fed up, and go his own way. He failed in politics; but he succeeded in that he ultimately did not let himself be sucked into the black hole of willed self-destruction. Perhaps he simply enjoyed himself and life too much. But it was probably because he was too serious that he did not let himself be trapped.

From Hitler's house at Obersalzberg Unity wrote as if from an English country-house weekend: 'I cannot tell you how wonderful the Führer was today copying a woman buying a hat! We all nearly died of laughing.'

★ *Inside the Third Reich.*

CHAPTER 9

William Joyce

The financial difficulties which came upon the BUF as a result of the withdrawal of the support of Lord Rothermere coincided with the hostile publicity resulting from Olympia. After a momentary upsurge in recruiting due to stories of violence, members, seeing more soberly the way things were going, began to fall away. Our District Inspector wrote:

> Public opinion was fomented against the blackshirts and physical assaults became more frequent and more dangerous. Open air meetings often ended in trouble, affrays and minor riots; public halls in areas controlled by Councils with Labour majorities were refused to the Movement on trivial pretexts. Now scrambled to safety all those erstwhile members who had been pleased to be identified with Mosley when the climate had been mild. Those worthy of the cause stuck it out, and found that the almost universal hostility put more iron into their souls.

Many who left were those who had joined on the Rothermere bandwagon and who were of the type of 'unmitigated nuisances to all new political movements – those crooks and adventurers who come in for what they can extract in the way of spoil'. But there was a number of those who had been with Mosley since New Party days who also left – amongst them Robert Forgan the Deputy Leader and F. M. Box the old New Party Agent. The inner circle of the movement became increasingly dominated by those who were by temperament idealistic fascists, whether propagandists or organisation men – William Joyce, Neil Francis-Hawkins. A new recruit during 1934 was John Beckett who came in as an admirer of William Joyce: he was a histrionic, pugnacious man who had been a left-wing MP from 1924 to 1931 and had gained notoriety by seizing the Speaker's mace and threatening to carry it out of the House of Commons. He was an anti-semite, but not so much in a doctrinaire way as in the way of someone who needed an enemy to fight. A good public speaker, in the hierarchy of BUF speakers he soon gained a position second only to Mosley and Joyce.

The falling-off in income was not noticed for a time: money from Mussolini was still coming in; Mosley himself was putting in more of his money (he estimated later that he spent in all £100,000 on the movement). There were a few other rich backers – Wyndham Portal and Sir Alliott Verdon Roe. There was a story that the eccentric Lady Houston once wrote out a cheque for £100,000 to give to the movement and then read in *Blackshirt* an article calling her a silly and vain old woman, whereupon she tore the cheque up. My father commented later – 'These things were liable to happen when I was constantly away touring the country and speaking at least four or five times a week, because often I did not see a line of what was written in our weekly press.'

The 30,000 to 40,000 members at the height of the movement's success had paid a shilling a month if employed and fourpence if un-employed: this probably brought in some £12,000 a year. The two weekly papers *Blackshirt* and the somewhat more highbrow *Fascist Week* roughly paid their own way: they cost a penny and twopence re-spectively and each had a circulation of around 25,000. Expenses at the Black House in London consisted largely of salaries: the top one or two executives were paid £750 a year; John Beckett as Director of Publicity was paid £600, the editors of the two papers – Rex Tremlett and W. J. Leaper – £400, and William Joyce as one of the chief speakers £300. There were the usual expenses of running a large headquarters, and the hire of halls throughout the country. In London the Albert Hall cost 150 guineas for a night and Olympia 250. Local branches were expected to pay their own way.

Mosley had, he said, been so busy making speeches that he had kept himself clear of financial arrangements and also from day-to-day super-vision of the papers; this had resulted in the somewhat anarchic style in which the BUF had developed. But in the wake of the hostile publicity about the Olympia meeting and of the withdrawal of Lord Rothermere some fundamental reappraisal of the way in which the movement was going was unavoidable; in particular, some decision had to be made about the BUF's attitude to anti-semitism. The old claim that fascists attacked only individual Jews for what they did and not for what they were was simply not believed. The chief culprit responsible for the fact that it was now being taken for granted by the public that the BUF was anti-semitic, was William Joyce.

Joyce was liable to slip into his speeches or articles in *Blackshirt* references to 'aliens imported from Palestine' or 'hairy troglodytes who crept out of the ghettos of Germany to seek sanctuary in the British Museum'. It was the style of these remarks, rather than that they expressed any deliberate policy, that seemed obviously to exhibit an obsessive anti-semitism; and the fact that Joyce apparently was not restrained nor even reprimanded seemed also fairly obviously to indicate that this was the sort of style that the leadership – despite its protestations – required. Joyce in fact had a hatred of almost any form of intellectual ('fascism is not a creed for the smug mice who choose to emerge from under Bloomsbury tea-cosies to have a nibble at it') but it was easiest to canalise this feeling into hostility to Jews. The question was now pressing: what was in fact the attitude of the leadership? There were enough responsible and moderate members in the BUF to insist that the predicament should no longer be ignored.

In the aftermath of Olympia G. S. Gerault wrote a report for the Leader:

> The Movement has become identified in the public mind with the Hitler movement chiefly through the fault of our own speakers, and the tone adopted in the *Blackshirt*.
>
> The original attitude of the Leader on the Jewish question was very sound and appealed much to the public mind; but of late it has been felt that the movement is going definitely in for the persecution of Jews on German lines, and that has produced very grave repercussions.
>
> In this connection it should be realised that the country as a whole is 95% against Hitler and all that he has done; and all the protests and explanations which may be made fall on deaf ears. We are definitely wasting time in any attempt to defend the Hitler regime, and we should have contented ourselves with saying that it is far too early for any intelligent man to form any sort of conclusion.
>
> There is an undoubted feeling throughout the movement that the leader is being jockeyed either knowingly or unknowingly into an impossible position by A.A.O. [Assistant Administrative Officer] Joyce; and there are those who say that he is now, to all intents and purposes, the Movement.
>
> This feeling is intensified when members see pamphlet after

pamphlet on policy appearing over this officer's signature; when they should either be anonymous or signed by the Leader.

Furthermore, older members can see quite clearly how issues upon which the leader spoke with perfect clarity in the early days of the Movement now appear to be modified in directions known to suit the personal predilections of this officer.

Intelligence and real thinking are definitely at a discount. Either the movement does not possess them, or no effort is made to find contributors who use them.

Far too many lies are cheerfully printed with a disastrous result. When a local branch reads a highly coloured account of what it knows was only a trifling business the immediate reaction is that the ordinary member considers the whole paper to be composed of similar lies and values it accordingly.

The only terms on which it is safe to lie in propaganda is when you cannot be found out, least of all by your own people; but this elementary truth appears to be beyond the understanding of some of the contributors to the *Blackshirt*.

Confronted by this, Oswald Mosley could hardly continue to claim that he was too busy to be able to know what was going on.

Amongst the numerous pamphlets by Joyce referred to in this report was one on India: this in draft form was seen by two BUF members who had personal knowledge of India – B. S. James and Leigh Vaughan-Henry. James sent a marked copy of the draft pamphlet to Mosley with the comment –

In my opinion should any of the portions I have marked come into the hands of knowledgeable Anglo-Indians, not to mention Indians, all sympathy for the BUF in India will be killed. In addition I consider that as India is such an important question, the distribution of the pamphlet in this country even will do us grave harm. The mind of the writer appears throughout to be superficial, pretentious and priggish – without real power. The pamphlet is a deplorable manifestation of a lack of even elementary insight into psychology (especially Asiatic).

The comments of Vaughan-Henry were –

Its tone from start to finish is wholly wrong. It is couched in a cheap, windy demagogic style which might go over as Hyde Park Corner

oratory. . . . there are transparently rhetorical touches of cheap lurid-
ness and journalistic sensationalism of the least convincing kind. . .
a continual touch of insufferable condescension. It it likely to irritate
the very kind of Indian who can be useful – the type who wishes
to support Britain because of its literacy and its care for Indian culture.

I know positively that it has alienated five potential Indian ad-
herents; I know equally that it has either infuriated or caused derision
among seven equally initially–sympathetic Anglo-Indians of some
experience and standing.

I respectfully submit that this pamphlet should be suppressed
immediately: I ask this urgently, with the interest of the movement
at heart.

About BUF policy in general Vaughan-Henry continued:

I feel that we need to take more care now than ever, not only in
all literature issued, but in the *Blackshirt* itself, to eliminate the kind
of dull, cheap clap-trap which has occasionally disfigured that paper.
The Movement has passed into a new phase. We can have the support
of fresh types from those initially supporting it. I am not for inclination to the Right; I am rather for a judicious incline to the Left
if the Corporate State is to work efficiently; and now it is our business
to be working to cement its fabric, for immediate operation of its
machinery when power is attained. I sincerely trust that you will
give your attention to this and find yourself able to carry out a sound
purge and reform.

The style and content of Joyce's pamphlet on India was indeed the
sort of stuff with which *Blackshirt* readers had often been regaled: it
began: 'True imperialism knows nothing of disintegration; true imperialism knows nothing of surrender; true imperialism knows nothing
of injustice, and Fascism is true imperialism.' It described Lord Irwin
as 'the phenomenal freak whom it would be indecent to describe as
Viceroy' and Stanley Baldwin as 'the steel merchant metamorphosed
into a squire by casual experiments in pig breeding'. It suggested that
'Indian education affords no source of justifiable pride' and that 'British
law and order had repressed and replaced chaos, violence, rapine and
habitual atrocity'. When Joyce was informed of the criticisms of him
and his pamphlet he reacted in a way which seems to have become
increasingly typical of those with influence at headquarters; he went to
the Deputy Leader and complained that there was a 'plot' against him.

There were two courses open to Mosley as a result of the crisis, particular but symbolic, aroused by this pamphlet. On the one hand he could suppress the pamphlet and demote Joyce and try to redirect blackshirt propaganda to appeal to a more sophisticated and responsible audience: the danger in this was that he might lose some of his most energetic and dedicated supporters and be left with nothing of the spirit that might make a revolutionary party work. On the other hand he could ignore the critics and back Joyce on the grounds that he, Mosley, had always said he was appealing to people who feel rather than to those who think: the danger in this was that he would be increasingly and inevitably seen as allying himself with the style of extremism that was becoming commonplace on the Continent. In the event, my father tried to pursue something of both courses: this was what he might have called a synthesis, but it was also a falling between stools. Announcements were made about reforms and the strengthening of discipline; but what the public saw was mainly the style of Joyce taking over.

The pamphlet on India was published; and in fact within a few months Joyce was promoted to be Director of Propaganda. As if in celebration of this, on 24th May 1935 Joyce published on the front page of *Blackshirt* an article on India which contained sentences which seemed to be epitomes of his style. Referring to the India Bill which would transfer powers to Indians, he wrote of the Tories who had backed it that they were 'one loathsome, fetid, purulent, tumid mass of hypocrisy'; behind them was 'the mean, narrow-souled, pig-eyed, comfortable employer of labour ... to this little beast all other issues are irrelevant ... [he is] unable to open his mouth lest the Jewish dictators of "Society" should foreclose'.

My father's backing and indeed promotion of Joyce can only be understood in terms of the situation that he had got himself into in which it was necessary, if he was to carry on at all, for him to believe that in some way he was hand in hand with destiny: that in spite of (or almost because of) the size of the odds against him, it did not matter much with whom he travelled because in the end his spirit and will could not fail. With this sort of vision and against the evident sort of odds what he needed was loyalty; since he was a gambler, he would not turn back but had to double up as it were on all his stakes. There were two occasions in the second half of 1934 which might have influenced him to support Joyce. The first was the rally in Hyde Park in September which I had watched from the roof of the Cumberland Hotel; this had been kept in order by the huge attendance of police but nothing of the BUF's message had been heard; the attempt to conform to respectability had resulted in the movement's being made to appear faint-hearted. The second incident was at Worthing a month later when there was a fight after a meeting at the Pier Pavilion: Mosley, Joyce and local organisers were confronted by a crowd shouting 'We want Mosley dead or alive' and 'Felix keeps on walking'; and singing 'Poor old Mosley's got the wind up' to the tune of *John Brown's Body*. As the fascists made their way through the crowd they had 'struck out with their fists' (the police alleged) and 'bodies had thudded against shop windows as people had been thrown aside by powerful rushes'. As a result Mosley, Joyce and others were charged with riotous assembly. When the case came up at Lewes Assizes there was the following exchange between Mosley and the prosecuting counsel:

Counsel: The whole idea of your movement on the streets is to hang together is it not?
Mosley: I trust not to hang together...
Counsel: Did you make any complaints to a policeman?
Mosley: It is not my habit to complain.
Counsel: Will you answer yes or no –
Mosley: I will give evidence in my own way, and I do not require any instruction from you.
Counsel: Don't be offensive.
Mosley: To be offensive is not the prerogative of a King's Counsel.

Members of the BUF were feeling both persecuted and belligerent: they were comrades-in-arms in a tough struggle: if they were to survive, they needed solidarity and courage. It must have seemed that now was not the time to think of casting out – of too severely reprimanding even – party stalwarts such as Joyce of whom there could be no doubts about their almost reckless courage.

Mosley was due to make his second large speech at the Albert Hall on 28th October 1934: before this it seemed imperative there should be decisions about policy. A report on the movement's attitude to Jews had been requested from A. K. Chesterton – a journalist and ex-public-relations-officer who had become a member of the BUF at the same time as John Beckett. Of this report, and of this time, Chesterton later wrote:*

---

* *The Tragedy of Antisemitism.*

Genuinely puzzled (I have the clearest mental picture of him at the time) Mosley ordered a thorough research into the Jewish question, especially into the financial and political activities which the movement attacked; and it was found that there was a very close identification between those activities and specific jewish interests. Rightly or wrongly, Mosley imagined that he had stumbled on the secret of Jewry's bitter attack on the movement.

What the report suggested was that the BUF was not in essence anti-semitic, but that when it had attacked as a matter of policy financial and political interests − such as those to do with banking, with advertising and with what is nowadays called the media − it had discovered almost as an afterthought that these happened to be run by Jews; and it was because of this that Jews were attacking the BUF; so was the BUF not now justified in more openly retaliating against Jews?

It was sometimes suggested (by John Strachey and Irene Ravensdale among others) that my father came to embrace anti-semitism openly for wholly cynical reasons − to maintain impetus in a party which for all the success of its first two years was by the end of 1934 running down: the expected economic crisis had not come and in fact the country was beginning to enjoy a small boom. But there was more at the back of BUF anti-semitism than simply a need to find a spurious crisis as a substitute for the expected real one to deal with which the BUF had come into existence: there was more to the BUF's anti-semitism, certainly, than what could be explained away by its Leader's skills in rationalisation. It was true that British Jews associated the BUF with German Nazism; it was true that Jews thus wanted to attack the BUF and could claim as justifiable the use of weapons such as those to do with publicity, banking and trade. But all this made it inevitable that there would be brought into the open what was anyway an intrinsic anti-semitism in the BUF, which up to now had only been partly restrained. The state of mind of people such as fascists who believe that they can and should set the world to rights requires scapegoats so that things may seem bearable when plans and hopes go wrong: this is a necessity if dynamism is to continue.

In 1934, Mosley seemed to accept A. K. Chesterton's report on the prevalence of a Jewish conspiracy in the attacks on the BUF: it was only years later that he wrote scathingly of people who −*

* *My Life.*

believe in a world conspiracy run by the Jews, which always seems
to me the most complete nonsense. The basic reason for my disbelief
in any such possibility is simply that from long experience I know
men are not clever or determined enough to organise anything of
the kind. Anyone who knows how difficult it is to keep a secret
among three men – particularly if they are married – knows how
absurd is the idea of a world-wide conspiracy consciously controlling
all mankind by its financial power: in real, clear analysis these deep-
rooted plots are seldom anything more sinister than the usual vast
muddle.

People who hold the conspiracy theory of history are those whose
minds work practically and logically: they cannot accept that there
are coincidences and occurrences simply by chance – that what appears
as a 'conspiracy' is just the fact that a great many people's minds happen
to work in common patterns, and thus patterns, if this is what is desired,
can be imposed on what is fortuitous. Not only bankers and Jews but
in fact most people like power: so (reason being the tool of what is
required) must there not be a vast conspiracy for power involving
powerful bankers and Jews? (Modern conspiracy theory sees a secret
alliance between Russian Communists and American Capitalists; both
sides, certainly, are united in their love of power). Conspiracy theory
depends for its devotees on those who feel themselves both to be rational
and to possess the power to effect things by will: marching with destiny,
they required scapegoats to explain the collision with reality.

The reason why Jews are so often picked as the heroes or victims
of conspiracy theory is because they have from the beginning seen themselves as involved as it were in conspiracy – even one with so grandiose
an aim as that of saving the world – and thus it is not difficult for
others to see them in some caricature of their own style. Also would-be
anti-semites can see that within the self-recognised Jewish conspiracy-
group there are both the enormously powerful and the apparently
abject: and so – how useful this is for those who wish for scapegoats!
They can explain their own failures as being caused by the enemy that
is all-dominating and threatening, and they can take out their envies
and rages on that which is helpless and abject.

At the Albert Hall meeting of 28th October 1934 it had become
known that there was to be some statement of policy about the BUF's
attitude to Jews; great care was taken by the police to keep fascists
and anti-fascists apart. Blackshirt stewards were detailed to see that only
ticket holders got in; as a result the hall was only two thirds full, and

Mosley spoke to an audience of blackshirt supporters. It was to them that he made what was expected, and what was taken to be, his declaration of open warfare against Jews. In fact (but who would see this and who would not?) this was still resolutely, almost absurdly enigmatic.

I have encountered things in this country which I did not dream existed in Britain. One of them is the power of organised Jewry which is today mobilised against Fascism. They have thrown down their challenge to fascism, and I am not in the habit of ignoring challenges. Now they seek to howl over the length and breadth of the land that we are bent on racial and religious persecution. That charge is utterly untrue.

Today we do not attack the Jews on racial or religious grounds; we take up the challenge that they have thrown down because they fight against Fascism and against Britain. They have declared in their great folly to challenge the conquering force of the modern age. Tonight we take up that challenge: they will it: let them have it!

CHAPTER 10

The Party

The other and apparently contrary steps that my father took to deal with the sudden aimlessness of the BUF in the second half of 1934 were to do with trying to re-establish discipline and decency. Although the movement had defended itself energetically with words after the fracas at Olympia, it was evident to anyone who cared to look beyond propaganda that things got out of hand amongst the stewards and the headquarters personnel who were supposed to control them. The District Inspector quoted earlier wrote:

> It must be admitted here that there were denizens of the Black House who would not have been welcome additions to any decent lads' club. . . They hoped to cash in in a big way eventually out of victory, but meanwhile were content with chicken-feed from petty theft and mean little rackets. Plain clothes officers from time to time showed interest in some of the individuals accommodated in the Black House. It took time to comb out these undesirable characters, but eventually the movement shook itself free of them.

Oswald Mosley set great store by the image of purity that he believed should be characteristic of his movement. It should be composed of men who were austere and incorruptible because it was only through such men – 'new men who come from nowhere' – that a fascist-type government could properly work; that power could safely be vested in the centrally dominated corporate state without traditional democratic safeguards. Years later he wrote of his vision of a fascist party:*

---

* *Europe: Faith and Plan.*

Oswald Mosley

B.U.F. hierarchy in 1935; Back row: J. H. Hone, E. Atherley, J. Thompson, R. Platten, R. Gordon-Canning, J. Beckett, B. Donovan, C. S. Sharp, W. J. Leaper; Front row: A. Raven Thomson, E. Piercy, I. Dundas, Oswald Mosley, N. Francis-Hawkins, W. Risdon, W. Joyce

Micky by Cimmie's tomb

The Leader speaking (*Fox Photos Ltd*)

Vivien, Micky, Baby and Oswald Mosley at Savehay Farm

Diana Guinness

Alexandra ('Baba') Metcalfe

Vivien, Florence the nursery maid, Nanny, Micky, Nicholas, Andrée – summer 1933

Fascists marching to Euston Station – 1933 (*BBC Hulton Picture Library*)

The Black House – Entrance (*BBC Hulton Picture Library*)

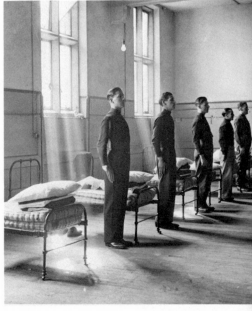

The Black House – Interior (*BBC Hulton Picture Library*)

Oswald Mosley with the 'I' Squad – Hyde Park 1934 (*A BUFPA copyright photograph*)

Crowds held back by police – Hyde Park 1934 (*BBC Hulton Picture Library*)

Lady Mosley (Oswald Mosley's mother) – Hyde Park 1934 (*A BUFPA copyright photograph*)

Oswald Mosley and Nicholas – Capri 1935

Diana – Capri 1935

Nicholas, Oswald Mosley, Baba – South of
France 1934

Baba, Oswald Mosley – South of France
1934

...ssolini and Oswald Mosley – Saluting base, Rome
1935 (*Keystone Press Agency Ltd*)

Unity Mitford and Diana – Nuremberg 1934

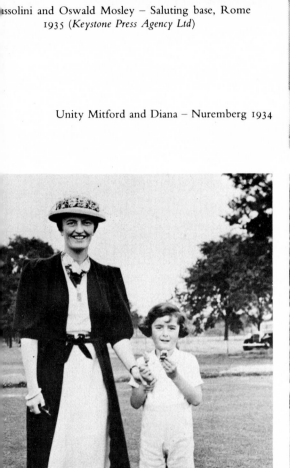

Irene Ravensdale and Micky – Eton 1936
Right: Nicholas and Micky – Eton 1938

The Battle of Cable Street – Crowds running (*BBC Hulton Picture Library*)

The Battle of Cable Street – Police chasing (*BBC Hulton Picture Library*)

The party can be the greatest influence in the modern world for good or evil... the party must be a party of men and women dedicated to an idea... its character should be more that of a church than of a political party... the old axiom that 'all power corrupts' has doubtful validity, because it derives from our neglect of Plato's advice to find men carefully and train them by methods which make them fit for heroes.

In 1934 it must have become unavoidably apparent that Plato's advice was not being attended to; that now was the time to repair this. Mosley wrote of this time: 'The supreme merit of defeat to a great party is that it purges the worst and preserves the best: not sweet, but vital, are the uses of political adversity.'

He called in to advise him Major General J. F. C. Fuller, a recent convert to the BUF. Fuller had been Chief of Staff to the British Tank Corps in 1917; he had then been Chief Instructor at the Camberley Staff College, and Military Assistant to the Chief of the Imperial General Staff. He had retired from the army in 1933 in order to devote himself to writing. He was a methodical and articulate man with a mind of his own; he could be trusted to be aloof from the in-fighting and accusations of 'plotting' that bedevilled the regular staff at BUF headquarters. Fuller wrote to Mosley in the summer of 1934:

... I am glad the position between you and Rothermere has been cleared up. The press is valuable, but as an instrument only; its danger is that it always aims at mastership, and that its principles are regulated by dividends. As it can only create great emotions and not great movements it cannot destroy a great movement. In fact its hostility is, I believe, as powerful an advertisement as its friendship; because, anyhow in the early days of a movement, it puts enthusiasts on their mettle and keeps out the jelly-fish. In fact hostility gives quality while praise, at its best, is of 24 hours duration in this age of ball-bangers and squeeze-and-kiss-me girls. Considering that the press is supposed to be almighty, which it isn't, it is strange that no press has ever created or even assisted any great national movement – e.g. the Salvation Army or even the Boy Scouts. Every great movement starts off in a minority of *one*. The strength of a new movement is in indirect proportion to the resistance offered to it.

This, in the circumstances, must have been just the sort of thing that the Leader wanted to hear. He asked Fuller to carry out research and to produce a report on the way in which he considered the BUF

should be reorganised. Fuller produced his report on October 8th, some
three weeks before the Albert Hall meeting.

> After two months close study at N.H.Q. I am of the opinion that
> the Movement cannot fail to succeed if certain radical changes are
> made in its organisation and discipline. It is obvious that the Move-
> ment has grown up on enthusiasm rather than to plan; that it is
> lacking in authority, requires pulling together, and needs to be guided
> towards a clear-cut and attainable object. Unless this is done, I am
> of the opinion that either the movement will decline or it will break
> up into hostile factions. The time has come when quantity should
> definitely give way to quality. This is very largely a question of
> organisation.
>
> *Object*
>
> As the ultimate object of the Movement is to establish
> constitutionally a new form of government, the immediate object
> is to win a number of seats in the next General Elections. Con-
> sequently all means should be directed towards this end.
>
> *Propaganda*
>
> Of the little I have seen of propaganda it appears to
> me to be somewhat crude. It lacks art and common sense. In place
> of being persuasive it is aggressive. I agree that to start with a
> challenging spirit is necessary in order to wake people up: but now
> that the Movement is on its feet, and seeing that there are at most
> but eighteen months to work in, tactics must be fitted to circum-
> stances. It should be remembered that for every one man and woman
> who applaud the words 'revolution' and 'dictatorship' there are ten
> who actively dislike them.
>
> *The BUF*
>
> I consider it imperative that what may be called 'Black-
> shirtism' is modified. It may appeal to the young and inexperienced,
> but if it is unchecked, it will lose more votes in the next elections
> than anything else. I consider this question a perturbing one. 'Black-
> shirtism' leads to coattrailing and gasconading, and if unchecked may
> develop into a Frankenstein monster. Though the wearing of the
> blackshirt appeals to young people, it must not be overlooked that
> this is an old country, very solid, stable and matter of fact. It is still
> instinctively a feudal country. The masses of the people will always
> listen to men and women of experience and importance, but they
> will seldom listen to boys and girls. They know that things must
> change, but their instincts are against violent change.

Most of the Blackshirts are too young to realise this. They are out for a game rather than to foster a Movement and consider that those who do not agree with them are old fashioned or lacking in energy. In a revolutionary country they would be right, but in a conservative country they are wrong. They do not see that attack, attack, attack, is a poor policy and a somewhat ridiculous one to assume in this country. It is not the Communists, Jews, etc., who are going to prevent the B U F winning seats in the next election, it is they themselves – not because they lack enthusiasm, but because they do not understand the conditions which exist in this country and, consequently, their enthusiasm is misdirected. This enthusiasm must be canalised towards the object. If it is not, I doubt whether a single seat will be won in 1935 or 1936.

The Defence Force must be limited to what it is intended for – the defence of free speech. It should be as inconspicuous as possible, whilst the mass of active and non-active members must be given a political outlook, and this out-look must dominate. So long as the Defence idea dominates, it is as if the police dominated the government. This is not dictatorship, but despotism. The Movement is sadly lacking in able men, and one reason for this is, that they are cold-shouldered out of it. Rothermere's support should have greatly benefited the Movement; in place it proved detrimental – why? First, because the organisation was not flexible enough to absorb a large number of recruits, and secondly, because the discipline was such that the more able recruits were not utilised; they joined up, became disgusted and then left.

There followed detailed plans for reorganising administration: these were mainly to do with ways in which the position of the Leader might be made less solitary and unapproachable – a Deputy Leader with more authority, or even a deputy 'triumvirate', were suggested – and ways in which 'political organisation' should be kept clear of 'general organisation'. Questions of policy, that is, should not be open to obstruction caused by fear of 'someone treading on someone else's toes'.

Fuller also sent to Mosley a letter in which he offered his own services for the job of getting 'the organisation pulled together' – presumably as one of the 'triumvirate'. Immediately at Headquarters there was the inevitable outcry that Fuller was plotting to take the whole movement over.

Mosley did not for the moment do much to implement Fuller's suggestions. He was occupied with matters such as the Worthing assault

charge, on account of which he seemed to feel it necessary to demonstrate loyalty to old comrades-in-arms; also with the libel action against
the *Star* which had finally come to court. The *Star* had reported, as
a result of his debate with James Maxton in 1933, that Mosley was
ready to take over the government with machine guns: in fact he had
said he would resist communists with machine guns if it was they who
tried to take over government illegally (see page 11). Here too in the
witness box he had a chance to demonstrate his contempt for conventionally cautious attitudes. The counsel against him was Norman
Birkett, who some five years later was to preside over the Tribunal
enquiring into his, Mosley's, imprisonment without trial. In November
1934 –

Counsel: If a Communist Government is called to power with the
              assent of the King, would you shoot them down?
Mosley: It is possible to put questions on ever increasing hypo-
              theses which lead at last to an absurdity. You might as well
              say that if His Majesty the King of England enacted the
              law of Herod that every first-born shall be slain, would
              you, in those circumstances, be a revolutionary?
Counsel: Who is to be the judge – you?
Mosley: When there is a condition of anarchy, it does not require
              much judgment. If you were shot in the streets it would
              not require any great condition of judgment to know you
              had been shot.

The Jury, still confident that words should mean roughly what they
say, awarded Mosley £5,000 damages. The Lord Chief Justice Hewart
in his summing up said of Mosley – 'Did he not appear to you to
be a public man of no little courage, no little candour and no little
ability?'

Within the movement however there was still the impression of
things being out of control. A. K. Chesterton was sent round provincial branches to report on conditions: he found in Coventry 'a snug
club with separate bars marked "Officers" and "Blackshirts" '; in Stoke,
which had the largest branch membership in the country, there was
an organisation which was 'part thieves kitchen and part bawdy house'.
A woman member wrote to 'Ma' Mosley complaining of the behaviour
of members of the 'I' Squad; people were apt to feel they were at
the mercy of any 'whipper-snapper in big boots.' The problem of what
fascists, brought together to deal with a crisis, in fact did when there

was no crisis, was now seen unavoidably to be coming to its own climax.

Eventually early in 1935 Mosley announced his decisions about reform in an article in *Blackshirt* entitled 'The Next Stage in Fascism'. Discipline, especially at National Headquarters, was to be tightened up: the atmosphere of headquarters would be 'that of a workshop rather than of a clubhouse or playground'. The organisation of the movement would be even more specifically on army lines. Every blackshirt was to be a member of a unit of five or six; units were to be part of Sections; Sections were to be part of Companies; and so on in a hierarchical structure up to the single Leader at the top. Only those who gave to the movement at least two nights a week would be entitled to wear a blackshirt; in this way there would be no need for a special Defence Force, because any blackshirt would be trained to steward meetings. Also –

Distinctive badges and dress will be worn by units giving more service according to the amount of time they give and to the degree of efficiency attained by certain standard tests which will be laid down. Units giving five nights a week will be permitted to wear the dress now worn by 'I' Division N.H.Q. provided they reach the required high standard of efficiency. Blackshirts will in every way be graded according to their service, and will be honoured within the Movement by the degree of sacrifice they make for the cause.

The most vital work in the future would be door-to-door canvassing; the aim once more was to have a BUF branch in every parliamentary constituency. There were complex instructions about methods of selection and promotion of group leaders. But above all –

I am determined to preserve pure and immutable the fine flame of the original Blackshirt movement. In the present great growth of our movement this can only be done by confining Blackshirt membership to those who prove, by real Blackshirt service, that they are inspired by the true blackshirt spirit.

The processes of weeding out were not always happy. 'Ma' Mosley had been leader of the Women's Section of the BUF since 1933; she had an office in the Black House and was responsible for the women who acted as secretaries and paper-sellers and even stewardesses at meetings: she would travel round provincial branches dispensing good cheer like a dowager queen. She had confronted danger: at Dumfries there had been a communist poster which exhorted people to 'Give Maud Some Bouquets', which referred to the throwing of stones. She was sixty: she had done her job with courage and with dignity. But there had always been something bizarre about her appointment by her adored son and Leader.

In February 1935 she was writing to him:

My Darling Tom,
You succeeded in making me look a complete fool this afternoon – and thereby justifying your shelving of me. You will always make an idiot of me by being rude to me in public; but it was not necessary to be quite so brutal. I would have 'gone quietly' and fully meant what I said some time ago – that in the cause of Fascism I would be ready to give way to a better woman at any time. It remains to be seen if Miss Shore is superwoman enough to do all she has undertaken. I hope so. So far I have shouldered all my officers' mistakes and done the *whole* of the work of the country branches since I came out of hospital six months ago. Lady Makgill did nothing but use the premises for her own business and told her secretary 'If Lady Mosley were fool enough to sweat over country branches she could'. Then came Miss R – with her dishonest inefficiency, later backed by Miss S – and Miss A – in sullen opposition to me. To them I was a stumbling block to collaring the machine and all its resources.

And a few months later she was writing:

I do not think you have any idea of the difficulties I had to face during the early months and when we moved to N.H.Q. Intrigue the whole time. Insubordination from people whose word you preferred to take to mine and who have since disappeared from the movement by your instructions.... No, Tom, it is not quite good enough; there is a limit to one's endurance.

Intrigue and back-biting are a recognised part of political machines: in the BUF they seem to have become exaggerated probably just on account of people dedicated to dynamism having so little chance to exercise real power. Regarding the Leader's handling of headquarter's court intrigues A. K. Chesterton, after he had left the movement a few years later, wrote of Mosley:

In order to back up his favourites there is no affront which he will refuse to offer to common sense and no specious excuse he will hesitate to advance. If a leader shows himself unable to maintain even the presence of a judicial attitude in dealing with his own organisation, he can plead with no convincing justification for the sacrifices which service to him imposes.

But then Chesterton had been writing of Mosley only a few months earlier:*

Oswald Mosley is a very kind man, far and away the kindest man I know ... Mosley's kindness is born of strong, tense generous emotions; of a sense of the innate decency of mankind; of a natural inclination to think well of his fellow men and of a very profound insight into the mainsprings of human action which enables him to understand when they fail... He is also one of the most patient and approachable of men... His extraordinary intellectual power often enables him to synthesise what first appears to be conflicting opinions... his own views are almost invariably confirmed by events. That is part of Mosley's real greatness: he has no need to dictate, for the good reason that his spiritual quality precludes the necessity of 'laying down the law' to men who share so completely his own outlook and serve him with so large a pride.

These two descriptions of Mosley are concerned with the same set of events: it seems to have been part of the atmosphere that he engendered that the attitudes of his followers to him should have been often so adoring, and then sometimes suddenly so alarmed and hostile. He seemed to give people the vision of being in touch with great events; then perhaps there was a glimpse of the vacuum.

What Mosley seemed to be trying to do with his movement at this time was to keep in existence as many different strands as possible: he recognised that the bravado of cheap propaganda and of the Defence Force had been overdone; but he wanted to maintain something of it in existence while he looked at other possible channels for the movement's future. He had by now accepted many of Fuller's recommendations: the party was to turn from being a movement ready to deal with a crisis to one with the aim of winning a parliamentary election; for this there had to be more emphasis on explaining what fascists were

* *Portrait of a Leader.*

for, apart from the demonstration that they would be able to maintain law and order. In fact for some time there had been two strands running side by side in the pages of the *Blackshirt* and the *Fascist Week* – on the one hand the virulent tub-thumping of which the chief exponent was William Joyce, and on the other a calm and comparatively civilised effort to explain fascist ideologies and policies of which the chief representative was Raven Thomson.

Raven Thomson was a free-lance philosopher and sociologist who in 1932 had written a book called *Civilisation As Divine Superman* in which he had suggested that civilisation itself should be seen as the higher form of entity such as was symbolised by Nietzsche's image of the 'Superman': in 1933 he had written for the *Blackshirt* an article on Smuts's 'Holism' in which he had elaborated this idea. 'An atom is more than a mere system of circling electrons, a molecule more than a collection of atoms and... the civilised state as a "whole" must be something more than the mere collection of individuals each working for his own end.' In the early numbers of the *Fascist Week* he was applying these ideas specifically to fascism: 'The Fascist call for national unity and a patriotic purpose is fulfilling that divine urge to wider life and nobler consciousness which is inherent in the whole scheme of existence.' This could be brought down to earth in the practical vision of the Corporate State:*

> The Corporate State is built up on the analogy of the human body which is composed of millions of cells all working harmoniously together and constituting the human personality... In order to enable the human individual to carry out his proper function in society, Fascism intends to reorganise the industrial life of this country under a system of discipline and control...
>
> Existing industries would be placed under Corporations on which would sit representatives of the employers through their Federations, representatives of the workers through their Trade Unions, and representatives of the consumers. These corporations would fix fair prices, eliminating cut-throat competition; and fair wages, preventing exploitation.
>
> All these Corporations would be under the control of a National Corporation whose duty it would be to direct the various industries to the best interests of the State and the Community.

* *Fascist Week.*

This was the vision of an ideal. The unasked question here was, as usual – who on earth would be these controlled and harmonious men, free from intrigue and back-biting, who would run such a Corporate State?

Next door to such articles in *Blackshirt* and *Fascist Week* William Joyce would be writing –

> Miserable pedantic intellectuals, who skulked in lecture rooms throughout the war, have now discovered that the Germans can commit atrocities. They chose to ignore the execution of Nurse Cavell, yet they twitter with execration because 'at Worms a number of Jews were arrested, shut up in a pigsty, and beaten on the buttocks...' When the spoilt body of capitalism is put into the straightjacket of the Fascist State, these little by-products of the political system which Capitalism had made possible will of course be cleaned up too.

This was the style of that part of the movement represented by Joyce. He would write: 'Our purpose is to crush all compromise out of existence ... the concept of right admits of no pollution by wrong... Just as democracy is a psychopathic expression of inferiority, so tolerance is the habit of countenancing in others the faults which we ourselves desire to develop.' (In many of Joyce's utterances the sense seems to come out not as intended.) But what had this got to do with Raven Thomson's vision of 'Holism'?

Another writer in *Blackshirt* was E. de Burgh Wilmot who announced: 'Our first duty to Culture is to destroy it... the slow insidious advance of its hateful poison is comparable to the destroying terror of the plague.' There were attacks on particular aspects of 'culture': Proust was one of the writers 'overcome by the neurosis of an effortless megapolitical life and the fragrance of their own personalities': also – 'it is time that Mr Eliot was told that mankind has plenty of use for courage and sense of direction, none at all for defeatism and disease'. Then – 'Who is this Korda who comes to England to make comedies and monstrosities of our Kings and Queens? Under a fascist government he would not find himself at liberty to make fun of monarchy.' A subject of repeated attack was psychoanalysis – a 'black magical art' which 'dabbling with the mysteries of sex, has elaborated from them an occult science which undermines self-confidence ... and therefore strikes at morality and the family and so at the foundations of Christian Civilisation'.

Anti-semitism was of course never far beneath the surface in this kind of writing. General Fuller had remained for the most part on the reasonable side of the fence in fascist propaganda: in his report he had warned –

The Jews cannot destroy fascism unless fascists create a fulcrum from which Jews can operate their financial lever: this fulcrum is anti-semitism in such forms as will lead to a popular outcry in their favour. What the big Jews yearn for is that fascists will knock little Jews on the head, so that non-Jewish popular opinion will be shocked. Then they will spend millions to exploit the situation.

But then in January 1935 in the first number of the *Fascist Quarterly* – a magazine in which a serious attempt was made to raise the tone of fascist propaganda – Fuller wrote an article entitled *The Cancer of Europe* in which he said:

For over a thousand years an obscure tragedy has been played on the stage of European history by that outcast race – the Jews. Having given Christianity to the world, this strange people have never ceased in their efforts to destroy Christian culture...

The predominant characteristic of the Jew is his materialism which endows him with a destructive social force when he is placed in a spiritually ordered society... By predilection a trader, a banker, a dabbler in the occult, like a mole he works underground, silently and hidden, and like a bat he flits through the night seeing things unseen by creatures of day...

He may be of diamond or of dirt, yet, whatever he is made of, he is like the grit within the oyster: pearls of wealth form round him, but only at the expense of the organism on which he feeds....

Self-defence has compelled him to rely upon craft and cunning, always the weapons of the weak, and to enter into alliance with every subversive movement. In these Jews see power – power to avenge their wrongs, and power to gain world domination under an avenging messiah – as foretold by Talmud and Qabalah.

General Fuller turned out, in fact, to be a fervent exponent of con-spiracy theory: it transpired from letters to my father of this time that he had once been an admirer or even some sort of associate of Aleister Crowley, the self-styled apocalyptic 'Beast'. He had once threatened a libel action as a result of some suggestion concerning this relationship, but had been advised by lawyers to withdraw.

In the pages of *Blackshirt* there appeared a jingle which seemed to epitomise the split in fascist mentality concerning many things but especially Jews; on the one hand, how rational on the other – did the left hand know at all what the right might be up to?

> There are Jews and Jews! and I refuse
> To condemn a man for his race.
> If he's born in this dear old land of ours
> If he loves her soil, her trees, her flowers
> And brings on her no disgrace
> That man is my brother!
> But not the other –
> The oily material swaggering Jew
> The pot-bellied, sneering, money-mad Jew
> Who sells his country and his soil for gain
> Who sweats his fellows, whose life's in vain. . .

use

In the summer of 1935 the BUF gave up the Black House in Chelsea and moved its headquarters to much smaller offices in Great Smith Street. This was partly for reasons of economy; also to put into effect the policy of running the headquarters 'as a workroom not as a clubhouse'. Then, in August, Italy began to threaten Abyssinia with invasion, and General Fuller wrote a front page article in *Blackshirt* entitled 'Britain Must Keep Out of War'. There was the question – had the BUF at last found a positive and worthy cause to fight for? Suddenly dozens of young men appeared in the streets wearing black shirts and carrying placards with a new slogan – *Mind Britain's Business!* Could a fascist movement appeal to a democratic electorate in the cause of peace?

CHAPTER II

Holidays

For the summer holidays of 1935 my father took my sister Vivien and myself to a rented villa at Posillipo on the bay of Naples. We flew from Croydon Airport in an aeroplane that my Aunt Irene described as 'the Mail de Havilland'; we landed at Rome; there, my father and my sister and I were photographed and were in the papers the next day – my father with his chin up like Mussolini and my sister looking normal and myself under one of those soft grey felt school hats that made me look like a toadstool. We stayed in the Grand Hotel and were given boxes of chocolates by the management and the next day we were in the crowd at a march-past of innumerable fascists while my father was on the saluting base with Mussolini. There had been some talk of our being up on the platform too: it had probably been decided, after a look at the photograph, that we might not add to the glory.

The house at Posillipo belonged to Sir Rennell Rodd who had been British Ambassador in Rome; it was said to have been built as a result of a competition amongst the young men of the Embassy to see who could design the most hideous villa and Lady Rodd had come in and picked up the winning design and said it represented her perfect house. It was dark and cool with wide corridors and arches; it was on the top of a cliff and looked out across the bay to Vesuvius with the Isle of Capri lying like a Sphinx in the sea to the right. This seascape and landscape were quite different from those of the South of France or the Lido at Venice where we had been on previous summer holidays: there, people seemed to have been spilled on to rocks and beaches as if from some shipwreck: here everything was bright and mythical and exact.

It was during this holiday that I began to feel in some stronger relationship with my father: I was twelve; I loved the place; my father seemed to be at home in it with us. We spent much of the time as a family – first with my Aunt Baba and then, for the other fortnight as in the previous year, with Mrs Guinness. Baba did seem to be a mother-companion to us: she swam with us, played; she and my father seemed happy. I was able for the first time to take on my father at some sports. There was a dusty deck-tennis court at the side of the house where we played with a rubber quoit; I had become quite proficient at this game since the time of our cruise to the Canary Islands two years previously. My father played, as he played all games, with a vast histrionic exuberance: he would fling the quoit, spin it, lunge, shout; go hurtling across the court yet so delicately on his injured leg. I found that for once in a game I did not care if I won or lost; the enjoyment was in the cunning; the laughter.

My father had bought a 30ft motor yacht which was moored in an inlet at the bottom of hundreds of steps down the cliff. The boat was called the *Vivien*: it had cabins at the front and in the middle and one at the back where the two crew lived – the Capitano, and a sad sailor who raised and lowered the anchor. No one else slept except occasionally on the boat: what my father liked doing was to sail across the bay to Sorrento or Capri, to eat there in the marvellous restaurants, to swim off rocks where no one else was swimming. If we felt bold, we would venture for the day as far as Ischia. I remember my father's ability to make almost any excursion seem an adventure: speeding round the Sorrento peninsula would be like going round Cape Horn; my father would stand in the prow as if he were Odysseus; he laughed at himself creating an atmosphere like this; his laughter would be part of the adventure.

We would swim and explore grottos; we would sit on rocks and my father would quote Byron or Swinburne to us; he would do his extraordinary joke quotation – 'and bluer the sea-blue stream of the bay' – which meant that while in the sea he was peeing. He had a way of making ordinary things seem hilarious: his liking for teasing in this context even seemed fitting. There is something about this particular land and this sea that makes it seem anyway like a place where gods might have come down; this is an impression that has never wholly left me.

One of the ways in which our father made his teasing contacts with us children (was not this somewhat godlike?) was by offering us bets or bribes in the way of challenges – one lira for the first one into the sea; five lire for her or him who jumps or dives off the cliff. My sister Vivien was much better than myself at diving: I perfected a rather crab-like technique of slithering more quickly into the sea. My father would recline in his chair on the deck of the boat and laugh: what mortal children would do for money! My sister and I chalked up quite a lot of winnings in this way; my father was slow at paying. One day my sister and I went on strike. We would accept no more challenges nor bribes until he forked out. He was amused at this: he offered us higher and higher prizes in order to try to break our strike: we grimly sat it out around restaurants and grottos. Eventually, still laughingly, he paid.

Sometimes the teasing went wrong. The relationship which he had with my sister Vivien was, I had noticed, different from that which he had with me: it was often characterised by what my Aunt Irene had called 'his insensate silly slapping "boppy" chaff'. Viv, aged fourteen, was almost the only person who did not seem to be in awe of my father; she answered him back; often she even got in a bit of 'chaff' first. She would tell him how ridiculous he looked when even for family snapshots he posed like Mussolini on the prow of the boat; how he cared too much about food. In return he would goad her when she was reluctant to do her dives off high rocks; he would tell her that she was fat. My Aunt Irene wrote of the 'pertness' with which Vivien seemed to be copying her father: all this went on amongst the rocks where it seemed gods must have come down; there was something between my father and Vivien like that between Wotan and Brünnhilde. Once at about this time Aunt Irene was looking for a boarding school for Vivien and she told my father that she had found a school that was 'enchanting' and my father replied – 'She doesn't need an enchanting school, she needs a barracks.'

My own role in this was to watch, I suppose rather like one of the Nibelung dwarfs from under the cover of whatever were symbolically my toadstools. My sister and I were in heart-felt alliance together; but there was also it seemed some quite solitary fight for survival.

My own characteristics were the opposite of those of Viv: I admired her courage: sometimes I felt I could hardly speak at all. That spring I had spent a term away from school in order to go to a stammer specialist in London. He taught me to speak in cadences so that I could declaim like a politician in front of an audience: I could do this quite well: then, when I was not with him, I would stammer as before. How could I explain – but I do not want to be like someone declaiming in front of an audience! My Aunt Irene recorded – 'Nick's stammer is quite unbelievable, and curiously he has no idea of how awful he is. Nanny tries to make him see his contorted face in the mirror and how hard it is for us to listen.'

At Posillipo for the first part of the holidays there was Aunty Baba with whom my father seemed at home. Then one day we had a rare visitor: the Crown Princess of Italy came to spend the day – she had been Princess Marie José of Belgium before her marriage, and had been Baba's childhood friend at Hackwood in the first world war. We all went for a trip on the boat from Posillipo to Ischia. Then in the evening back at the villa and after we children had gone to bed there seemed to be strange comings-and-goings in the grown-up world; doors banged here and there; but what might one expect with Crown Princesses? But then the next morning when I was prowling about hitherto un-inhabited parts of the house to try to find out what was happening I was stopped in the passage by Andrée, my mother's ex-lady's maid who was with us on the holiday as usual to 'look after us'; and Andrée said in the stage-French accent that she never lost after all her years in England – 'Do not go in there, eet ees Mrs Guinness.' So – was this or was it not a surprise? Was it not the sort of thing, after all, we knew went on in the grown-up world?

What in fact seems to have happened – people inevitably have slightly different memories of this story – was that Diana, who had been due to arrive somewhat later in the week when my Aunt Baba had moved on to continue her holiday in Tunisia, had arrived in Naples early. She had recently been injured in a car-crash in London and had had to have plastic surgery; she had so longed to get out of the nursing-home and into the sun that she had persuaded her father to help her to escape from the nursing-home and to put her on an aeroplane; the telegram announcing her early arrival coincided with her actual arrival at the house at Posillipo in the middle of dinner. This was, of course, a social and a personal challenge worthy of the mettle of someone like my father – on his tightrope, as it were, juggling with his plates above Niagara. My sister Viv remembers a row in the middle of the night: then it was with Aunty Baba that we set off the same day on the boat on a three-day trip to Amalfi for the remaining days that had been planned of her holiday. I remember this occasion because it was the one time during those holidays when Viv and I slept on the boat: my father and Baba were in the hotel on the cliff. Mrs Guinness was left in charge of the house, being looked after by servants.

While Diana had been in the nursing-home my father had written to her:

Hurry up and get better as this place is lovely – no great horrors
been revealed except the ancient truth that 'Rodds never wash' – also
1,000 steps down to the beach – soon get used to them – we run
up them now – saying 'Won't they be fun when Diana arrives!'

I feel so badly about being away while you are so bad, why is
it? .... You may think this place too picture-postcard – being so
precious – but it is very enchanted.

It is in relation to this holiday that my memories properly begin
of my future stepmother Diana. At first because of her injuries she
did not venture far from the house; she would sit under a sunshade;
there were faint scars on her face, like the trails of snails, which were
healing. Viv and I would approach her cautiously like animals looking
for food; after a time she was playing games with us; she taught us
poker, and I think bridge. Then she was venturing down the hundreds
of steps with us and coming on the trips to the islands. Her relationship
with my father was different from that of other people; she did not
argue with him, did not reply in kind to his teasing; she did not enter
into any sort of contest really: either she seemed to like what he was
saying or doing, or else she would close her eyes for a time with a
look on her face that my father came to call 'tired' or 'patient'. And
then he would laugh, and she would laugh; and when she opened her
eyes whatever it was she had not liked had usually (but not always)
disappeared. She would sit on the boat and there would be an air of
stillness about her like that of the sphinxes and classical statues that
looked out over the sea from the terraces of villas on Capri. My father's
way of teasing her – I suppose he had his ways of teasing nearly
everyone – was to tell funny stories that were in fact in praise of her.
There was the story of a press reporter who had got into her room
in the nursing-home just after the operation on her face; he had asked
her what were the results of the plastic surgery; there was a headline
in the papers the next day – 'Mrs Guinness says "I am more beautiful
than ever."' There was a story of how my father and she had been
driving once on a mountain road in France and he had had to back
the car to turn it and he had asked her to look out of the window
to tell him when to stop; when the back wheels were half over the
precipice she had murmured – 'Vaguely wo.' My father would tell
such stories giving an exaggerated imitation of her *cor anglais* Mitford
voice: Diana would listen with her 'tired' look and at the end would
say, 'Oh you are silly!' Then she would smile at him with her huge
blue eyes and he would do his strange clicking laugh behind his teeth.

There were the strange names that they each had for the other: my father always called Diana 'Percher' (pronounced persher) which was a reference to a breed of golden and heavy Flemish carthorses called Percherons; and she, for some reason, called him Kit. On the boat she would take photographs of him and would not object when he posed like Mussolini; she would sit on the prow like a mermaid, and indeed sometimes play a small piano accordion and sing sad German songs such as the *Lorelei*.

One conversation that I remember having at this time with Diana (I think this was the following summer, 1936, when we were all together again in a hotel in Sorrento) was concerning my schoolboy passion, cricket. There was a day when my hero, W. R. Hammond, scored 317 runs for Gloucestershire against Nottinghamshire; Diana asked me why I looked so pleased; I showed her a newspaper headline which said – 'Sublime Hammond'. I could not understand why she laughed so much. She reassured me – Yes, she was sure, Hammond had been sublime: it was only – well, what was it? I imagined I understood. I wondered if there would ever come a time when I might laugh at W. R. Hammond's being sublime.

Before this 1936 holiday at Sorrento there had as usual been a good deal of jockeying about who would be where and when and with whom: there had been some plan by which my father and we children would as in previous years be for a time with Baba; then at the last moment my father had to have an operation for appendicitis, so Vivien and I had gone to Cornwall with Irene and Micky, and then when we did get to Italy our father had been accompanied there by our grandmother, and it was Diana who was there with them, having come on from the Olympic Games in Berlin. I have a memory of Granny in the boiling heat always seeming to be equipped with her full complement of hat, scarf, frilly blouse, black suit and chain-mail bag – like the character of Grandma in Giles's cartoons. She was kind and gallant and did her best with us children; but she used to cheer herself up with phrases like 'It's a poor heart that never rejoices' which was apt to send at least mine into my boots. Perhaps my father and Diana needed her as a sort of chaperone: these were the days in which it was still thought that if the two of them were seen together staying in a hotel, it might do him political harm.

Viv and I had some notable quarrels during these holidays: we would play chess, and she was liable to hit me over the head with the chess board. She was under a certain stress because she was waiting for a telegram which would tell her the results of her School Certificate

Examination: when the telegram came she opened it and rushed out of the room in tears. We got ready to commiserate with her; but of course the telegram had said that she had passed.

It was probably good of my father and Diana to have us children with them in these holidays; they could have left us with Nanny and Micky in Cornwall. They did not have many chances to have holidays on their own together; and we were now of an age to be staying up for dinner.

Some time during or just before the summer holidays of 1936 my father and Diana decided to get married. They wanted to keep the marriage secret because, my father explained later, his first wife Cimmie had suffered much public hostility due to his politics and he did not want Diana to be in an even more exposed position now that he was a notorious fascist. He and Diana worked out that the only place where they might be married and where there might be a chance of this remaining secret was Germany: there was an agreement between England and Germany by which the nationals of each country could be married in the other by a registrar and not – as was the rule in other countries – at the Embassy. And Hitler himself could be prevailed on, they thought, to ensure that news of the marriage did not get into the papers.

Diana's and Unity's relationship with Hitler had prospered since the time they had first met him early in 1935. In September of that year, after the summer holiday at Posillipo, Diana had joined Unity in Munich and they had gone for the third time to the Nuremberg Parteitag; they were known now as Hitler's friends; when they told Hitler of the difficulties that Putzi Hanfstaengl had made for them in previous years when they wanted to meet him – especially over his, Hitler's, reputed horror of lipstick – Hitler laughed, and said that Hanfstaengl usually bored him by introducing him to old American women. Diana and Unity were taken to a village rally by Unity's new friend Streicher; he asked them to stand up in front of the crowd and he announced 'They may be taller and more beautiful than we but they have the same blood'; and then in English – 'They are not Angles but angels.' In the autumn their mother visited Unity in Munich and was introduced to Hitler: she got the impression that Hitler had 'plenty of leisure. . . . in congenial company he would stay and talk for ever. . . . he gave the impression of doing always whatever he wanted at the moment, unhampered by any set time table or urgent work waiting to be done'.

In March 1936 when Hitler's troops entered the Rhineland Diana and Unity were in Cologne to greet him; he recognised them in the crowded foyer of a hotel and came over and asked them to tea; then he asked them to be his guests at the Olympic Games in Berlin. They stayed in the Goebbels' house and were driven to the games each day: they also went with Hitler to the Wagner Festival at Bayreuth. Diana found the latter 'an experience as heavenly as the Olympic Games were boring'. She told Hitler that *Parsifal* was the only opera of Wagner's that she did not like. Hitler told her that she would feel differently as she grew older.

Diana made friends with Goebbels' wife Magda: she told her of her and my father's hopes to get married. Magda suggested that the wedding should be in her and her husband's house, then secrecy could be ensured. She wrote to Diana at Sorrento after she had heard of my father's operation for appendicitis:

Schwanenwerder 14th August 1936

Dearest Diana,

A thousand thanks for your lovely letter, but how sorry I was to hear of your and the Leader's bad luck... I sincerely hope that you have now got over it all and that the Leader very quickly recovers.

Here the beautiful but exhausting days of the Olympics will soon be over. I shall be back on 1st September and we will then settle your problem. The date of the 17th is a good one and we will be able to do all the paperwork etc. in peace. Your stay in Germany will be a little longer and the whole business settled in Germany.

Have a good rest. You are taking on difficult tasks, and just as in the past, so even more in the future will you need your strength and health. Give my best wishes to the L [Leader]. A thousand best wishes and kisses to you too. I am so fond of you.

Your Magda.

My father and Diana were married on October 6th in the Goebbels' house in Berlin. Of their families only Unity was present. Diana told how★ –

Unity and I, standing at the window of an upstairs room, saw Hitler walking through the trees of the park-like garden that separated the house and the *Reichskanzlei*; the leaves were turning yellow and there was bright sunshine. Behind him came an adjutant carrying a box and some flowers.

★ *A Life of Contrasts.*

Inside the box was Hitler's wedding present – 'a photograph in a silver frame with A. H. and the German eagle'.

My father had travelled to Berlin on October 5th; this was the day after the traumatic event in East London that came to be known as the Battle of Cable Street, which is described in the next chapter. On the night of the wedding, October 6th; Diana recorded that in the Kaiserhof Hotel she and my father had 'a quarrel of which, try as I will, I cannot remember the reason: we went to bed in dudgeon'. Next day they flew back to England.

No one in England was told of the wedding except Diana's parents and her brother Tom. It was thought, probably correctly, that others could not be trusted with the secret.

One odd result of my father's links with Hitler through Diana was that his relationship with Mussolini was broken. For some time Mussolini had seemed to be rather aloof. There had in fact been Count Grandi's letter of the previous year advising Mussolini to reconsider the question of payments to my father: by now, in 1936, the payments had stopped. When my father was in Rome later that autumn and he tried to arrange his customary meeting with Mussolini he was interviewed instead by the Foreign Minister Ciano who asked him pointedly whether or not it was true that he had been just previously in Berlin. When my father said that he had, Ciano said that Mussolini was too ill to see him. Mussolini was at that time envious of Hitler. My father never saw Mussolini again: nor, for that matter, did he again see Hitler.

In his autobiography my father wrote:

Clearly, my normal relations with him [Mussolini] would easily have been restored if I had gone back to Rome a year or two later because he and Hitler were then on good terms. But for the last three years before the war I never left England at all; I was held fast by the growth of our movement and the ever increasing intensity of our campaign.

CHAPTER 12

The Battle of Cable Street

Towards the end of 1935 Oswald Mosley found himself with a movement somewhat pruned and reorganised: the Black House had been given up, and attempts were being made to fit the style to the policy of putting emphasis on the winning of elections rather than on demonstrations of toughness. The Italian-Abyssinian war which had begun in October 1935 had provided the movement with a slogan – 'Mind Britain's Business' – and this for a time had concentrated members' energies. But then the Prime Minister Stanley Baldwin, who six months earlier had taken over from MacDonald as head of the National Government, called for a general election in November, a year or so before it might have been expected: the BUF found itself in a difficult position. The election it had been working for was at hand, yet its electoral organisation was clearly still inadequate – it was short of funds and had few suitable potential candidates. Two years earlier the BUF had boasted of putting up four hundred candidates at an election: now, Mosley must have remembered the débâcle of the New Party in the 1931 election when all but two of the twenty-three candidates had lost their £150 deposits. What should be done by a movement that had so recently decided that its *raison d'être* was the putting up of candidates?

Mosley hit on the original idea of trying to make it seem a positive move in the electoral game to put up no candidates at all: he announced –

My advice is not to waste a vote for a farce. Wait for the real battle. This election is a sham battle, which at the next election will be followed by the real battle: for not until Fascist candidates enter the field as challengers for power will any reality be introduced into British politics.

And indeed the 1935 election was rather vapid, because both the National and the Labour parties were adopting the same indecisive attitudes towards the crisis that mattered – that of the Italian–Abyssinian war. They were advocating sanctions against Italy but that these should not occasion any threat to European peace. Baldwin was restored to power as the head of a new so-called National but in effect Conservative Government. Mosley wrote in *Blackshirt*:

> It was the lowest poll of the last thirty years with the single exception of 1918 when the men had not returned from France... the old force and the old system are a dying force in Britain... Fascism alone emerges as the triumphant challenger... the future is with us.

Fascists were becoming adept at arguing that whatever happened was probably for the best. They were still searching, however, for some practical cause to harness their energies to.

During the course of 1935 there had sprung up in East London a movement which, almost uniquely in the history of the BUF, gained a large and spontaneous local following without direction from head-quarters or at first the impetus of the Leader as a speaker. Up till now the BUF's outgoing energies had been directed mainly at industrial parts of the country where unemployment was highest and at country districts where government agricultural policy might be felt to be ruinous: the fount of these energies was central London where it was felt that political influence resided. The East End had seemed to be a political backwater – a world of its own, a hive of small industries, a slum. A large proportion of the population were immigrants; a large proportion of these were Jewish.

In October 1934 at the Albert Hall Mosley had thrown down, or taken up, the challenge concerning the Jews; but the enemy had re-mained somewhat amorphous, mythical. In April 1935 he was reiterat-ing – 'I openly and publicly challenge the Jewish interest in this country commanding commerce, commanding the press, commanding the cinema, commanding the City of London, commanding sweatshops': in response to this he had received a telegram of congratulation from Streicher in Germany to which he had replied, 'I greatly esteem your message in the midst of our hard struggle: the forces of Jewish corrup-tion must be overcome in all great countries before the future of Europe can be made secure in justice and in peace'. (Mosley later explained that this was a sort of routine reply sent out by his office in response to congratulatory telegrams and he did not remember being personally responsible for it.) Then in September, as part of the run-up to his 'Mind Britain's Business' campaign, he was saying: 'Over the whole of this Abyssinian dispute rises the stink of oil; and stronger than even the stink of oil is the stink of the Jew.' (He later explained that unfortunately one did sometimes get carried away in the heat of speeches by phrases that one later regretted.) But not much of this rhetoric was directed against the sort of Jews that were in London's East End.

The first BUF branch there had been one at Bow, opened in the winter of 1934/5. Then a branch at Bethnal Green was opened by District Officer Mick Clarke. Clarke was a Cockney, a powerful and vituperative speaker; it was he who built up a political following almost independent of Mosley. Fascism in the East End became directed specifically against Jews. There were about 20,000 Jews in Bethnal Green; about three times as many in nearby Stepney; somewhat less in Hackney, Shoreditch and Bow. There were about 150,000 Jews altogether out of a total population of about half a million.

These Jews had come for the most part from the ghettos of Russia and Poland and Hungary as a result of the pogroms at the end of the last century. They had brought with them their distinctive clothes, their distinctive food and their distinctive language (Yiddish). They observed their day of rest on Saturdays instead of Sundays; they were opposed to intermarriage with non-Jews; and they kept themselves to themselves. There was no district of East London in which they were in an actual majority, but it seemed as if in many places they were in positions of power: they worked hard – mostly at the tailoring and furniture trades – and saved money. They often became landlords, and were apt perhaps understandably to give preference to their people in matters both of accommodation and of jobs. Surrounding them were people of a more free-and-easy, almost anarchic tradition, often Irish; but who themselves were dependent on a feeling of group-solidarity if they were not to lose identity in their hard-pressed lives. This was a situation that would seem to have been only too ready for the introduction of a racialist type of fascism: what is of interest is the slowness of BUF headquarters to have taken any advantage of it.

At first there were the usual street-corner meetings with Mick Clarke's men on soap-boxes and a flag or two: there began to be phrases like 'hook-nosed unmentionables' and 'yiddish scum'. The accusations were mostly about conditions of employment in local businesses: there were sexual overtones too in the charges of non-Jewish girls being 'sweated' in back-street tailor's shops. Sometimes the style of this remained within the knock-about tradition of British street corner politics:

there were protests for instance by non-Jewish ponces against Jews who had cornered the prostitution industry: slogans appeared on walls – *British Streets for British Cows.*

Mosley addressed his last huge meeting at the Albert Hall in March 1936: in it he repeated (according to *The Times*) that 'it was the intention of British Fascism to challenge and break for ever the power of the Jews in Britain'. He also went into one of his more rousing flights of peroration –

> We count it a privilege to live in an age when England demands that great things shall be done, a privilege which learns to be of the generation which learns to say: 'What can we give?' instead of 'What can we take?' For thus our generation learns that there are greater things than slothful ease; greater things than safety; more terrible things than death.

William Joyce and Raven Thomson had begun to go down to the East End and add their voices to those of Mick Clarke and his followers. Then, in June 1936 Mosley himself appeared on the scene. He marched at the head of what *Blackshirt* described as 'a half-mile column': he spoke in Victoria Park, Bow, to a crowd that was variously estimated at anything from 5,000 to 100,000. He announced that from now on fascist effort would be concentrated in the East End: the BUF would put up candidates for the municipal elections in 1937. This was a new departure for the movement: so far, there had only been talk of fighting parliamentary elections. To lead the march Mosley and other members of headquarters staff had appeared in a completely new uniform – jack-boots, breeches, military-style jacket, Sam Browne belt and officer-type hat. The uniform was seen by many to be in emulation of the Nazi SS. One caustic member of the BUF said that it seemed to him more like that of 'King Zog's Own Imperial Dismounted Hussars'.

Soon after this Mosley had his operation for appendicitis; then there was the holiday in Sorrento; he was out of the fray for nearly two months. But the campaign in East London had been given its impetus. From now on, and for the next nine months, the BUF seemed to have found a cause and an actual enemy to fight.

For night after night there were meetings often in the same streets; fascists would arrive with their drums and loudspeaker vans; the crash of fascist oratory would go on for hours; it would break up old patterns of social life. If protests were made there was the likelihood of a fight and broken windows: if protests were not made there were jeers about Jews being 'on the run'. All this, it was claimed, was being done in the name of 'free speech' as part of a run-up to democratic elections. Before he had temporarily left the arena Mosley had again laid down the rule – 'Mere abuse we forbid... it is bad propaganda and alienates public sympathy.' But there were always fascists who seemed to care little about alienating public sympathy. Gangs of youths went through the streets chanting 'The Yids, the Yids, we've got to get rid of the Yids'. William Joyce's favourite phrase for Jews at this time seems to have been 'sub-men with prehensile toes'.

BUF speakers played a game with the police to see how far they could go in the matter of abuse without breaking the law. The law at this time was that it was an offence to use threatening words with intent to provoke a breach of the peace, but it had to be shown that an actual audience was being provoked. This led to prevarications such as are loved by barrack-room lawyers: words like 'Oriental' and 'Simian' were defended as being geographically or physiognomically descriptive: a word 'Licean' was introduced as if it referred to a middle-eastern race; it was understood by those who used it and most of those who heard it to refer to lice. An animal called the 'She-Neelouse' was described which had 'a large hook-beaked protuberance and vile smell when it clusters'. The police would painstakingly write such stuff down and try to decide whether or not to instigate a prosecution. During the three years from the beginning of 1936 to the end of 1938 there were in fact brought by the police 39 cases of insult, 61 cases of insulting slogans chalked on walls, 60 cases of alleged assaults by fascists or fascist sympathisers on Jews, and 100 cases of damage to property – largely the breaking of windows. During this period there were 29 cases of alleged assault by Jews on fascists – but this statistic applied only to such cases in which there was evidence that the assailants were Jews. A reporter in the *Evening Standard* at the end of 1936 wrote that in fact 'most of the back-street assaults seem to have been directed against Blackshirts'. One part of the criminal gang life of East London seems to have been run at this time by Jews: they would have been skilled both at violence and, presumably, at the covering up of their traces.

One of the self-confessed leaders of the opposition to the BUF was Jack Comer (known also as Jack Spot for his propensity for being 'on the spot') who later became notorious as a leader of London's under-world and an expert (and victim) in razor fights. In 1937 he was sent to prison for six months for causing grievous bodily harm to a fascist. Another gangland leader sentenced in 1936 for assault was Barnet Becow of whom the magistrate said – 'He is a man trading in violence and is more likely to lead to the destruction of the Jewish community in the

East End than the fascists are'. But in all the carefully kept police records there is, again, no evidence of a crippling injury or death. It is understandable that the Jewish community, with its memories of eastern European pogroms, must have feared that it was about to be subjected to a persecution such as had already begun to be perpetrated by Hitler: it is also just possible that non-Jewish toughs might have seen the style of violence as not much more than that which had traditionally been perpetrated from time to time in the East End.

Very occasionally in fascist publications there was some discussion about where, if the 'Yids' were to be got rid of, they might go: Mosley in his last Albert Hall speech had made it clear that under a fascist regime Jews who did not 'put Britain first' would be deported. It was not suggested that they should go to Palestine because of the local Arab population. Sometimes Africa was mentioned; a writer in *Blackshirt* pointed out that there were 'many waste places of the earth possessing great potential fertility'. But for the most part it was recognised that the East London campaign was not concerned with such distant practical questions; it was a contest for local mastery. Virulence increased confusingly when Arnold Leese's Imperial Fascist League turned up in the area; Leese was explicit that all Jews should be sent to Madagascar and the world's navies should be assembled to see they did not get out – even that a more 'permanent way of disposing of the Jews' (this was in Arnold Leese's paper *The Fascist*) 'would be to exterminate them by some humane method such as the lethal chamber'. To the inhabitants of the East End, it must often have seemed not worth while to attempt to distinguish between one set of fascists and another.

Perhaps in order to try to remove from his movement the effects of the excesses of other fascists Mosley had decided early in 1936 that the word 'Fascist' should be demoted in the title and that the movement should be known from now on as 'The British Union of Fascists and National Socialists' or just 'British Union' for short. This was possibly in some deference to the National Socialism of Germany: but in the main the emphasis was from now on to be on the Britishness of British Union. And it was true that 'National Socialist' might have a patriotic ring: a slogan was coined – 'If you love your country you are national, if you love your people you are socialist'. The old emblem of the Roman or Italian fasces was dropped and in its place there was introduced a home-grown symbol of a flash-and-circle. This represented (in my father's words) 'the lightning of action based on the circle of comradeship'. To the enemies of the British Union it became known as 'the flash in the pan'.

In October 1936 when Mosley returned from the holiday at Sorrento there was planned for his re-appearance in the East End the biggest demonstration yet: a march would start by the Royal Mint near the Tower of London and would proceed through Shoreditch, Limehouse, Bow and Bethnal Green: in each district there would be a halt and a speech by Mosley. This was an occasion such as that of the meeting at Olympia two years earlier when the opposition also decided to make their biggest demonstration yet: as before, the technique would be to try to discredit British Union by making out that they were simply trouble-makers and thugs.

The march had been well publicised: both fascists and anti-fascists rallied their forces. The anti-fascists (this was shortly after the outbreak of the Spanish Civil War) coined for their slogan that of the defenders of Madrid – 'They Shall Not Pass'. On the day itself, October 4th, bus-loads of communist and left-wing militants arrived in the area from outside: the local leader was Jack Spot; he had armed himself (so he told a newspaper reporter) with a 'type of cosh shaped like the leg of a sofa but filled with lead at the end which had been made for him by a cabinet-maker in Aldgate'. Before Mosley's arrival there was chanting and stone-throwing by the anti-fascists; the fascists were in orderly ranks; there were 6,000 police to keep the protagonists apart. When Mosley arrived – with a motor-cycle escort and standing up in the open Bentley doing the fascist salute in his new uniform (Jack Spot called this 'the rummiest sight I've ever seen in the East End') – he walked up and down the columns of blackshirts inspecting them while the crowd, beyond the lines of police, tried to charge, were pushed back, but here and there broke through. There were some arrests. The Police Commissioner Sir Philip Game told Mosley not to start his march before the police had set about clearing the streets across which barricades had been erected. The largest barricade had been built across Cable Street, on the route of the intended march going east from the Mint towards Limehouse. A lorry had been used to construct a formidable defence work.

Sir Philip Game saw the whole occasion as primarily one concerning the police: he seemed determined to show that the streets would be controlled by his men and not by rival gangs. The police tried to push their way through Cable Street; they failed; they charged the barricade and captured it only after a battle with the defenders in which stones, bricks, truncheons and iron bars were used. The defenders, however, withdrew to further barricades, scattering broken glass in their wake to discourage the police on horses. After two hours of this sort of fighting

during which 83 anti-fascists were arrested and there were over 100
injuries including those to police – and during which time the fascists
remained out of the action lined up by the Royal Mint – Sir Philip
Game telephoned to the Home Secretary, Sir John Simon, who was
in the country for the weekend, and asked for his permission to give
orders for the march to be called off. Sir John Simon agreed. Sir Philip
Game came to Mosley and said, 'As you can see for yourself, if you
fellows go ahead there will be a shambles.' Oswald Mosley asked (this
was according to newspaper reports), 'Is that an order?' Sir Philip Game
said, 'Yes.' Then Mosley gave orders for his men to turn and to march
the other way – back down Great Tower Street and Queen Victoria
Street towards the Embankment. Newspapers reported that amongst
his ranks there were 'cries of disappointment'. Before Mosley dismissed
his men near Charing Cross Bridge he made a short speech:

> The Government surrenders to Red violence and Jewish corruption.
> We never surrender. We shall triumph over the parties of corruption
> because our faith is greater than their faith, our will is stronger than
> their will, and within us is the flame that shall light this country
> and shall later light this world.

The London District Committee of the Communist Party announced: 'This is the most humiliating defeat ever suffered by any
figure in English politics.'

In popular mythology it came to be thought that the Battle of Cable
Street was a battle between the fascists and anti-fascists – that fascist
thugs had tried to march through a Jewish area of the East End and
residents had heroically prevented them. In fact the battle was between
the police and left-wing militants to some extent brought in from outside: the fascists did not become involved in the fighting at all. They
had behaved obediently according to the law.

Two years previously at Olympia the BUF had taken on the left-
wing militants and had 'won' the physical battle but had been branded
as thugs and the meeting had been a propaganda disaster; now it seemed
that they were to suffer a similar fate by having remained passive. There
was something just in their style that made people imagine they had
been violent even when they had not: and when they were law-abiding,
there was the added impression that their violence had been defeated.

It is conceivable that Mosley might have instructed his followers
not to conform to police orders in such a way as to have brought
upon them neither ignominy nor a reputation for lawlessness – nor

indeed the chance of serious charges being laid against them. They might have marched – in some sort of formation or in none – along another route; they might, if this was the way things went, have got themselves fairly honourably arrested. It is doubtful what charges the police could in fact at that time have brought: but even if they had the BUF might at least have appeared as martyrs.

As it was, they appeared to be a revolutionary movement prepared for a crisis who in a crisis did exactly what they were told by the authorities. People wondered – what on earth then was Mosley doing in his jackboots? He was due to be in Berlin the next day for his wedding: but then, hardly anyone knew this.

The next Sunday in the East End there was a 'victory' parade by anti-fascists; the police now had to make baton-charges to clear the way for them. While the police were thus occupied, a gang of about 200 pro-fascist and mostly teenage youths ran down Mile End Road smashing Jewish shop windows and attacking anyone who might be thought to look Jewish: a hairdresser and a four-year-old girl were reportedly thrown through a plate-glass window. British Union officials denied responsibility for this; they said as usual that such behaviour was strictly against orders.

Then during the following week British Union held a series of what it claimed to be its largest and most peaceful meetings ever held in East London. In Stepney, Shoreditch, Bethnal Green and Limehouse huge crowds listened attentively: the meetings were orderly, the speakers claimed, because no agitators had been brought in from outside. On Wednesday October 14th Mosley himself addressed a crowd of 12,000 at Bethnal Green and then marched to Limehouse: police reports noted that there was little or no opposition whereas 'in contrast, much opposition has been displayed at meetings held by the Communist movements' speakers'. Mosley said in his Limehouse speech – 'We make no appeal to violence because we have behind us the British people. . . I challenge and expose tonight the corrupt power in England of international Jewish finance.'

He might seem, as usual, to be winning the particular argument; but also, as usual, other impressions were what remained in the public mind. *The Times* referred to the activities of both fascists and anti-fascists in East London as 'a tedious and pitiable burlesque' which made the lives of East Enders 'unbearable'. Beverley Baxter MP wrote – 'Here is a picture of Sir Oswald Mosley surrounded by his bodyguard just like a dictator or a gangster: he is wearing riding breeches and riding boots though I cannot see any horse.'

There were arguments in the press about what was, or was not, the duty of the police in the matter of ensuring that citizens should be able to march through streets: it seemed to be generally accepted that it was the appearance of British Union in the uniforms of a private army that caused provocation.

The Government decided to push through a Public Order Act which would prohibit the wearing of military-style uniforms. Mosley protested that the British Union was being discriminated against while all the evidence showed that it was their opponents who were causing the disturbances. He also pointed out that without the uniforms it would be difficult for British Union to maintain the discipline that had enabled them to be law-abiding till now. In later years, however, he would admit that the wearing of military-type uniforms had resulted in a propaganda disaster.

The campaign for the municipal elections of 1937 continued. British Union were putting up candidates in three districts – Bethnal Green, Shoreditch and Limehouse. Fascist publications kept up their anti-semitic tone. The doggerel verses increased in unpleasantness –

> His hair was sleek and full of oil
> And so his manner too
> His hands were far too soft for toil
> The son of a son of a Jew –

and bands of drummers went through the streets singing to the tune of *Daisy Daisy* –

> Abie Abie now that we've tumbled you
> You'll go crazy before we have done with you.

The British Union election manifesto, however, tried to put it more reasonably:

We guarantee that, if elected, we will oppose all grants and donations for foreign causes of whatever kind. No more Basque children will be supported in luxury at 10/- per week while the children of the unemployed get only 3/-; nor will we give away facilities for collections for foreign wars while the war against poverty and bad conditions at home is neglected.

We ask you to return us as your watchdogs on the Council to keep a sharp look-out that no grafter of Right or Left takes advantage

of the present rotten system to fill his pockets pending the great
National Revolution for which we are all waiting.

HONESTY THE BEST POLICY

On 6th March 1937 the election results were announced. Mick Clarke
and Raven Thomson in Bethnal Green got 3,000 votes each or 23%
of the votes cast; Charles Wegg-Prosser and Anne Brock Griggs in
Limehouse about 2,000 or 19%; and in Shoreditch William Joyce and
Jim Bailey 2,500 votes or 14%. In other parts of the country where
British Union had put up candidates – Edinburgh, Leeds, Sheffield
and Southampton – their results were insignificant.

Immediately after the announcement of the East End results Mosley,
according to John Beckett, sat down with a pencil and paper and worked
out how British Union had done better than Hitler had done in Germany
a few years before he had come to power: in 1928 in a general election
Hitler had polled only 2.7% of votes cast and in 1930 18%. It could
also be pointed out that in the East End municipal elections only house-
holders had been eligible to vote, so much of the support for British
Union amongst the young had not been represented.

However two weeks after the poll Mosley summoned all his senior
staff to headquarters and told them that most of them would have
to be dismissed; salaried staff had to be cut from 143 to 30: there was
now just no money to pay any more, though he hoped that some might
carry on in an unpaid capacity. Two of those who did not choose
to stay were William Joyce and John Beckett – the Director of Propaganda and the Director of Publications – both leading anti-semites.
They were angry at having been dismissed, and started a movement
of their own – the National Socialist League – in which they were
heavily critical of their once so admired Leader. But it was while they
had been with him that they had done him much damage.

Years later my father was asked by a journalist whether it was true
'that your reason for dismissing Joyce was less a financial one than
a personal and political one'. My father replied: 'He gave no trouble
in our movement until he was dismissed. . . he resented that in financial
difficulties we dismissed the speakers and retained the organisers.' This
was long after Joyce – by then better-known by his war-time nickname
of 'Lord Haw-Haw' – had been executed as a traitor in 1945. My father
seldom noticed the damage that people on his own side did to him:
he seemed to float above such things: but then, what was it in the
clouds that he had his eyes and heart on?

CHAPTER 13

Wootton Lodge

In the autumn of 1936 my father and Diana rented a very beautiful house, Wootton Lodge, in Staffordshire. It was an early seventeenth-century house with an imposing front with huge windows. Some of the back was said to have been knocked away by a bombardment by Cromwell.

During 1937 my father was spending much time speaking in the Midlands and in the North: it suited him to have somewhere within driving distance where he could spend nights. Also now that he and Diana were married they needed a home: but because their marriage was secret, my father could also keep going to the family home at Denham without anything much appearing to have changed.

At Wootton there was a long drive through beech trees and then suddenly the house below with two lodges and a circular lawn in front, very formal like the backdrop to a ballet. The ground fell away sharply behind the house to a ravine with trees and a semi-circle of lakes; beyond this again was a curve of green hills so that the house seemed both to be high and solitary on a rock and yet protected. It was the most beautiful house I have ever lived in: like a castle in storybooks.

You went up a wide flight of steps into a panelled hall; the drawing room was to the left where there were Chippendale chairs and a settee shaped curiously like sea-shells; here Diana would sit like someone in a painting by Botticelli. There was a bow window full of light and a round table on which would be set out tea. In a smaller room towards the back there was a gramophone with an enormous horn, also like a shell; you sharpened triangular wooden needles with an instrument like a cigar-cutter; out of the horn came tiny pure music as if from a homunculus. This was music I had never heard before – *Das Rheingold*; *Götterdämmerung*; Marlene Dietrich singing two sad German songs called

Peter and *Johnny*. From this room you went out on to a terrace which looked down over descending gardens to the chasm at the bottom with woods and caves and lakes. On a platform at the back of the house, where the part knocked away by Cromwell had been, there was a deep lily pond or a shallow swimming pool – according to my father's mood. At the back of this, on the cliff-face, were paths slanting down between rocks and trees that were haunted by wild cats like those of witches. In the lakes there were a few old and very large trout that seemed too sophisticated to be interested in such things as flies. Beyond the lakes were the hills with huge warrens of rabbits; beyond these again wild woods of elm and beech and oak.

I was often at Wootton without my sister and brother; they remained for the most part at Savehay Farm. Because it was not known that my father and Diana were married there was some difficulty about us children going to Wootton: Irene wrote in her diary of my father: 'He has no right to put growing Vivien in such a position: oh dear God help us!' I do not remember any pressure being put on me. I loved being at Wootton; I liked splitting the holidays between it and Savehay Farm.

At Wootton there were the woods, the mysterious lakes, the disused shafts of lead mines going deep into the hills. These I could crawl along until I seemed to have found the ultimate hidey-hole from the grown-up world; yet I did not need this at Wootton because no one was now trying to stop me being alone. My father would return from his speaking tours; he taught me how to shoot rabbits with a .22 rifle; I would sit quietly at the edge of one of the lakes in the evenings while he fished. Then he would be away again, and I could carry on doing such things on my own. One had to stalk the fish as one stalked the rabbits, crawling to the shelter of a tree and casting a line as if threading a needle.

I would have meals quite often on my own with Diana, the two of us in the large panelled dining room to the right of the hall. There were servants of course – a cook and a housemaid and a footman – but I was old enough now (thirteen and fourteen) to feel myself as no longer part of the servants' world; and besides, my father and Diana treated me as if I were not. They, on holidays or at Wootton, were the first grown-ups I knew who treated human relationships straight-forwardly: others were liable to use words to attack or to defend or to complain; my father and Diana seemed to listen, and to reply to each question on its merits.

I do not remember talking much with my father at this time; perhaps he was too often away; when he was with me in the woods or by the lakes we liked to be quiet. But with Diana in the huge dining room, in which I suppose we were like tiny figures at each end of a table in one of those joke cartoons, I would ask about politics, about Germany, about Hitler. I had fairly conventional English attitudes towards Hitler: neither my father nor Diana had ever tried to influence us children in our political views – much more vocal had been aunts, schoolfriends, schoolmasters. I would say to Diana – But surely, I mean, look – Hitler just can't be a good thing, can he? Diana would say – But you see, there are all the things he has done for Germany. We would go thus to and fro – this is his style, but this is his achievement. Then once she said – To understand, you would have to come to Germany and look. I said – Would you take me to see Hitler? She said she would ask my father, and write and see. But then this was the year of the Munich crisis, and there was no chance of my going to Germany.

One summer holiday (I think this must have been the year after the news of my father's and Diana's marriage had been made public) I had two schoolfriends to stay with me at Wootton: we camped out on the green hills: in the evenings we would all take up the arguments with Diana. This was a time when my father was reiterating his claim that Jews were a dominating influence in advertising, in films, in the press. When one of my friends, my future brother-in-law, came to write his thank-you letter to Diana he ended his formal, schoolboy phrases with – 'P.S. My father says the *Yorkshire Post* is not run by Jews.'

I, returning to Savehay Farm, would write to Diana:

Thank you so much for having me to stay. I always enjoy myself so much at Wootton. Everyone was very cold to me when I got back as they were teased that I had stayed on till Wednesday. I told them of the great Dramas in the fishing, and of the Wailing Woman in the cave; but all they did was to say 'Oh' in a very bored voice. By the way, I left Mummy's picture in my room so would you be so kind as to send it on to me.

Life at Savehay Farm continued as before with my sister Vivien, my brother Micky, Nanny and Andrée the housekeeper. Aunt Irene would come down when my father was not there: Aunt Baba would come down usually when he was – until she learned about his marriage. My father would visit Savehay Farm when he was seeing to things at his headquarters in London. This was the time when there was trouble with the Courts about the provision of our – the children's – money for Savehay Farm: a judge had reduced the payments on the grounds that they would enable my father to spend more of his own money on fascism. My father approached Irene to see if she would make up the amount withheld; he suggested we children could pay her back when we came of age. She agreed to this: she still complained that she was not consulted about arrangements.

During Christmas 1936 all of the family for whom it might be thought proper were at Savehay Farm – my father and Irene and Granny and we three children: Baba and her family came over on Boxing Day. Diana was not there: we did not yet know that she and my father were married. On Boxing Day at dinner my father was rude to all the grown-ups in turn; one by one they rushed out of the room in tears or to give each other comfort. Irene recorded – 'Viv got more and more scarlet, and tears ran down from behind Nick's spectacles whilst Granny talked madly about any piffle.' I remember this scene quite well – though not my own tears. We were fairly used to my father's roaring off like this: he was like someone fighting against being trapped. What he might feel himself trapped by, we did not know.

My grandmother wrote to him afterwards –

Dear lad, I know very well how hard Xmas is for you and how you miss Cim – the very spirit of Xmas. I think the way you work to make the children's Xmas as happy as she would wish is wonderfully brave and very like you.

The continuing feud between the one part of the family and the other was still mainly due to what my aunts and grandmother had felt about my father's relationship with Diana at the time of my mother's death. But it was now kept going by a growing divergence of feelings about Hitler; also by a divergence of attitude towards the conventional upper-class world. My father kept up the house at Denham, he said, because of us children; he himself showed less and less interest in the traditional sort of arrangements that my Aunt Irene made about schools or occupations for the holidays, and in particular he paid almost no attention to his youngest son Micky. Irene, with her warm-hearted but sometimes ponderous style, had for long been a butt to my father's teasing (he used to refer to her as 'flying nose-heavy' – a reference to a tendency of aeroplanes in the first world war). But now his impatience with things at Denham seemed to influence even his feelings

about the elaborate tomb that he had constructed for Cimmie: he did
not often visit this, and his reluctance seemed to increase.

However, in the summer of 1936 it had been Irene who had been
as an official guest of the German government at the Nazi Parteitag
at Nuremberg: she had come home with stories of the occasion 'breath-
taking in its splendour and its gaiety'. In her diary she had thanked
God 'for bringing me here and guiding me through an evening of
delirious enjoyment'. When she had been introduced to Hitler she had
been struck, as Diana had been, by 'the freshness of his skin, the beauty
of his smile, the frankness of his eyes'. She too had felt 'the aloneness
of that man in his colossal undertaking'. Also – 'It is quite shattering
and makes one gulp and say – What was the war all for? – with this
tremendous, spiritually inspired people with one heart and mind – their
Germany above everything'.

1937 was a difficult year for my father: there had been the financial
crisis and the dismissals of headquarters staff at the BUF; the turning
against him of people who previously had been almost sycophantically
loyal. He had recently brought another libel action on much the same
grounds as those on which he had won £5,000 from the *Star* two
years earlier; now he was awarded damages of a farthing – such was
the change in the public mood about him. He continued to get large
audiences in his meetings up and down the country: sometimes the
audiences were attentive and enthusiastic and sometimes they still
became involved in the violence with which his movement had become
associated in the public mind. But always after he had gone the local
enthusiasm he generated seemed to wane, and there were left just groups
of people wondering when he would return – as if he were a famous
actor in the business of undertaking tours.

Inevitably it was still the meetings at which there was violence that
were reported in newspaper headlines; meetings that were orderly were
not recorded at all. Indoor halls were now almost all banned to him
because the owners or trustees feared violence (or such was their excuse);
and many public places such as parks were withheld for the same reason
if local authorities had the power. And with the banning of the uniform
it was true that discipline and thus also self-protection had become
more difficult. In Southampton he was hit in the face by a stone and
had to be rushed away by the police in a tram; at Hull a bullet was
fired through the window of his car. Another march through East
London was banned; then one through South London was so controlled
by police that there were fights again simply between police and anti-
fascists as there had been at Cable Street. And then in Liverpool, in

October, my father was hit on the head by a jagged brick and was quite dangerously injured; he was lifted down from his van and carried to hospital half conscious; a minor operation was performed on a 'punctured wound of the skull'. He remained in hospital for a week, then went to Wootton to recuperate. My grandmother professed herself outraged by this, in the light of her belief that he and Diana were not married.

While he was in hospital a libel case came to court against the British Union newspaper *Action*. *Action* had taken the place in 1936 of the now defunct *Fascist Week* as yet another attempt to run a paper which would have a more sophisticated appeal than that of *Blackshirt*. Its editor had been John Beckett: he had written an article in April 1936 in which he had suggested that Lord Camrose, the owner of the *Daily Telegraph*, was (in the words of the plaintiff's Counsel) 'a Jewish international financier with no loyalty to the Crown and no sense of patriotism, and that in his conduct of the *Daily Telegraph* he allowed his duty to the public to be subordinated to his own financial interests'. Lord Camrose sued for libel and the case came to court on 14th October 1937. For the defence it was argued that the words did not have the meaning implied by the complainant – for although Lord Camrose was not in fact a Jew it was no offence to be called Jewish. John Beckett was not called as a witness: but after he had heard the case for the defence he asked if he could make a statement from the witness box. He said, 'When I wrote that article I honestly believed it to be true because I had the information in it given me by people on whom, rightly or wrongly, I placed great reliance ... To me, to tell a man that he is a Jew and that his financial interests are far greater outside this country than in it are two of the greatest insults that can possibly be offered to any man ... When I discovered that so far from the information my titled friend gave me about Lord Camrose being a Jew being true – he was a Welshman and, if I may say so, an obvious Welshman – I did not want to go into the box to justify that.'

The 'titled friend' of Beckett's statement was evidently Mosley: Beckett suggested that the article had been approved by Mosley himself. In the course of the trial Mosley's secretary George Sutton said that he 'could not confirm this' and that he believed Mosley had been 'ill at the time'. Lord Camrose was awarded £20,000 damages and costs: John Beckett could not pay; *Action*, owned by a company with £100 capital, went bankrupt. Beckett made a statement to the press in which he referred scathingly to a man who would 'send his secretary into the witness box to say he had had influenza'; he announced that he envied the editor of the *Daily Telegraph* whose 'chief, at any rate, was man enough to say he was the chief and did not hide behind a £100 company'. British Union issued a statement – 'The company laws of this system were devised by capitalists for use against the people, and no one can complain if the people now use the company law for their own purposes'.

Several more of those who had been Mosley's most loyal and outspoken supporters turned against him at this time. Charles Wegg-Prosser who had been the BUF candidate at Limehouse wrote to him:

> You are side-tracking the whole issue of social betterment by the anti-semitic campaign. Anti-Jewish propaganda, as you and Hitler use it, is a gigantic side-tracking stunt – a smoke-screen to cloud thought and divert action with regard to our real problems. Our people are fair, tolerant and humane. You introduce a movement imitating foreign dictators, you run it as a soulless despotism. You sidetrack the demand for social justice by attacking the Jew, you give the people a false answer and unloose lowest mob passion.

Jim Bailey who had been the BU candidate for Shoreditch also resigned but for somewhat opposite reasons: 'I am a disillusioned man, and have lost faith with our Leader ... from being a party with great ideals and a great future it has become a children's Sunday School outing: they have guyed a great ideal.'

Then early in 1938 A. K. Chesterton resigned. In 1936 he had published a hagiographical biography of Mosley called *Portrait of a Leader*. In it he had perorated –

> Now he moves forward to a still greater destiny, an implacable figure looming ever more immense against the background of his times: through his own eager spirit, so full of aspiration and boldness, symbolising the immortal spirit of his race ... Hail Mosley, patriot and revolutionary, and leader of men!

Now two years later he was writing –

> I have been amazed that a man so dynamic on the platform should prove so unimaginative, so timid, so lacking in initiative and resource ... the public aspect of this shows itself in his refusal to deal objectively with the movement's fortunes. 'Flops' are written up as triumphs, and enormous pains are taken to titivate reports so as to

give the impression of strength where there is weakness, growth where there is decline, of influence where there is only indifference. In a recent issue of his journal there were two major attacks on the veracity of the National Press and yet in this very issue, to my knowledge, there were several statements which were sheer lies. National Socialism should have some nobler inspiration than to oppose one kind of corruption with another still less pleasing to the nostrils.

One of the characteristics of my father's career had always been his trust that he could charm people and keep them loyal to him by his use of words: that if one made an argument sound convincing enough, then one need not be too anxious about the relationship of argument to events. This was, indeed, a general tendency of fascism and national socialism: Mussolini claimed that he had 150 front-line divisions when in fact he had 10; that he possessed the largest airforce in the world when in fact he had no idea how many planes it contained. Hitler did not boast like this; but he did use arguments as if words might dominate the people whom they concerned – Germany needed room for its population and for raw materials *therefore* it had to move into the Ukraine; a homogeneous nation must feel disturbed by its minorities *therefore* the solution was to get rid of them. All this happened at the one time in history when politics in fact was dominated by the disembodied voice – radios were in every home and loudspeakers blared on the street corners – there was as yet no television, on which the oddities of often uproarious human beings could be seen. But the efficacy of words being used like this depended on those who spoke them having power: people then wanted to believe the words, because they wanted to hand over their trust to leaders with power. Mussolini in Italy and Hitler in Germany, however, had come to power by more savage and even more subtle political means than simply the use of words: my father did not have power; but he still seemed to use just words to pin his faith on.

People adored him because of his fluency: but then some turned against him perhaps just because they felt he was more interested in words than in power. This was felt by people like William Joyce: in 1934 Joyce had said, referring to Mosley, 'There is no greater man that God has ever created!'; after his defection, he referred to 'the Mosley group ... who never dared to say boo to a goose except when coppers were in front of them'. It seemed to be the accusation of such people that Mosley would not in fact, in a crisis, be contemptuous enough to treat people as if they were just words.

My father was never in the same sort of business as Hitler: he would appear half to hypnotise people with his talk and flashing eyes; there seemed about to be thunderbolts; then he would switch off, become himself again, as if after all life was too precious for there to be time for more of the boring chicaneries of manipulation. He had an instinct perhaps about the way in which human beings who did obsessively act like this might destroy themselves: he had read, after all, poetry, tragedy. He did not often read novels (Hitler did not read novels) but he had read one or two which he loved such as Stendhal's *Le Rouge et le Noir* and he knew something of the ironies of human nature. If it gave my father pleasure often to be carried away by words he also had the wit sometimes to see himself being carried away: if he was Mephistopheles seeing that good can come out of evil, at least he knew Mephistopheles laughed at this.

When he became exhausted or ill – such as the time he had been hit by a brick at Liverpool – he would return to Wootton as if it were his fairy castle and Diana was his princess – as if after all this was his reality. Only a few of the old friends of either of them came to stay at Wootton: my father was apt to be jealous of Diana when he was away. Diana's sisters came – though her sister Nancy was in bad odour with my father as a result of her novel *Wigs on the Green* in which she had made mock of a fascist called Captain Jack the Leader of the Union Jackshirts. My father always liked to keep separate the different compartments of his life: perhaps this was one reason why he did not announce his marriage – he wanted somewhere to return to which could remain in some way mythical. Diana never had much money at Wootton; she paid for the house largely from what she got from her first husband: she once said that sometimes she had difficulty in paying the servants, and even in buying Christmas presents for her family. My father was often obstinate about handing out money; he thought that he needed all he had for politics. But Diana managed to create an atmosphere of extraordinary beauty and stillness at Wootton. There was an aura around her and my father such as there is around people who are in love.

While he was away she would write to him –

My beloved Darling: it is a long time since I wrote to tell you how much I love you because my letters are bad and stupidly written. But today as my heart is full of love I shall write what is always in my thoughts; and that is, that I love you more than all the world and more than life; that to be with you is paradise, and each parting from you a little tragedy which does not become less with the years. Thank you my precious wonderful darling for the loveliest days I could possibly imagine and for the happiest love. I wish I could write as I feel. God bless you and keep you safe.

And my father would write to her –

Darling Dimpler,
Tried to ring you late Saturday but told no answer – nothing special – just love!
Nothing like plump Percherons for pulling the loads of life. . . .

Sometimes when he returned to Wootton Diana would suggest that he might give up – not exactly politics, but the apparently endless round of meetings at which crowds cheered or booed but at the end of which there was little to show except as it were the litter and flowers of a stage performance. At moments he would get dispirited and almost agree: then his energy would return – there were people who needed him after all – and what else should he do with his enormous talents and his idealism?

The one time in my childhood when I myself was taken from one to another quite frightening of the separate compartments of his world was when, in the summer holidays of 1937 (just after my first term at Eton) I was transported as if on some terrible magic carpet from the commodious double-compartment of life at Savehay Farm and Wootton to that of the British Union Holiday Camp at Selsey, in Sussex. I had heard of the plans for this with unutterable alarm: I was to spend a night or two incognito in a tent with four or five other boys; how could I be incognito! how could I not – or indeed how could I – open my mouth? What I remember about the fascist Holiday Camp at Selsey apart from the pots and pans and bugle calls and sad songs round camp fires at twilight was the way in which, in our tent at night, the other boys brought out photographs rather portentously as if they were indecent or of film-stars; they passed them round: this was so-and-so, this so-and-so: they were of my own family! – Granny, Viv, Aunty Baba – good heavens was there, or why was there not, one of me? A wrong name was attributed to one of the photographs: I thought – well, why not correct this? The boys observed me. I thought – I might either be, or not be, the son of the Leader?

The other instance I remember from this weekend was when my father made his spectacular entrance into the Camp the next day – he had been staying in a near-by country house – and we all went off to have a ceremonial swim in the sea. But there was a very low tide, and the shallow water seemed to go on for ever; and it seemed to be protocol, as it might be with royalty, that no one should immerse themselves until my father had immersed himself first. But there was not enough water to allow him to do this; we seemed to be proceeding across the English Channel like the Children of Israel through the Red Sea. Eventually my father flopped down in a foot or two of water; we all flopped down; then he laughed; we all laughed; I think he caught my eye. What a joke! Was not this the sort of thing he was good at – laughing at himself laughing in a foot or two of water – and was it not this that I was learning from him?

That week the *Blackshirt* reported –

Clustering round the Leader, chanting the songs of the National Socialist struggle, the whole twelve hundred left the Blackshirt camp and passed through the encampment of the general public in one huge procession. The holiday makers tumbled out of their tents in amazement and, apart from one or two offensive remarks by women spectators, stood watching the proceedings very quietly.

Some of us discovered that a boy named 'Smith' who had slept in one of the tents overnight was in fact Nicholas Mosley, the Leader's eldest son. He showed himself to be a fine swimmer.

CHAPTER 14

'Tomorrow We Live'

In two months during the winter of 1937/38 while he was staying at Wootton to get his strength back after the wound to his head my father wrote *Tomorrow We Live* – a 35,000-word book which put a slightly different emphasis on his brand of British fascism.

In *Tomorrow We Live* the enemy is 'money power': it is the lure of money that drives financiers 'firstly to supply backward nations with the means to undercut us in the markets of the world and secondly to draw a high rate of usury from the transaction in the shape of cheap sweated goods which enter the British market to the complete displacement of British labour because they are balanced by no form of export . . . so in the final frenzy of the system finance drives the West to produce the means of its own destruction'. The remedy for this is, as before – 'to build a home market in which the British can consume what the British produce by the joint method of excluding sweated products from without and the prohibition of sweated products from within'. This can be done by an authoritative fascist government by the manipulation of high wages and reasonable prices, and by the keeping of the countries of the Empire as sources of raw materials without their being allowed to become producers of manufactured goods.

Under the present system of industrial investment abroad there 'may develop in the Dominions an economic self-sufficiency which may lead in time to the complete inability to accept our exports. Great Britain will then again be faced with the retribution of internationalism in dependence on foreign supply . . . We have to choose between Empire and Usury: British Union chooses Empire'.

But this concept of 'Empire' depended on Dominions and Colonies being kept as non-industrialised areas.

The question is sometimes asked whether we can rely on the co-operation of the self-governing Dominions with whose self-governing status we have no desire in any way to interfere. The question does not arise in the case of the Crown Colonies, because their control changes with the Government of Britain. In the case of the Dominions it surely follows that they will co-operate in the policy for which they have always asked. It is they who have demanded a market for their raw materials and for such foodstuffs as we could not produce in this country, and it is the Government of Britain who have refused in order to accept goods from foreign countries for reasons above stated. It is inconceivable, therefore, that the Dominions for any political reason should refuse a policy for which they have always asked and that offers to them such a great advantage. If any Dominion Government for any purpose of political spite adopted such a course, we would rely with complete confidence on the Dominion producer at an early election to sweep them from power; for he would not tolerate the sacrifice of his economic interest to any political prejudice. Our appeal for Dominion co-operation is based not only on kinship and on history, but on an over-riding mutual economic interest.

This was the appeal once more to human beings as if they were rational: but it was a statement of belief that the highest rationality would involve a yielding to money-power – which had previously been seen as the enemy. What if a Dominion, or Colony, were imbued with the same sort of non-materialistic, regenerative spirit such as was supposed to be at the heart of British Union?

In *Tomorrow We Live* British Union is spoken of as an 'instrument of steel' that will cut through old economic interests: 'the struggle of a National Socialist movement is a necessary preliminary to the exercise of power, because the bitter character of that struggle gives to the people an absolute guarantee that those who have passed through that test unbroken will not betray their people or their country'. The appeal is specifically to a sense of 'greatness' that is spiritual.

Are we really to believe that a great people cannot make up their mind that they do not like a Government and give a vote to that effect without a lot of little politicians bawling in their ears that they do not like it and asking them to vote for a dozen confused and contradictory policies? . . . In physics the influence of the external to matter, the unknown, in short the spiritual, provides phenomena for which the purely material can afford no explanation. In fact, every tendency of modern science assures us that in superb effort the human spirit can soar beyond the restraint of time and circumstance.

In *Tomorrow We Live* the only Jews who are mentioned as specific enemies are Marx and Freud: the one 'tells us that man has ever been moved by no higher instinct than the urge of his stomach' and the other 'supports this teaching of man's spiritual futility with the lesson that man can never escape from the squalid misadventures of childhood'. The characteristics of these enemies are materialism and determinism. Against these is projected a spirit given confidence by interpretations gleaned from modern science – such as that reality is composed of what might be called mind and will, rather than of matter.

One of the themes in *Tomorrow We Live* is an attack on concepts of 'class' – especially those held by the *nouveaux riches* who exercise power without a balancing sense of responsibility. 'The act of birth and the mere fact of being their "father's son" is held by these miserable specimens of modern degeneracy to elevate them without effort of their own above their fellow men'. What characterised these people as members of some spiritual lower order was simply the fact that they assumed for materialistic reasons they were higher. What was advocated in *Tomorrow We Live* was that 'the award of honour, as the award of money, may go to great service and may be transmitted to children, but will be liable to be removed if the children are unworthy'.

The arbiters of all this would be, of course, members of British Union as represented by their Leader. Much of what my father advocated at this time seems to have been the outcome of the position in which he found himself: he was gravely short of money but need not feel defeated if it was true that material circumstances were subservient to will; the people who felt they might have defeated him were themselves in fact the slaves of economic materialism. And it was during this time of the late 1930s that people in British Union, tempered by adversity, did apparently feel most confidently at home. Their aim had always been to take part in what seemed to them an almost religious crusade; the actual outcome, as with everything properly to do with religion, seemed a secondary consideration.

My father wrote in later life of the atmosphere within his movement at this time:*

* *My Life.*

We were a band of companions wholly given to the saving of our country for purposes in which we passionately believed and by methods which we became convinced were entirely necessary. In action all command depended on me, but in the common room of headquarters or in the local premises of something over four hundred branches throughout the country I was just one of them. I joined in the free discussion of politics which always prevailed among us, in the sports to which our spare time was largely given, in the simple club-room gatherings where we would drink beer together or cups of tea. This was the most complete companionship I have ever known, except in the old regular army in time of war.

In war the spirit of soldiers is maintained without too much emphasis being placed upon who wins and who loses; this attitude is necessary for the maintenance of spirit. All through my father's career he had the vision of politics being run as if by an army; the quality of this army would be judged by its heroism – as at Thermopylae, as in the valley at Balaclava – rather than by its immediate results. In this respect he was indeed not materialistic; and it is a fact that there is historically something effective in legend. Of those involved in the Charge of the Light Brigade, for instance, it is the cavalry who are remembered and not their killers behind the Russian guns.

What was extraordinary about British Union was that it kept up its martial spirit while at the same time reaffirming that its aim was to prevent war: it was a quality of my father's leadership that he was able to contain this sort of paradox. He was also able to maintain the impression that he and his men were getting somewhere when to out-siders they seemed beset by defeats. What they were getting – and this was what was provided by my father – was just the sense of belong-ing, of finding meaning, of being involved in 'greatness' just by having him at their head.

When my father talked about himself and his movement being 'class-less' this did not mean that he deluded himself about the hierarchical nature of what he believed in: armies usually work best when distinctions are maintained between officers and men. What is aimed at is a style of camaraderie in which each man shall feel satisfied by his own place and thus shall not resent the places of others. My father continued to accept the social patterns of his time: a symptom of this was indeed his keeping separate his political and his private worlds. No members of the movement called my father by his Christian name unless they were on some sort of social terms: few of them came to stay at Wootton.

There is a story of how Neil Francis-Hawkins was once dining at
Wootton and in the course of making conversation he asked one
of Diana's Mitford sisters – 'What make of bus do you run?'
After this remark had been interpreted, it duly passed into Mitford
legend.

Some time during 1937 it struck my father that if indeed he was
on some crusade rather than in the business of trimming ideals to catch
the winds of political power – and if moreover one of his ideals was
that he should not be corrupted by the strings attached conventionally
to requirements about money – then either very soon he would be
reduced to penury, so much money of his own was he now spending
on his movement, or he had to find some fresh source of money
over which he would have control and which thus would not be cor-
rupting. In a piece dictated years later for his autobiography and typed
out but then not used, he wrote of this time:

> The growing hostility of the capitalist, which had begun with my
> public refusal of Rothermere's suggestion to adopt a more con-
> servative policy and to abandon anti-semitism, appeared to have
> resulted in the entire hostility of the money world and a practically
> complete boycott of our funds. Capitalism had discovered we were
> a genuine revolution and were not to be bought off or used for
> their own purposes. It was plain to them that our victory meant
> the end of the capitalist world; and for once the fools were right.
>
> I was therefore confronted with the classic problem of the revolu-
> tionary: lack of money. So far the problem had been solved in one
> of two ways. (1) The Socialist way: to take money from capitalism
> and stay bought. (2) The Fascist way: to take money from capitalism
> and to double cross the capitalists in the interests of the workers.
>
> Naturally of these two methods the latter was the only one open
> to me. It was no use (a) because I do not like double crossing anyone
> even a capitalist; (b) because the same trick had been worked twice
> before and could not be worked a third time – even the capitalists
> had woken up to it. I had, therefore, either to conceive a new method,
> or to witness the exhaustion of my own fortune before my object
> was achieved. I did not object to spending all my own fortune, but
> I did object to failure.

What he 'found fascinating', he said, was 'the possibility of leading
a movement with a revolutionary idea to power while at the same
time making the necessary money in business without financial depend-

ence on anyone; this achievement would be unique in history; but what a labour to undertake!'

During 1937 one or two business schemes were bandied about. One that I remember — perhaps because it was not very serious and so it could be toyed with over the dinner table at Wootton — was to do with the manufacture and marketing of a pill that would take smells away from breath; this was before the days of mass deodorants. There was a young scientist who came to Wootton and I remember conversations between him and my father and for some reason my grandmother on the amazing fortune to be made by someone who found the magic touch of deodorising breaths — how many marriages might be saved, for instance, by the removal of the smell of whisky! I found all this very mysterious — was it really true about marriages — let alone the enormous fortune. Then there was another scheme — I don't think this got very far — about the concession for the organisation of football pools in France. But by far the most serious scheme, and one which indeed it seems might have come off if there had not been war, was one to do with the launching of radio advertising over Britain.

My father founded a company called Air Time Ltd which was financed largely by his own money but which was hedged around by legal and accountancy smokescreens so that in the early days at least his connection with the business should for obvious reasons not come to light. The person responsible for most of the front organisation was W. E. D. (Bill) Allen, who it seems likely had been involved in the handling — and in the keeping of the secret — of the Mussolini money: he was chairman of his family firm David Allen & Sons who were an advertising company based in Northern Ireland. By a system of loans and guarantees and agreements (including a document by which the signatories undertook not to divulge that my father was involved) Air Time Ltd was set up, and negotiations began in the matter of acquiring stations. The BBC of course had a monopoly of broadcasting stations in Great Britain: there were two foreign stations — Radio Normandie and Radio Luxembourg — who put out a mixture of entertainment and advertising from the Continent, but these were not aimed exclusively at Britain and in any case their range did not extend very far. My father's plan was to set up and run a network of radio stations which would cover much of Britain from the south and from the west and from the east; these would not only put out advertising but would (in his words) 'provide the people with an entertaining alternative to the dreary schoolmasters at the BBC'. One of these stations would be sited in the Channel Island of Sark, whose semi-autonomous ruler, the Dame of Sark, was an admirer of my father and with whom he had come to some preliminary understanding: it was thought that legally Sark could be shown to be outside the area of the BBC monopoly, though in fact later this proved not to be the case. Another station, it was hoped, might be set up in the Republic of Ireland, where my father was still a popular figure as a result of his stand fifteen years ago against the Black and Tans. But by far the most important location, because it was thought that if this station could be set up the others would follow, was planned to be in Germany, in Heligoland, from where most of the east of England could be covered. The Germans, if they came in, could provide much of the technical and constructional assistance.

My father had in partnership with him a radio expert called Peter Eckersley who was in charge of technical affairs: Eckersley was sympathetic to British Union, and had been a chief engineer at the BBC. In order to get the Germans interested in the scheme Diana began to travel to and fro between Wootton and Berlin; she would sometimes take with her a young barrister, Frederick Lawton, whom my father had had instructed by his solicitor to advise him on the legal side; he too was in some personal sympathy with my father. Diana had discussions in Berlin with officials in the Ministry of Propaganda.

From time to time Diana would see Hitler. The hope was that Hitler himself would give his blessing to the scheme. At first there were difficulties. Hitler's adjutant, Captain Wiedemann, wrote to Diana –

> Obersalzberg b. Berchtesg.
> Berghof Wachenfeld, den 9.10.1937
>
> Dear Mrs Guinness,
> I have today finally reported to the Führer the whole matter concerning the advertising transmissions. I had also in this connection to report to the Führer that apart from considerations of the technical matters and so on that the Ministry of Propaganda has raised – considerations which under some circumstances could have been disregarded – the greatest objection was raised from the side of the appropriate military authorities.
>
> The Führer regrets that under these circumstances he is not able to agree to your proposal. I am very sorry that I cannot give you any other answer.

Diana however persevered. Because so very few people knew what in fact was going on, it might have appeared that Diana's frequent visits to Berlin and indeed to Hitler were due to the close relationship that the Nazis had with my father: this might have told against him (the security people must surely have known of the visits) in 1940 when he was locked up. In fact Diana's visits were aimed, even if optimistically, at trying to make my father independent of any sort of outside influence. During 1938 she saw Hitler several times in Berlin; she succeeded in re-awakening his interest in the plans; Wiedemann wrote to her in February – 'The Führer took the documents himself some time ago: whether in these last few stormy weeks he has got round to reading them, I don't know. I would advise you to come again to Germany when things have settled down and then get your decision from the Führer himself.' This was the time when Hitler was on the brink of annexing Austria. Frederick Lawton knew nothing of Diana's meetings with Hitler. But by 1939 the prospects for Air Time Ltd were from a legal point of view looking good.

Diana would try to time her visits to coincide with periods when Hitler was in Berlin; she would let him know of her arrival, and he would send a message to her hotel usually late in the evening asking her to come round to see him in the Chancellery after he had finished work. When he was in Berlin he saw officials and made speeches; in the evenings, he would find it difficult to rest. He suffered from insomnia and liked to stay up half the night talking; he liked talking to Diana. He and she would be left alone in his private room in the Chancellery by officials who were grateful that they themselves could get some rest. Years later I would say to Diana – But what did you talk about with Hitler? and she would say – Oh, we chatted: about what was going on in England, what was going on in Germany, your father, the state of the world. I would say – But what was his charm? What was his power? She would say – Can you describe charm? Then – Of course it has something to do with power.

By the summer of 1939 the arrangements for the launching of the radio station in Heligoland were almost complete: it seemed, my father wrote later, that he was on the edge of making 'an immense fortune'. The organisation was purely commercial; it had nothing to do with the German Government – except that it was they who gave permission, and provided the vital wavelength. Profits were to be split between the shareholders of Air Time Ltd and an independent German company in the same sort of proportion – 45% to 55% – as was in operation between Radio Normandie and the French Government. One reason why the German Government approved of the scheme was probably because they needed foreign currency. But above all, from his side, my father wrote – 'Our money would have been clean money, made by our own abilities and great exertions'. He would have achieved his ambition to be 'the first revolutionary in history to conduct a revolution and at the same time to make the fortune which assured its success'.

This attempt was defeated, he said, only by the 'accident' of war. I don't think my father ever quite believed there would be war. It would have been difficult for him to credit that human beings could be taken over by such patterns of self-destruction.

CHAPTER 15

Schoolboy Patterns 2

In the summer of 1937 I left my pleasantly anarchic school of Abinger Hill and went to Eton. This move from prep school to public school was traditionally held to be a release from infancy: one was supposed to find oneself on a training-ground for what life was actually like.

It seemed to me that I moved from a society in which people for the most part learned how to go their own ways and to keep out of the ways of others going theirs, into a society in which lip-service was paid to individuality and freedom but in practice this involved looking for means of imposing oneself that were glamorous; of making rules so customary that they hardly seemed to be there.

A new boy at Eton had to learn, during his first fortnight or so, a mass of local information such as the names of the twenty-five or so 'houses' and their 'colours'; he had to become versed in the peculiar jargon that it was imperative for Etonians to use ('half' rather than 'term'; 'sock' rather than 'food'; 'm'tutor' and 'm'dame' rather than 'housemaster' and 'matron'); he had to demonstrate his knowledge of tribal taboos such as those to do with which shops one could visit and which one could not, which side of the street it was permissible to walk on and which clothes were *de rigueur* at what places and at what times. One had not only to learn this information but to find out what it was that one had to learn: what was being inculcated was not just a list of rules, but a habit of knowing the areas in which such rules might have to be observed.

After I had been at Eton a week I wrote to my father – 'Darling Daddy' (my father and I addressed each other as 'Darling' in letters up to the end of the war) 'Eton is very nice and I like it, except that it is rather dull as nothing exciting ever happens. The boys are all awfully stupid and dull. I am very disappointed in the cricket here, as there is no master looking over us and there are one or two boys in our game who are very bad and hate cricket and who fool about the whole time and spoil the game'.

Every boy had a room to himself; this was one of the privileges of Eton. Curiously, I do not remember having much appreciation of this. Some boys hung up pictures and decorated their rooms to try to make themselves feel at home: I hung up two sporting prints that had been given to me by my Aunt Baba. I do not think I really wanted to feel at home; this might have seemed like setting up one's household gods in the camp of the enemy.

I wrote to my father: 'Fagging is rather a bore, but it is not very hard. The person shrieks "Boy!" and we all have to run to him, and whoever gets there last has to do the job. I am not often last as my room is in such a convenient position.'

I remember little of the academic work at Eton; I was quite clever; I worked hard when it seemed sensible to do so, which was just before exams. But there was anyway never the impression that one was at Eton mainly to do academic work: in so far as the accustoming of oneself to rules and jargon was aimed at making oneself feel part of a tribe, the superiority of one's own tribe over others would be demonstrated by the effortlessness by which one did not even have to work much to be superior.

In each house there were about forty boys of whom the top six or eight were known as 'the Library': this was with reference to their having a special sitting room of their own. It was usually from the door of this room that to summon fags they uttered their shouts of 'Boy!': it was here that new boys came, one by one, to be tested on what they had learned of the rules of the game. In the library there was a hot, languid atmosphere as if of men separated by plate glass from the girls of eastern brothels. It was in the library and by 'the Library' that boys were beaten when they failed to perform satisfactorily the tasks of fags, or to have discovered what were the areas of the game.

At Abinger Hill sensuality had been shameless and a bit of a joke: we had experimented languidly when we wished like pubescent Trobriand Islanders. At Eton it was like an enormous genie inside a bottle, liable to erupt portentously if rubbed. There was comparatively little about sexuality that boys at Eton seemed actually to do – even the eighteen-year-olds in 'the Library'. Running after girls was very much taboo; and the hankering after small boys seldom got beyond the accepted form of loitering romantically in passageways or on street

corners. There were certain socially acceptable jockeyings for position
concerning, for instance, who might sit opposite whom in school chapel:
who might follow or precede whom in the house roster concerning
baths. But for the most part the outlet for sexuality was in talk: the
talk was bawdy-romantic as it must have been I suppose at the time
of Boccaccio when girls were locked up in towers: there were dreams
of what one might do in a world in which dreaming was not the
convention. But one way in which sexuality came down to earth in
a socially acceptable form was in the matter of beating.

Boys in the library would loll about in their wicker chairs as if on
the verandahs of empires; would twiddle canes between their legs
looking down on native populations. It was their very frustration, I
suppose, that gave them their air of control – as it must have been
over empires. Canes became the emblems of school rule like orbs or
sceptres: there were three kinds of cane – an ordinary cane which was
smooth, a sixth-form cane which was thicker, and something called
a Pop cane which had knobs on. 'Pop' was the exclusive, self-electing-
club of boys who were the arbiters of school conventions; they had a
super-library in a building of their own. They were further distinguished
from the populace by being able to wear coloured waistcoats and
sponge-bag trousers (as opposed to dark ones with or without stripes);
they could even put sealing-wax in their hats, as if they were cattle
specially branded. The actual business of beating – performed by
boys in House Libraries and by Pop – did not, as with sex, in fact
too often occur; what was prevalent was the image of beating that
seemed to hang over the place – a sort of soft bald genie looking
down on small boys in what were known as their 'bum-freezer'
Eton jackets.

My own feelings about sex at this time were romantic and
comparatively straightforward: the boy with whom I had been in love
at Abinger Hill had come on to Eton: we were in different houses – there
was a suggestion of social indecency about being friends with a boy in a
different house on the grounds that personal predilections should not
take precedence over the social structure – but we would go out walking
on Sunday afternoons: we were still very innocent; I see us even at
Eton as some sort of illustration to *Winnie the Pooh*. (We would in
fact spend part of our Sunday afternoons playing the game called Pooh-
sticks which involves dropping bits of wood into a river by a bridge
and seeing which comes out first on the other side). But the places
where it was pleasant to walk on Sunday for the reason that in such
places one would be apart from the crowd were those which, pre-

sumably for the same reason, were themselves considered somewhat improper. Known as 'Arches' and 'Butts', the former was the place where the railway viaduct of the Slough-Windsor line went over the meadows, and the latter was where there was the school shooting-range. And around these places there were apt to lurk the sort of gangs that often hang around, and take their toll from, whatever it is that society thinks is improper. My friend and I had made for ourselves a hidey-hole within a hedge by a stream; here we would recline for an hour or two like hares; we would talk – about the meaning of the world, I suppose; about how we would always be immune from absurd rules and temptations such as those to do with the putting of sealing-wax in hats. Then one day when we were walking back over the fields, I was shot in the face. The projectile, which felt like a stone, was a pellet fired from an air pistol by a boy from one of the gangs; the pellet had gone between the inside of my spectacles and my eye and had come to rest in the side of my nose, which bled profusely. The boy who had shot me and a companion came up; they explained that they had been aiming at my top hat, as if this of course was a valid pastime for a Sunday afternoon. They apologised for their bad marks-manship, and said they hoped no physical damage had been done. When it had been established that I was not blind, the question was – would or would not my friend and I tell? But of course, unless the physical damage proved to be too bad, the rules of the game were that we would not tell. We reassured them about this. Also – might it not be to our advantage to be in favour with a gang of toughs?

My 'dame' (house-matron) wrote to my father 'Nicholas had a very fortunate escape this afternoon. . . . the doctor can find nothing beyond a bruising on the eyelid . . . he is a dear boy and no trouble'.

My father asked me later whether or not I thought the incident might have been some sort of demonstration against fascism. I told him I did not think Etonians thought much about things like that.

One of the things that thirteen- and fourteen-year-old boys did think about (is not enough known about this now for it to be treated with amusement rather than with disgust?) was – apart from who sat opposite whom in the school chapel and so on – the question of lavatories. At Abinger Hill lavatories had been restful places where one could lock oneself away and read the *Wizard* or the *Modern Boy*: at Eton they were in a row and had no doors, and were apt to become like a bear-garden. It was probably thought that lavatories might be the sort of place where, behind locked doors, Etonians might at last get

up to what was thought of as no good: with the doors removed, what
was provided was an arena for concentrated ragging and badinage.
There was only one lavatory in the house which had a door; this was
set apart like a loose-box next door to stables, and was for the exclusive
use of the Library. I thought some heroic stand on principle should
be made about this: I determined to try not to use any lavatory except
the secluded, discreet one of the Library. This of course, was very much
taboo; it meant much spying-out-of-land; much use of odd hours.
Perhaps because such sacrilege was almost unheard of, I was never
caught.

There were other incidents in the guerrilla warfare that I felt for
one reason or another should be carried out against the school. Some
time during my first year – I still had the reputation of being a meek
little boy – I took down, or altered, or played some joke upon (I cannot
remember) one of the notices that were pinned on the notice-board
at the head of the stairs of my house: this was of course also the breaking
of some heavy taboo. All the tribe were gathered together and it was
announced (no one had seen me do the deed) that either the perpetrator
owned up, in which case nothing much would happen to him (such
was the game), or else – some fearful punishment would descend on
the whole tribe. I did not know what were the rules about this: I did
not want to harm my innocent image; but was I not someone anyway
who was beginning to be interested in what might be beyond accepted
rules? This otherwise trivial incident has stuck in my mind with such
clarity because, I think, it was the first time I was struck with the idea
that if life was not to seem meaningless there had at moments to be a
regard for something beyond either the conventions of games or self-
interest; there had to be what might be called – for want of a better
phrase – an effort at truth. We were told that the Captain of the House
would come round to each boy's room that evening and would ask for a
confession. The question seemed to be – was there, or was there not,
any actual virtue in truth? Now it happened that this Captain of the
House was in some sort of particular relationship with me: he, as part
of the roundabout of things such as who sat opposite whom in college
chapel, had taken to coming to my room in the evenings (this was
the appointed time for Captains to deal with administrative matters)
and would sit and watch me and chat; sometimes we would play chess.
I had thought of myself as an unattractive little boy; now, amongst
my own age-group it was suggested – Well, there's no accounting
for tastes! This evening when the Captain of the House came round
asking for confessions he stood in my room and said with heartfelt

eyes – Of course I need not ask if it was you! I said – Well yes, it was, actually. I did not know quite why I said this. Perhaps it was because I wanted to confirm (I think I did) that, at such moments and perhaps in any such relationship, there was importance in truth.

In formal areas of school life the question of honesty seemed less pressing. One of the routines was that each week one had to show to one's 'tutor' something called an 'order card': this was a piece of cardboard on which were written one's marks and the comments of masters one was 'up to' (was being taught by). One's house tutor thus kept an overall eye on one's work; each week he signed his initials on one's order card. He did this in the evenings after supper; there would often be a queue outside his room. One wanted to go to bed oneself: he, very probably, wanted to get back to his dinner: it often seemed more sensible and even more charitable not to join the queue but to learn how to put his initials on one's order card oneself. Since the remarks on my card were usually favourable, it seemed to me that in no area of importance was I cheating. I became quite proficient at this forging of my tutor's initials: of course one had to join the queue from time to time or else one's behaviour would be noticed; so the previous forgeries had to be good enough to take in the tutor himself. I think he must sometimes have had an inkling of what was going on; but he was an intelligent man: he saw occasionally that I was getting good marks, so why should he not at other times have had a chance to get back to his dinner?

As for masters one was 'up to' – they used to sit behind desks on platforms in front of classes and life would drone like flies trapped between window panes. Myself and my cronies would sometimes liven up the time by playing paper games such as *Consequences* or a more highbrow version of this called *The Poetry Game*: this involved writing the first line of a rhyming couplet, passing it on, then the next person writing the second line, folding the paper over, writing a new line, passing it on, and so on – until at the end there would be unfolded like a Japanese flower a whole sonnet. The pleasure of this of course was in trying to make it funny; when we opened the bits of paper and read them – all this going on under the sleepy but ever-present buzzing of trigonometry or Latin construe – there would be the agonising and ecstatic business once more of suppressed laughter – the whiff of the beatific vision – the knowledge that even if trigonometry and Latin construe were the surfaces of life there was yet something that could break through, like a pin through a bubble, towards enormous and proper events elsewhere.

There was one master whom we were 'up to' for Greek and with whom we were 'doing' the *Medea* of Euripides: this master was a rather formidable man with steel spectacles and close-cropped hair: he announced one day that he was going to read aloud to us what was, in his opinion, one of the most beautiful speeches in all literature – that in which Medea says goodbye to her children just before she murders them on account of their father, Jason, having been unfaithful to her with another woman. The master read this speech to us in a soft voice standing in front of class; he swung his watch-chain to and fro like a water-diviner; he seemed to have found, at the end, the fount in himself of tears. Afterwards he asked for our comments. I said – I did not often have the courage to put such questions into words – how was it that he found this speech so beautiful, when it was about a mother on the point of murdering her children? He said – That is an interesting question. The class discussed it. It was agreed – But it's poetry, isn't it? I wondered – But what is poetry?

I got a terrible dislike for the *Iliad* at this time: all those ridiculous people bashing one another: the gods standing round like seconds with towels and buckets. One could see why people liked it; but was not the interesting question why people liked it?

About boys in my house bashing one another, I remember two instances. The first concerned almost the only boy of my generation who did not seem obsessed with the talk about sex: he declared one day he had never masturbated; he was laid on his back across a table – he appeared about to have a fit. The second concerned a boy who was held to be 'sucking up' to older boys: he was put in a bath, had oil poured over his head, and was beaten. There was the terrifying impression – was it going to be difficult not to be part of conventional bullying?

Violence, sexuality, at fifteen, sixteen – if they were to go anywhere decent, it seemed, had to go inwards. But what on earth did this mean? In the privacy of one's room there were – the bed that folded into a cube, a Dali-like chest of drawers, a padded object called an ottoman. Somewhere about this time I had come across amongst a pile of unshelved books in a back room at Wootton – amongst the Proust and the Henry James and other intimations of the vast complexities of the grown-up world – a book called the *Encyclopaedia of Sexual Practices*. This contained mostly of course stuff I already knew: but there were one or two stories of a kind I had not heard before. These concerned people in dire and solitary straits: the one that I remember was of a man who had got himself stuck in the overflow pipe of a bath. How amazing: and yet how apt! Were not human beings indeed like things helplessly propelled towards the overflow pipes of baths? But why were we not taught about this – rather than the *Iliad*?

The highest dignitaries that bobbed about like ships' figureheads on the ocean of the school's unconscious were, in ascending order, the Lower Master, the Headmaster and the Provost. The Lower Master was a huge, bony man who was in charge of Lower Chapel choir; I was for a time a member of this; his way of criticising choirboys (I used to sing sharp) was to give them such an enormous hug that they were lifted off their feet and pouched like a baby kangaroo in his cassock. The Headmaster was a stately, shiny man who walked up and down the aisle of College Chapel preceded by a man with a wand like a lamplighter. The Provost was a very old man who read the lessons in College Chapel and when he was at the lectern his hands used to shake so much that the pages of his Bible went off against the microphone like machine guns.

One day my father came down to take part in a fencing contest against the school: he was one of a team from the London Fencing Club. I wrote to him – 'I will be working all Tuesday morning till 1.45 and in the afternoon I will be playing cricket but I will try to come to the gym and see if you are there.' This is the only time that I remember my father visiting the school. For the most part I was visited by Nanny and my sister and my two loyal aunts.

In November 1938 the news suddenly broke that my father had, for the past two years, been married to Mrs Guinness: there were headlines in the papers – 'Mosley Secretly Married' and 'Hitler was Sir Oswald's Best Man'. The papers said that my father and Diana had been married in Munich a year ago: my father issued one of his categorical denials, saying that he had not been in Munich during the last two years. The papers also said that Diana had just given birth to a son. When I had been at Wootton in the summer I had noticed that Diana had seemed large, but this had aroused not much curiosity in the mind of a fifteen-year-old schoolboy. It made sense now however that Diana and my father should be having a baby; what did not make sense was that my father should not have told any of his family of his marriage even if he had wanted to keep it secret from the world. So after breakfast – what apprehension there had come to be about what might be seen in the papers about one's father after breakfast! – I explained to my school friends: Of course, it is rubbish that my father and Diana are married; you think it is shocking that they are having a baby? But then the next day (why the next day?) there was a message from my father that, yes, he had indeed been married all the time to Diana. To this letter I replied:

Darling Daddy,
I was naturally very surprised when I got your letter as I had gone round telling everyone that it was not true. The only thing I really felt was that it was a pity you had not told us, for although I had no idea that you really were married I was always wondering if you would be. You know that I have always liked Diana very much, so I had no feelings on that part of it; but I am longing to have a talk with you about what you feel about Mummy and Diana. I have always loved Wootton and the life at Wootton, and I at any rate would always love to come up there when you are there.

The last three days have been terrible here as everyone has been asking me about it all, and they think I am mad as first of all I said it was rot, and then said it was all true.

Granny told me that you had had a baby boy and apparently it looks just like Grandfather Mosley with a bull neck and a great red face. I am longing to see it.

I was confirmed yesterday and Granny, Nanny and Aunty B came down for it plus a long confirmation letter from Aunty N all the way from America. In the afternoon we went over to Denham.

Are you going to spend Christmas at Wootton or at Denham? Do try and be at Denham just for that day.

Yesterday I had an awful puff with Aunty Baba about having a dog at Christmas and also about Micky going to Abinger. She was against both of them; but I think that Abinger is the nicest private school I can imagine, and there is absolutely nothing against the dog.
                    Much love from
                    Nicky.

In fact, I found a way of dealing with the mocking looks of friends; I explained that of course I had known about the marriage all the time, but I had had to keep up the secrecy until I was officially as it were absolved.

My father put out to the press his own justifications: 'My first wife was subject to the most blackguardly abuse from some sections of the Press and it was my strong desire that no woman should again be subject to such treatment merely because she happened to be married to me.' Also – 'We [in British Union] believe in real sex equality, and therefore both men and women perform their own service in their own way without reference to the purely private fact of marriage.'

My Aunt Baba read of my father's and Diana's marriage in the newspapers while in a train between London and Paris. Years later I said to her that I thought one of the reasons why my father had kept his marriage to Diana secret was because he could thus during these years maintain his relationship with her, Baba, whom he often saw in London while Diana was at Wootton. Baba said that she thought this interpretation was probably correct.

From this time on, occasionally and briefly, my father did in fact talk to me, as I had asked him to, about what he felt 'about Mummy and Diana'. He used to say – as if he were making a special point of this – Of course his second marriage was very good, but his first marriage had been perfect.

CHAPTER 16

The Fight for Peace

There were three stages in the history of British Union: the first was when there had been enthusiasm and genuine hope about being carried to power within a few years: the second had been characterised by the anti-semitic campaign in East London; and the third was when efforts came to be concentrated on the prevention of war.

Throughout his political career Mosley had made stands against war: in 1919 he had spoken against an expeditionary force being sent to Russia; during the twenties he had criticised signs of British imperialist expansion; then when Mussolini had invaded Corfu he had asked that the League of Nations should take positive action to prevent further aggression. In this sense it was a coincidence that now, in the late nineteen thirties, his demonstrations against war should be seen as moves in favour of Hitler or Mussolini: it was they who happened at the time to be driving other people to think of war. He had no faith now in action by the League of Nations; he simply wanted Britain to stay out of trouble. His slogans were – *Mind Britain's Business* and *Britain Fights for Britain Only.* He advocated the creation of a large navy, army and air force for the purpose of enabling Britain to defend herself if attacked. He was never a pacifist.

The first *Mind Britain's Business* campaign got under way when Mussolini invaded Abyssinia. Then in March 1936 when Hitler marched into the Rhineland, which had been demilitarised according to the provisions of the Treaty of Versailles, Mosley made a statement that such a reassertion of natural German rights was justified: however – 'Whether it proves in the result to be the best or the worst thing that has happened in European relationships since the war depends on whether or not the steady will to peace of the British people is maintained.' Then in 1938 there was the German occupation of Austria and Mosley wrote – 'What on earth does it matter to us if Germans unite with others of that race? If all Germans outside the Reich were added to Germany their population would only increase from seventy to eighty millions: has the British Empire sunk so low that we have to shut up shop if another ten million Germans enter their fatherland?' When later in the same year the crisis came to a head about the Germans in Czechoslovakia he praised Neville Chamberlain's peace-keeping efforts; he wrote: 'I don't care if $3\frac{1}{2}$ million Germans from Czechoslovakia go back to Germany, I don't care if 10 million Germans go back to Germany, Britain will still be strong enough, brave enough, to hold her own.' British Union coined a more recondite slogan – 'Nineteen fourteen echo, we will not fight for Czecho'. Mosley never saw much in the argument that Hitler's moves should be resisted because they were immoral; the Treaty of Versailles had not been moral; the tensions in Europe were now largely the result of the Treaty of Versailles; people only talked about morality in international affairs when they lacked national power. And anyway, what could be more deeply immoral than moves towards the starting of another war between England and Germany – which Hitler said he did not want?

What had stayed in my father's mind was the senselessness and horror of the 1914 war: when he spoke of his companions who had been killed in the Royal Flying Corps, tears used to come into his eyes. In the 1930s he saw no logical reason for conflict between England and Germany. As early as 1936 he had written in the *Fascist Quarterly*:

More than any other European nation at present the objective of modern Germany is the wealth and happiness of its own people. It is true that in order to secure that happiness and wealth it is necessary for her to possess an adequate supply of raw materials and full outlet for expanding population. But less than any other great nation of today her philosophy leads her to think of limitless colonial Empire – which to the Nazi mind suggests loss of vital energy, dissipation of wealth and the fear of detrimental admixture of races. Her natural objective lies in the union of the Germanic peoples of Europe in a consolidated rather than a diffused economic system which permits her with security to pursue her racial ideals. In fact, in the profound difference of national objective between British Empire and the new Germany rests the main hope of peace between them. Our world mission is the maintenance and development of the heritage of Empire, in which our race has displayed peculiar genius and which in our vast experience we may pursue not only without fear of racial

detriment, but with the sure knowledge that in this arduous duty
the finest and toughest characteristics of the English are developed . . .
British power throughout the world and German power in Europe
can together become two of the main pillars of world order and
civilisation.

This was almost precisely the attitude that Hitler himself professed:
ever since he had written *Mein Kampf* in 1925 he had said that he did
not want war with England: he needed England as an ally to control
the world's trade-routes while he marched east to get access to raw
materials and more 'living-space' for Germans. There were no secrets
about this. To my father it seemed inconceivable that this would not
be the sort of programme that would appeal to serious English politicians: was not politics about power? and was there not the chance
here for politicians, English and German, hand in hand to wield a
uniquely far-reaching form of power? For English politicians suddenly
to be talking about morality seemed to my father so bizarre that it
could not be taken seriously; it seemed that it must be a cover for
some other form of power – that of the international financial conspiracy.

Then in November 1938 there was the *Kristallnacht* in Germany in
which, as retaliation for the murder by a Jew of a German Embassy
official in Paris, there was a widespread smashing of Jewish shops and
burning of synagogues throughout Germany; there was no effort to
disguise this activity nor to hide that it was encouraged by the authorities.
The argument that German anti-semitism was an attempt to deal
rationally with the 'Jewish Question' no longer made sense; it began
to seem to English people that what had to be faced in Germany was
the power of something irrational. Mosley, however, wrote in *Action*:

Supposing every allegation were true. . . . supposing it were a fact
that a minority in Germany were being treated as the papers allege;
is that any reason for millions in Britain to lose their lives in a war
with Germany? How many minorities have been badly treated in
how many countries since the war without any protest from the
Press or politicians? Why is it only when Jews are affected that we
have any demand for war with the country concerned?

Then in March 1939 Hitler moved his armies into the main part of
Czechoslovakia in contempt of the Munich Agreement which with
such difficulty and in the face of such criticism had been worked out

the year before. This made nonsense of Hitler's claim that he was only concerned with bringing de-nationalised Germans back into the national fold. Almost immediately he seemed to be making threats against Rumania and against Poland; his activities now seemed not only irrational but insatiable. But still, Mosley argued, what better could Britain do than to see that she herself was well armed so that she could defend her own interests against even what was irrational?

Years later he wrote in his autobiography:

Was this policy more immoral than a war which killed twenty-five million Europeans? Was it more immoral than a war which killed 286,000 Americans and 1,500,000 Japanese? Was it more immoral than Hiroshima? ... Was it more immoral than the cold-blooded killing of prisoners in German concentration camps on a vast scale? ... None of these things could have happened without the Second World War.

At the end of March the British Government gave a guarantee to Poland that, if its independence was threatened, 'His Majesty's Government and the French Government would at once lend them all the support in their power'. There was little pretence that this guarantee made practical sense: no efforts were made to prepare any material 'support' for Poland. What was being made was some gesture that might inform Hitler that if he went any further in the way he seemed to be going, there would be war. Hitler in fact made no further moves for a time. But from now on, Mosley wrote in *Action* – 'any frontier incident which excites the light-headed Poles can set the world ablaze: British Government places the lives of a million Britons in the pocket of a drunken Polish corporal'.

Few other politicians seemed to be thinking about what a European war would actually be like. But then – a vision of the horrors of war has seldom been a deterrent either to the bellicosity or to the nonchalance of politicians.

The run-up to war during 1939 coincided with what was known as the 'coming-out' of my sister Vivien: this was the complex of rituals by which eighteen-year-old girls were initiated into membership of the upper-class tribe. Vivien's relationship with her father had developed in its ding-dong style: as she grew older he liked at least the thought of visiting her at school: he initiated a 'tease' with her by which he suggested that all her fellow schoolgirls must be longing to have a glimpse of him as he drove up in his Bentley. (Vivien wrote: 'I loved

going out with you on Sunday . . . you must have had a great disappoint-
ment when there was nobody looking out of the End Room window'). She went to finishing schools in Munich ('It is Wagner that you like isn't it?') and in Paris where here he took her out once on the town: he behaved as if he felt again (as a French journalist had once described him) like 'the young Alcibiades . . . trailing after him many entangled hearts . . . . a few confidences'. But when Vivien returned to England he made clear his aversion now to rituals of upper-class life: these were not in keeping with the image of classlessness that he was trying to inculcate with his fascism. Aunt Irene became Vivien's mentor in the round of cocktail parties, dinner parties and balls by which eligible neophytes could become acquainted with one another and those already in the tribe; there were Ascot, Henley, the Eton and Harrow match: as a climax to the 'season' was something called Queen Charlotte's Ball in which dozens of vestal virgins cut an enormous cake. Then in the middle of the summer there was a full-page piece of gossip about Vivien in the *Sunday Express* − it went on about her wealth and her grandfather having been called Levi Zebidee Leiter − and her father felt driven to reply to this in a statement published in *Action*.

It has ever been the American habit of the Beaverbrook Press to attack the Leader of the British Union through his relations, prefer-ably female. His daughter, Miss Mosley, is the latest object of their chivalrous attention.

As Miss Mosley is a Ward in Chancery whose every arrangement is in the charge of her aunt, Lady Ravensdale, her father has nothing whatever to do with her present activities. Therefore, the Beaver-brook malice shoots very wide of the mark, as an attack on a man who has neither the time nor the inclination for any social life at all.

On the other hand, it should be stated in fairness to this pleasant but ordinary girl, whose appearance in the world would have at-tracted no extraordinary attention if the Press had not detested the person and politics of her father, that not one word written about her in the national Press should be believed without verification.

Our father was still at this time our legal guardian: his statement in *Action* was not true (only the income of our money was in the hands of the Chancery Court); nor indeed was it chivalrous.

One of the high points of my sister Vivien's (and indeed my own) social season occurred on July 15th when, in the Eton and Harrow cricket match at Lords, Harrow won for the first time for thirty-one years. My Aunt Irene recorded that thereupon –

A most disgusting riot and shambles took place. It was not mere 'top-hat bashing'; middle aged men rushed in and were bestial and savage in their onslaughts on boys and older youths alike; one small boy was badly hurt and was carried off; the savagery shown was sickening, even trying to debag people! Eyes teeth and noses risked being smashed.

The next day, Sunday 16th July, was the occasion of my father's last and greatest indoor meeting in London. He had been able to hire the vast and new auditorium at Earls Court – the management not having believed, it was said, that any political leader would be so rash as to try to fill it. On the night it was 95% full with an audience of more than 20,000. The family was there – myself, Viv, Irene, Granny – we listened to the fanfares and watched the parade of flags: there were the usual banners of *Britain First* and *Mind Britain's Business*: and then there was my father marching alone up the aisle and climbing to the top of a high rostrum like a rocket as if he were an astronaut. He spoke for two hours: as usual, without notes. He said:

We have shown over and over again in infinite detail how the money and credit of the British people, created by the exertions of the British people and by no other force on earth, has been used for their own destruction in the equipment of the Orient with its sweated labour to undercut and to destroy the West; in order that usury, international usury, may draw its dividends and its interest by destroying the country of its origin through the equipment of our world-wide competitors against us. We have shown again and again how the British Empire, as well as the British people, the British industrialist and the British worker, has been relentlessly sacrificed to this international power; how the whole of our international trading system, how our conflicting party system, and our foreign policy above all, is maintained for one reason and for one reason alone – that the money power of the world may rule the British people and through them may rule mankind.

It is almost impossible to recreate the effect of one of my father's speeches; there was such certainty and such passion; one felt one's mind being taken over – either this, or one had to be ready to turn away as if from a fire.

I am told that Hitler wants the whole world. In other words, I am told that Hitler is mad. What evidence have they got so far that this man, who has taken his country from the dust to the height in some twenty years of struggle – what evidence have they got to show that he has gone suddenly mad? Any man who wants to run the whole of the modern world with all its polyglot population and divers peoples and interests – such a man is undoubtedly mad, and I challenge my opponents to produce one shred of such evidence about that singularly shrewd and lucid intellect whom they venture so glibly to criticise. 'Oh,' they say 'any man who gets to such a supreme position must go mad.' Well, of course any democratic leader would; but we knew before they told us that they had got weak heads.

Somewhere about this point Randolph Churchill, the son of Winston, got up and walked out: he had been pointed out to us by Aunt Irene in a row in front, in the company of the dancer Tilly Losch. My father went on to describe an incident in which British citizens had been molested by Japanese troops in China about which the British Government had made no protest:

Why is it a moral duty to go to war if a German kicks a Jew across the Polish frontier but no moral duty to lift a finger if a Briton is kicked in Tsientsin? Is it only because English men and English women are being insulted that the Parties are indifferent? ... We are told that this is the policy of the Conservative Party which stood for security, for prestige and for Empire. The Empire is sold and war is bought in British money today, in British lives tomorrow ... My friends, can we conceive of a policy of greater insanity, heading more straight for suicide, than this: to be prepared to fight a world war over a few acres which do not belong to us, but to make a present to the whole of mankind of the land which was won by the sweat, blood and heroism of our forefathers?

One could tell when my father was arriving at his peroration; his voice and his personality seemed to change; it was as if the count-down was beginning; he was ready to take off into space. For his audience there was a tingling up and down the spine –

I ask the audience here tonight whether or not we are going to give everything we have within us, not only material resources but our moral and spiritual being, our very life and our very soul, in holy dedication to England that she shall not perish, but shall live in greatness. We are going, if the power lies within us – and it lies within us because within us is the spirit of the English – to say that our generation and our children shall not die like rats in Polish holes. They shall not die but they shall live to breathe the good English air, to love the fair English countryside, to see about them the English sky, to feel beneath their feet the English soil.

This heritage of England, by our struggle and our sacrifice, again we shall give to our children. And with that sacred gift, we tell them that they come from that stock of men who went out from this small island in frail craft across storm-tossed seas to take in their brave hands the greatest Empire that man has ever seen; in which tomorrow our people shall create the highest civilisation that man has ever known. Remember those who through the centuries have died that Britain might live in greatness, in beauty and in splendour. Remember too that in the spiritual values that our creed brings back to earth, these mighty spirits march beside you and you must be worthy of their company.

So we take by the hand these our children to whom our struggle shall give back our England; with them we dedicate ourselves again to the memory of those who have gone before, and to that radiant wonder of finer and nobler life that our victory shall bring to our country. To the dead heroes of Britain in sacred union we say – Like you we give ourselves to England: across the ages that divide us – across the glories of Britain that unite us – we gaze into your eyes and we give to you this holy vow: We will be true – today, tomorrow and for ever – England lives!

For some time before the end of this my Aunt Irene, on the seat beside me, had begun to sway as if she were a snake being lifted up out of a basket; she was murmuring half under her breath over and over – 'Oh this is very good!' People around us had begun to cry; there was a stir as if in undergrowth on the edge of a forest fire; we were sparks swirling up in the wake of my father's chariot-rocket to heaven. I can still, when I read this speech, get some tingling in my spine. We were most of us at the end standing on our seats and cheering.

Much of my father's argument against war with Germany was based on his assumption that human beings were rational: it was rational that Germans should want to re-join the main part of Germany to East Prussia that had been arbitrarily split from it by the Polish Corridor

at the Treaty of Versailles; it was rational that Britons should not feel
threatened if Hitler marched in the opposite direction to them – and
in any case, what on earth did Britons think they could do to help
Poland? What my father did not see – which he might have seen because
it was so much part of his own technique to sway people as if they
were hypnotised – was that human beings are not rational when they
feel themselves either charmed or threatened by a force that is taking
them over like flames.

Politicians talked about things like the guaranteeing of Poland's
independence or the balance of political power because this was the
way in which they were accustomed to talk: there was no tradition
of talking about fear of a massive psychic invasion or paralysis. But
in fact what people felt about Hitler at this time had little to do with
rationality or even political self-interest: they felt that with the Nazi
regime they were on the edge of being in the presence of things like
devils and witches; these had to be fought, because tingling changed
to shivers of alarm down the spine. And in fact, it is usually for this
sort of reason that people go to war: there is always some excuse for
war in terms of the breaking of a guarantee or an unbalancing of power;
what makes people choose this instant rather than that to fight is best
described in terms of the prevalence of evil – possibly the evil in oneself,
of course, as well as that in others.

After the Earls Court meeting the family went back to Ma Mosley's
flat for supper: we waited for my father. Suddenly he put his head
round the door so that he was like a clown popping his head through
curtains; he looked mock-penitent. Someone said 'You promised!' He
came into the room and gave himself a pat on the behind and said
'Naughty!' This was a reference to a promise he had given to my Aunt
Baba that in his speech he would say nothing unpleasant about her
friend Lord Halifax: he had in fact said that it was Lord Halifax's 'particular genius' that 'when you are walking down in the street and
someone comes up and gives you a hard kick behind you can pretend
not to notice it'. At Ma Mosley's he then laughed; we all laughed.
Diana arrived with her brother Tom and her mother Lady Redesdale.

Next month, August 1939, Diana went to Germany for the last time
and saw Hitler. He was at Bayreuth. There he told her that he thought
war between Britain and Germany was inevitable, because of the
guarantee that Britain had given to Poland. He said that this guarantee
made no sense rationally, except in terms that it was Britain who was
determined to go to war.

CHAPTER 17

War

During the summer holidays of 1939, as war approached, most of the family went to Wootton: this was probably considered to be safer than Savehay Farm from the threat of bombing. My Aunt Irene and Nanny with my brother Micky arrived at Wootton treading warily: Irene recorded that she recoiled from a photograph of Hitler by Diana's bed: that she 'removed from the sitting-room mantelpiece photographs of Goering and his baby (she probably meant Goebbels). Diana herself was in London with my father. My father was stepping up his campaign for peace.

The old spirit of British Union seemed to have come alive again: Mosley held large meetings up and down the country: the feeling of being on a crusade, always crucial to the movement, now seemed a reality. There was an appeal to members to give bits of jewellery to provide much-needed funds: a lady from Harrogate wrote: 'I am sending you my wedding ring to hasten the day when all Britain will hail Mosley!'

The Leader orated:

There are thousands of women living in East London today with their husbands, their brothers, their children who may be doomed by this war conspiracy to the bitterest tears that a woman can shed. What good does it do to such a woman to know that German women too are doomed by us striking back at a foreign city? War is a crime against the people of all lands.

For moments, it seemed that my father might attract more solid support than that which he usually inflamed by his oratory. After listening to the Earls Court speech Major Yeats Brown, a recent convert to the

British Union, wrote to Lord Elton, who was trying to form a group dedicated to preserving peace:

> Personally I agreed with $\frac{3}{4}$ of what he said, but the other $\frac{1}{4}$ is the stumbling block. He declares that there can be no compromise nor conciliation with any of the old parties, and this is absurd in England ... I listened in vain for any word that would have shown that if a crisis came suddenly he would be behind the government. I suppose he wouldn't be, and that he would use the opportunity for political ends.

This had been the stumbling block about much of my father's politics: people could not understand how, if he saw himself as a politician, he would not play the political game of manoeuvring for the successful outcome of his policies by making use of such forces and alliances as were available. People could not understand that he might not be interested in power on such terms; that more important to him might be just the announcing of his policies like some sky-sign – Listen to what I say and take it or leave it – and then leaving the rest to fate. In fact his peace campaign of 1938 and 1939 did often have an apocalyptic ring about it. In April 1938 he had written in *Action* in a style that seemed almost knowlingly to be parodying the *Book of Revelation*:

> Facts will then be brought to light which are partly known to many already but are hidden from the people as a whole by the machinery of the system ... Then all things will be known and at last will be revealed to the people. Mighty on that day will be their wrath, and justice shall be done.
>
> Let the rats of this system not think that any land will safely shelter them, nor any sewer of the world provide them with a refuge. For revolution sweeps across the earth and will overtake them in the furthest cranny that the fugitive criminal can reach. The victory of British Union will seal the doom of their world power.
>
> So to the jackals of putrescence we say today 'Beware!' Britain will have no mercy on you and the world will find you no refuge! The cleansing flame shall pursue you to the uttermost ends of the earth.

Hitler marched into Poland on 1st September 1939; Great Britain declared war on Germany on September 3rd. My father and Diana were still in London: my Aunt Irene, Nanny, my brother and sister and I heard Neville Chamberlain's sad, tired voice making his announcement over the radio in the nursery at Wootton. My aunt recorded that she 'expressed to Nanny my pain and horror if Diana turned up here with her adulation of Hitler, and that she and Unity were two of those who had so inflamed his vanity that in the end he thought he was invincible'. I remember going out on to the lawn to practise football. I explained to Nanny – You see, this war is all a game: there is something impregnable called the Maginot Line, and there is something impregnable called the Siegfried Line, so nothing can happen; and after a time the war will stop.

My father, in London, put out another of his apocalyptic calls containing echoes from the past –

Stand fast, my comrades and companions. Come what may, you have lit a flame in Britain which all the dark corruption of Jewish money-power cannot extinguish. Alone you stand undaunted in the face of the war conspiracy. Alone British Union marches to this decisive struggle, for all lesser things are gone.

However he also wrote and distributed a practical 'Message to All British Union Members' which is of vital importance in any assessment of his attitude to the war – and of the attitudes of others concerning him and the war.

The Government of Britain goes to war with the agreement of all the Parliamentary parties. British Union stands for peace. Neither Britain nor her Empire is threatened. Therefore Britain intervenes in an alien quarrel. In this situation we of British Union will do our utmost to persuade our British people to make peace.

Before war began, in our struggle for peace, our thousands of members had awakened great masses of the British people to demand peace. But sufficient of the people could not be awakened in time without the money which we did not possess. The dope machine of Jewish finance deceived the people until Britain was involved in a war in the interest of the Money Power which rules Britain through its Press and Parties. Now British Union will continue our work of awakening the people until peace be won, and until the People's State of British Union is born by the declared will of the British People.

To our members my message is plain and clear. Our country is involved in war. Therefore I ask you to do nothing to injure our country, or to help the other Power.

Our members should do what the law requires of them; and, if they are members of any of the Forces or Services of the Crown, they should obey their orders and, in every particular, obey the rules of the Service. *But I ask all members who are free to carry on our work to take every opportunity within your power to awaken the people and to demand peace.*

The italics are in the original. To my father, it would have been inconceivable that there need be any contradiction in being at the same time completely loyal to orders to fight, and occupied in work for peace.

A few days before the declaration of war, at a huge street meeting in Hackney, he had (according to *Action*) 'asked those to hold up their hands who wished to fight for Poland: in all those tens of thousands of closely packed people only two raised their hands to the derision of the crowd'.

At Wootton, my Aunt Irene continued to write in the strain of – 'I wonder what my brother-in-law and his wife and her sister Unity Mitford are thinking of their hero Hitler now?'

In Munich Unity Mitford, one hour after war had been declared, went to the office of Gauleiter Wagner, put a sealed envelope on his desk, then went out into a park called the English Garden and shot herself in the head. When after some time Wagner opened the envelope he found in it the signed photograph that Hitler had given to Unity the first time they had met, Unity's Nazi Party badge, and a letter to Hitler in which she said that since war between England and Germany would be the end of the hope to which she had dedicated her life – that of friendship between the two countries that she loved – she would kill herself. Wagner instituted a search, and his men found Unity in the hospital to which she had been taken from the English Garden. The bullet had entered her skull, but she was not dead. Hitler came to visit her three times in a clinic in Munich: she recovered partially. Once when the wife of one of Hitler's adjutants visited her and put on her bed her party badge and her photograph of Hitler, Unity frowned and placed them under the bedclothes. When she was well enough Hitler arranged for her to be moved to Switzerland where she was met by members of her family and brought home. At Folkestone there were hordes of reporters offering money for an interview. Unity lived for another eight years before the bullet moved in her skull and killed her. She remained something like a child.

During the first autumn of the war, after the defeat of Poland, nothing

much happened: this was the time known as the Phoney War: Britain
and France had gone to war to preserve the independence of Poland,
but Poland had been very quickly overrun not only by Nazi Germany
but also by Communist Russia which just before the war had entered
into an alliance with Germany. Britain and France had done, and could
do, nothing to prevent any of this. The situation seemed to my father
so grotesque that he thought anyone reasonable must now want peace.
Hitler in fact made peace proposals which, if accepted, would leave
Britain and the Empire much as they had been before; these proposals
were rejected. It seemed that people in England were feeling, without
much obvious reason, quite cheerful about the war. In the press there
were the usual fantasies – all Britain had to do was to sit tight and then
Germany would mysteriously collapse because of internal dissent or
because of the shortage of this or that vital material. My father wrote
articles in *Action* pointing out that in such respects time was on the side
of the Germans: war materials were now available to Germany from the
east, whereas it was Britain, being an island, who was vulnerable to
blockade by aeroplanes and submarines. So, if we refused to make peace
now, what could be at the back of this except madness or conspiracy?

   Then in November Russia invaded neutral Finland for not much
reason other than that she might want a lump of border territory or
training for her army; so if international morality was being talked
about, should not Britain logically declare war on Russia? There were
in fact some voices in Parliament that advocated this; ministers in France
talked about an anti-bolshevik crusade; there were suggestions about
turning the flank of the immobile western front by an attack through
Norway and Finland and Russia into Germany; or perhaps the Germans
might suddenly overthrow Hitler and come in on an anti-bolshevik
crusade themselves. My father must have thought all this indeed evidence for his theory that the western democracies had gone mad: such
fantasies were outside the range of what could even be explained by
conspiracy. In fact during the winter of 1939–1940 an Anglo-French
force was assembled to come to the help of the Finns against the
Russians; but then in March 1940 Finland made peace with Russia.
The British and French governments felt themselves under impetus
however to go ahead with some sort of activity in the area; it was
decided that Norwegian coastal waters, through which iron ore was
brought to Germany should be mined. Neville Chamberlain announced,
apropos of nothing much in particular, that 'Hitler had missed the bus'.
My father wrote – 'Can anyone pretend much longer that these men
are fit to govern a great nation in a great age?'

During the winter he had announced that British Union would fight two Parliamentary by-elections: he had been encouraged in this perhaps by the large and apparently enthusiastic audiences that had been attending his meetings. But then at Silvertown in East London in February 1940 Tommy Moran, the British Union candidate, got 151 votes against the Labour candidate's 14,343; and in North-East Leeds in March the British Union candidate got 722 votes against the Conservative's 23,882. About the Silvertown result *Action* made what was, for it, an almost unique admission that the British Union vote had been 'very poor'. About the North-East Leeds result it argued that since 1,000 people had come to a meeting addressed by Oswald Mosley, this was evidence that 72% of them had been won over by the British Union message.

On April 8th the British Government decided to mine Norwegian waters: the same day Hitler set about taking over the whole of Norway. This he did within a few days. The British planned landings in Norway here and there; while they were carrying these out, and having to withdraw them, Hitler, on 10th May invaded Holland and Belgium. Neville Chamberlain resigned: Winston Churchill became Prime Minister. My father reiterated the message which he had made to his followers at the beginning of the war – 'I ask you to do nothing to injure our country or to help any other power.'

By 19th May the Germans were approaching Paris; the British army was retreating towards Dunkirk; Mosley went to Middleton, in Lancashire, to speak on behalf of his third British Union parliamentary candidate at a by-election. He was attacked by a mob when he tried to speak from the top of a van and was escorted from the area by police. The British Union candidate polled 418 votes and the Conservative 32,063.

On 23rd May Mosley wrote in *Action*:

The question has been put to me why I do not cease all political activity in an hour of danger to our country. The answer is that I intend to do my best to provide the people with an alternative to the present government if, and when, they desire to make peace with the British Empire intact and our people safe ... I can conceive no greater tragedy than the British people desiring to make such a British Peace and having no means to express their will.

The next day, May 24th, Hitler gave orders that the pursuit of the British army in France should cease; the result was that much of that army was able to get away at Dunkirk. There is evidence that this

order was given in the light of Hitler's genuine desire to make peace
with Britain; he still hoped that Britain might look after the sea-routes
of the world while he, Hitler, turned to the East. It seems that he thought
this might be feasible if the British army was not humiliated. But there
was no one in England both willing and in a position to make this
sort of peace that was also envisaged by my father.

On May 22nd the British Government rushed through an Emergency
Powers Act which gave them almost unlimited power over all British
citizens and their property. Just before the outbreak of war there had
in fact been an earlier Emergency Powers Bill which had empowered
the government to make Regulations by Orders in Council for the
Defence of the Realm; this had, ironically, given to government the
sort of powers that my father had advocated in 1930 in order to deal
with unemployment. One of the regulations suggested in 1939, however, had gone beyond anything ever advocated by my father: it was
labelled 18B: it empowered the Home Secretary to detain in prison
'any particular person if satisfied that it is necessary to do so'. There
had been parliamentary protests about the unparalleled scope of this:
the regulation had been amended to the Home Secretary's being able
to detain anyone whom he had 'reason to believe' to be 'of hostile
origin or associations'; or to have been recently concerned in 'acts prejudicial to public safety or to the defence of the realm'. Now, in May
1940, the Home Secretary John Anderson reported to the Cabinet that
under the existing Regulations he had no power to detain Oswald
Mosley or other members of British Union. He admitted that Mosley
had given explicit instructions to his members to obey the law and
to do nothing to injure their country or to help foreign powers; but
he also reported, according to Cabinet minutes – 'Two officers of MI5
have given it as their opinion that a certain proportion of the members
[of British Union] ... say 25–30%, would be willing, if ordered, to
go to any lengths': and that although he, the Home Secretary, was
of the opinion that Oswald Mosley 'was too clever to put himself in
the wrong by giving treasonable orders ... he [the Home Secretary]
realised that the War Cabinet might take the view that, notwithstanding
the absence of such evidence, we should not run any risk in the matter
however small'.

Accordingly the Cabinet (consisting of just Chamberlain, Attlee,
Halifax and Greenwood; Churchill was in France) authorised Anderson
to have the Regulation 18B amended in such a manner that Mosley
and his followers might be detained. It was this Emergency Powers
amendment that was rushed through on the evening of May 22nd:

Regulation 18B (1A) now gave the Home Secretary power to detain any members of an organisation which in his view was 'subject to foreign influence or control' or whose leaders 'have or have had associations with persons concerned in the government of, or sympathetic with the system of government of, any power with which His Majesty is at war'. Thus my father became liable to arrest and imprisonment because he had met Hitler twice and Mussolini five or six times before 1937; and for this reason all his followers became liable to arrest too. The Regulation did state that the Home Secretary had to be satisfied 'that there is a danger of the utilisation of the organisation for purposes prejudicial to the public safety, the defence of the realm, the maintenance of public order, the efficient prosecution of any war in which His Majesty may be engaged, or the maintenance of supplies and services essential to the life of the community': but these considerations had only to be in the mind of the Home Secretary. The way in which the Regulation had been specifically amended was evidence of just what in fact was in his mind.

On May 23rd my father and Diana were at Savehay Farm: Wootton had been abandoned when the Phoney War came to an end because my father felt it was necessary to be near the centre of events. He and Diana drove in the afternoon to London to the flat at Dolphin Square which they had rented: (during the mid-thirties my father had moved from Ebury Street to a house on the river at 129 Grosvenor Road: this was too large for wartime, so in 1940 he and Diana moved to Dolphin Square). Outside the block of flats Diana noticed four or five men standing on the pavement 'aimlessly staring into space': my father recognised one or two of them as policemen who had been on duty at his meetings. They said they had a warrant for his arrest. He was allowed to go up to the flat to pick up some clothes. Then he was taken to Brixton Prison.

That evening Diana, back at Denham, was having dinner (I was at school) when the garden gate was pushed open and policemen poured across the lawn. They said they had come to search the house. They leafed through many of the books in the library; some of them began to dig up the garden looking for arms. After a time they left.

The British Union Headquarters was searched for three days: crates of papers were carried away. The last number of *Action* appeared on May 30th: it reported that between 70 and 80 members of British Union had been arrested including Francis-Hawkins and Raven Thomson. Some of those arrested had fought in the last war. *Action* made a statement that 'not a shred of evidence had been found to support any allegation that British Union was, or ever had been under foreign influence'; that there had been 'a clear violation of British justice, which is that a man (or for that matter a body of men) is deemed innocent until he had been proved guilty'. There was a biographical account of Mosley's career showing him to have been a steadfast and passionate patriot. During the following days British Union members were arrested as they came back from the beaches at Dunkirk; one was arrested as he returned from a bombing mission over Germany.

Up to the time of Hitler's invasion of the West, British Union's advocacy of peace had been tolerated if not electorally supported: now, with the threat of invasion, all had changed. Diana recorded – 'There was an indescribable air of panic, barely suppressed; and wherever I went I was met with glances not so much hostile as terrified.' After my father's arrest the Mosley family solicitor refused to help Diana with her enquiries: Diana's friend Gerald Berners, when he told some Oxford friends of his intention to visit her at Savehay Farm, was warned that if he did so he would be putting himself in the way of arrest. Nanny and my brother Micky left Denham and went to stay with Irene and Vivien in London; Diana remained at Savehay Farm with her one-and-a-half-year-old son Alexander and her six-week-old baby Max, and their Nanny. Diana received anonymous letters from people saying they were coming to murder her, and to pour vitriol over her babies.

People were afraid, and they needed scapegoats: they argued – Mosley has been arrested; does not this prove he is a traitor? The writer Henry Williamson, a friend of my father's and an outspoken supporter of British Union, wrote to Diana describing how he had been banned from the local Defence Corps for having 'blasphemed against King and Country': when he had protested that this was a 'damned lie' the local organiser had said, 'I don't care if it is a damned lie, I believe it.'

But Henry Williamson also wrote:

I thought of writing to the Times saying that as a non-active member I wanted to know if it had been discovered that funds had been received from any foreign country; for if so, thousands of people like myself would then immediately disclaim all connection with such a party; that there was a considerable and harmful amount of rumour going around and for the sake of public *morale* a Govt statement about the existence of such contributions to the funds, or non-contributions, should be made public. If such funds had been received,

then I and thousands like me were gulled fools and deserved imprisonment at once; if not, the air of Britain should be cleared of at least
that amount of enervating rumour.

Rumours about these funds were now rising up to haunt my father.
Vengeful passions were anyway running high. On May 16th, shortly
before my father's arrest, my Aunt Irene had recorded in her diary:

> I had to go on to Sir John Anderson: he wanted to ask me if I
> had any evidence that Tom Mosley would betray his country in
> its peril with the 5th column. I said I had no evidence of that, and
> Sir John told me *Action* had become milder. But I told him that
> if Tom thought such a thing was good for England in conjunction
> with Hitler's regime then he might do anything if he got angry
> and thought we were mucking the whole thing. I gave him bits
> of conversation from Tom and Diana and I said I had been useless
> as we had not met for weeks. He said I had given him all he wanted.

And then on May 25th, just after my father's arrest, Irene wrote in
her diary:

> I asked Vincent [Massey] if he did not think that Diana Mosley was
> as dangerous as Tom and I wanted to write that to Sir John, and
> he entirely agreed.

And then the next day:

> I wrote to Sir John Anderson on Diana Mosley.

Diana was arrested on June 29th: it was reported in the papers that
it had been intended from the first that she would be arrested, but
she had been left for a month on account of her baby. A gang of
police came to Savehay Farm: she was given the choice of either taking
or not taking with her eleven-week-old Max whom she was still breast-
feeding. She was told she would not in any case be able to take with
her one-and-a-half-year-old Alexander, so she decided not to separate
the children but to leave them with their Nanny. She arranged for
them to go to stay with her sister and brother-in-law Pamela and Derek
Jackson in Oxfordshire. On her way to Holloway Prison Diana asked
to be allowed to stop at a chemist in Wigmore Street in order to buy
a breast pump to get rid of the milk that should have been for her
baby.

On the evening of my father's arrest I was in my room at Eton; I was visited by my amiable and intelligent house tutor; he told me my father had been arrested – he had been telephoned by my stepmother Diana. I said – I see – or some such. Then my tutor hung about my room as if he wanted to say something more; I wondered what it was; eventually he said – Do you think there might be anything – I mean – in it? I could not make out what he was implying. Then I realised – He was asking me if I thought my father might in fact be some sort of traitor. I said – Oh good heavens no! Then – It is just, you see, that he doesn't think there's any sense in this war. My housemaster seemed to accept this. But it was as if he still felt there might be something more to be said. I wanted to ask him – Do you think it's wrong to wonder, then, whether there's any sense in this war?

CHAPTER 18

Background to Imprisonment

The story behind my father's detention in May 1940 and his imprisonment for the next three and a half years has remained obscure because
of the refusal by the authorities to release their papers about it. In July
1940 my father appeared before an Advisory Committee set up by
the Home Office to examine the validity of the reasons for people
being detained under Regulation 18B; my father was questioned for
sixteen hours over a period of five days; the chairman of this Advisory
Committee was his old adversary from the *Star* libel case – Norman
Birkett KC. The transcript of this cross-examination apparently exists:
it is in 'a category of Home Office records which are closed to public
inspection for a period of up to 100 years by order of the Lord
Chancellor'. This statement was made in a letter to myself, the author,
from the Departmental Record Officer of the Home Office when I
applied in July 1981 for permission to see the transcript. Normally
public records become available for inspection after thirty years. The
letter said that the Lord Chancellor has powers to impose a longer
ban under 'section 5(1) of the Public Records Act 1958'. This act
describes the circumstances under which such powers can properly be
exercised as those in which there might be a 'breach of good faith';
'distress or embarrassment to living persons might be caused'; or the
papers might be so 'exceptionally sensitive' that their disclosure would
be 'contrary to the public interest on security or other grounds'. Further
correspondence with the Departmental Record Officer established the
fact that the papers concerning my father's imprisonment were being
'retained by the Home Office on security grounds'.

The idea that publication of my father's cross-examination in July
1940 might be a danger to security in 1981 was so bizarre that further
representations were made to the Lord Chancellor himself, and a ques-

tion was asked in the House of Lords by my father's old friend Bob Boothby. Nothing further could be elucidated other than that, yes, the information was being withheld because it might be a threat to present security.

The question at stake in 1940 had been – what were the justifications for arresting and imprisoning people indefinitely without trial as a result of a regulation which was invented the evening before their arrest and of which they had never heard, and which rendered them liable to imprisonment on account of matters which at the time of their happening had been quite legal? This was an exceptional departure from traditions of English justice. Moreover the amended regulation was used mainly against people who had publicly reaffirmed their patriotism. But the added question at stake now is – what on earth happened in 1940 the disclosure of which even in 1981 might be a threat to public security?

On 9th May 1940 when Neville Chamberlain realised he might have to resign as Prime Minister the Labour leaders Attlee and Greenwood had been approached about whether or not they would serve under him in a coalition Government; they said they would have to consult their national executive at Bournemouth, where the party was assembled for its annual conference. At the Bournemouth Conference one of the delegates, Hugh Ross Williamson, remembered – 'One of the main subjects of conversation which I heard at unofficial talks was whether or not the Labour Leaders had made the arrest and imprisonment of Mosley a condition of their entering Government. The general feeling was that they had – or at least, that they ought to'. On May 10th Attlee and Greenwood, back in London, said that they would serve under Churchill but not under Chamberlain. They became members of Churchill's coalition Government. The amendment to 18B which enabled Mosley to be arrested was made on May 22nd on the orders of the four-man Cabinet group that included Attlee and Greenwood.

Labour politicians – perhaps because their feelings of loyalty are apt to be divided between party, nation, internationalism and class – sometimes seem vengefully to need the scalps of those who they feel have betrayed them. They had not forgiven Mosley for having been what they called a 'traitor' to their party in 1930; they now had a chance to suggest he might be a traitor to his country.

What members of British Union found objectionable in this was the fact that so many of them who were arrested had been members of the fighting services either in the first world war or indeed in the second – one officer in 1940 was arrested in front of his men on the parade ground – while many of those responsible for their arrest had chosen not to fight in the first world war (Greenwood; Morrison) and indeed many of those who were to be future Labour leaders remained out of the fighting services in the second.

It could of course be said that members of British Union just by dressing up in black shirts and making aggressive noises in the cause of peace had invited retaliation. But it seems likely in fact that there were more pertinent influences at work than any of these at the back of the decision to detain them.

My father kept a record of what he intended to say to the Advisory Committee: this was in the form of 'answers' to suggested 'reasons for detention' that his solicitor had put to him in anticipation of the sort of questions the Advisory Committee might ask. My father seems to have been at least partly aware of what might be at the back of decisions concerning regulation 18B – even possibly to have had an inkling about why these might be kept secret.

His statement began –

The police have raided my flat, my wife's flat, the London house we used to occupy and my children's house in the country. They have raided the offices of British Union. At the end of this process what shred of evidence can they produce to support the allegation that I would play traitor to my country?

I believe that I was one of the first two Cavalry officers who volunteered to go to the Royal Flying Corps in 1914. I served with the R.F.C. in France in the winter of 1914/15. The following winter I was back with my regiment in the trenches. I have since been a member of Parliament for some twelve years and am an ex-minister of the Crown.

It is apparently suggested that I want my country to be defeated. Yet for the last seven years I have spent much of my time demanding that Britain should properly be armed to resist attack, and have violently attacked the old parties in and out of season for neglecting our defences. In particular I have demanded air parity with the strongest other country – which was Germany.

I opposed this war on two grounds: (a) the members of my movement are ever prepared to fight in defence of Britain but do not think that Britain should go to war for the sake of Poland or any Eastern European question: (b) they were more than ever opposed to intervention in a foreign war when Britain was not properly armed for war.

I admit quite frankly and have always admitted that I hold the high ambition to make a great country even greater. I cite my whole record and whole career in refutation of the charge – as absurd as it is vile – that any aim which I have ever held can be achieved through disaster to my country.

I desire to advance one concrete argument and one constructive suggestion. If it is considered that we were wrong to state our opinions in time of war and openly to advocate Peace why were we not told to shut up? The Government had ample power at any time to close our mouths. The Home Secretary possessed powers to give publications such as *Action* a warning and after the warning those responsible would be liable to prosecution with heavy penalties. A warning was never given.

I make the suggestion that we be told to live in any place or to act in any way that the Government may specify and that we shall be forbidden to speak, write or communicate with anyone without permission. I further suggest that if possible we shall be permitted whether on the land or elsewhere to do useful work instead of being an incumbrance to the nation in gaol. I offered again and again in public speeches to fight if the nation was invaded. Now this situation appears to be imminent, I ask to be permitted to do something useful for my country rather than be a nuisance to it, even if I am not to be trusted with the weapons with which in my early life I was brought up.

The statement went on to deny the charges that the names 'Fascist' and 'National Socialist' implied that British Union was under foreign influence; that what might be called its brand of anti-semitism had anything to do with German anti-semitism; that its officials ever made official contacts with members of foreign governments. But then – the possible charge that my father was at most pains to be ready to refute was that concerning funds. He seems to have expected that he might be faced with the charge that British Union had received funds from Italy during 1932–1935: the Committee might even have got hold of some evidence about this. He was ready to reply –

I personally had nothing whatever to do with the finances of the organisation during that period because I had divorced myself from that side in our original constitution on the grounds that it was improper for the Leader of the Movement to be familiar with those who subscribed. My general directions were that no money should be accepted except from British subjects and that no conditions should be attached.

The allegation is denied: but even if it were true, I ask why it should be a reason for holding me or my colleagues in gaol? It was stated in Lord Snowden's biography that the *Daily Herald* was started by money from Russia and that the late and highly respected Mr George Lansbury was the principal figure in the transaction. He was afterwards Leader of the Labour Party in the House of Commons.

Then my father described how after support by British capitalists had been withdrawn and he himself had subscribed £100,000 of his own money, he had become involved in the radio advertising business in which agreements had been under negotiation with Sark, Ireland and Germany. He emphasised that the dealing with Germany had been purely commercial:

I finally got the German concession some fifteen months after the Sark concession: I eventually secured an interest of over 90%. The terms were much less favourable than in the case of Sark; they were roughly the same as I have always understood the French government gives in the case of Normandie. The German company got 55% of the profit and the British company 45%. The Directors of the German company are businessmen and are not in the government of Germany.... If we get radio advertising in Sark, all this money will stay within the Empire; why oppose it?

At the end of the actual hearing, the details of which are still taboo on the grounds that their publication would present a threat to present security, my father asked the chairman Norman Birkett (this is my father's publicly stated recollection which has never been challenged), 'Is it suggested that we are traitors who would take up arms and fight with the Germans if they landed?' and Norman Birkett replied 'Speaking for myself, you can entirely dismiss that suggestion.' My father then said, 'I can only assume that we have been detained because of our campaign in favour of a negotiated peace?' and Norman Birkett replied 'Yes, Sir Oswald, that is the case'.

It seems possible that this Advisory Committee recommended that, once it had been effectively decreed that all further political activity by British Union must stop, there would no longer be a sensible or legal case for British Union members such as Oswald Mosley to continue in gaol. If so, such a recommendation was overruled. Such an overruling might itself be a reason for the papers continuing to be withheld. There is evidence that the Advisory Committee did in certain cases make such recommendations which were indeed overruled on the authority of a more powerful and secret body; and it may be in order not to divulge anything about this body that the papers are still banned.

In May of 1940 there was set up a Defence Security Executive whose job it was to investigate 'suspicious political activities' and report directly to the Prime Minister. Winston Churchill said in the House of Commons in July 1940 – 'I take full responsibility for the control, character and composition of this committee'. This 'Executive' was the effective power behind the legalistic façade of Birkett's Advisory Committee. It consisted for the most part of men to do with 'security' – with MI5 and MI6 – who by the nature of their trade are concerned to keep their activities secret.

The chairman of this Defence Security Executive was Lord Swinton, a Conservative politician and ex-minister and a director of multi-national corporations. Other members included Sir Joseph Ball, known to be a high-ranking officer in British Intelligence, and Alfred Wall, a leading trades unionist and a communist activist in South London. The Executive was formed at a time when the Hitler-Stalin pact was still in force: security people, again by the nature of their jobs, are sometimes arbitrary about matters of loyalty. One thing they could all agree on perhaps in 1940 was their dislike of British Union. My father would have been anathema to such men – if for no other reason than that they, in their respectably treacherous world, would have been anathema to him.

Questions were asked by Aneurin Bevan and Richard Stokes in the House of Commons about the composition of this Executive; and whether it was true that there was a government directive prohibiting newspapers referring to it. Churchill replied that it was accepted 'that it was not in the public interest that questions should be asked and answered about. . . . . Secret Service work'. In November 1941 Conservative MPs were bringing the subject up again. Sir Irving Albery asked – 'Has not the Home Secretary some advisor other than the independent Advisory Committee? And was not the advice on which the Home Secretary relied that of the Security Department, the body which originally advised the detention?' Sir Archibald Southby said that it seemed –

There was no obligation on the Home Secretary to accept the advice of the Advisory Committee, and in numerous cases he had

rejected their advice. The only reason could be that the Home
Secretary had not disclosed all the facts and suspicions in regard to
the detained person to the Advisory Committee. Undue state control
on the individual, if allowed to go unchecked, must inevitably lead
to something approaching the tyranny of Nazism.

It is inevitable perhaps that security people should have the last word
in war – even if it means that people are innocently at the mercy of
such men. In 1940 it might have been the case that the Home Secretary
had 'suspicions in regard to the detained person' fed to him by the
Defence Security Executive which were not divulged to the Advisory
Committee let alone to the House of Commons. In particular, there
were the continuing rumours about the money from Mussolini. My
father had taken great care that no hard evidence concerning this money
should be procurable (it was stated in the House of Commons on 11th
December 1940 that 'the Advisory Committee and the solicitors had
had to admit that there was no foreign money coming into the British
Union') but he must have known that security people do not work
in areas to do with hard evidence.

As early as 1935 Robert Forgan had written to my father: 'I wonder
if you realise that one source of income is known to a number of people
who are not in our confidence – I mention this merely so that you
may be on your guard'. Even earlier a BUF member in Rome trying
to get an increased expense allowance had written 'I am sure that the
powers that are here will thoroughly approve of this payment as the
sums being transmitted to you are for the general expenses of the BUF'.
My father had replied – 'I am at a loss to understand the reference
in your letter' and had 'forthwith suspended' the member from his
duties. But the most bizarre fact that has come to light concerning
the possible ways in which such information might have come to the
notice of the security people is to do with W. E. D. Allen, who was
not only likely to have been my father's go-between in the matter
of the Mussolini payments but was certainly his front-man in the radio
advertising deal: Allen himself, my father divulged later, worked for
MI5 in the 1930s – and my father even knew of this at the time. In
a statement he recorded in later life he said of Bill Allen – 'Very much
involved with MI5, made no bones about it, that is why he wasn't
imprisoned in the war, of course, because he had done so much for
them.' Also, when asked whether he thought MI5 had used Allen to
find out what was going on in the movement my father replied – 'To
some extent: probably reporting conversations with me which were

probably largely fictitious: he was a tremendously boastful man ...
one of those men who simply lived in a dream world – a Walter Mitty
world, as we would call it now'. In addition, my father had quarrelled
with Allen in 1938 on the subject of loans that the latter had made
to Air Time Ltd, and Allen had told him he was in danger of losing
his 'one surviving friend'. In the light of all this, it seems more than
likely that the Defence Security Executive must have been fed some
information about the links with Mussolini; and then they could, owing
to my father's intransigent denials of the whole affair, make from it
whatever they liked. And they might according to their custom have
wanted to keep their sources secret: it might even conceivably be considered advisable on 'security grounds' not to have the nature of these
sources, and such elaborations as were made from them, spelled out
now.

Whatever the nuances of the truth about this, it seems probable that
the very skill with which my father had operated in the business of
keeping the payments secret worked in 1940 to his grave disadvantage:
it could be argued by his opponents that if he had gone to such lengths
in the matter of this form of secrecy, what other kinds of contact with
foreign governments might he have covered up? There were of course
Diana's visits to Berlin on the radio advertising business: my father
had been at pains to keep his own connections with this secret. He
had been ready later to give an account of this to the Advisory Committee; but still, what he had been involved in was the setting up of
a radio business of which a German company would own over 50%;
and more than this, Diana's visits to Hitler's Chancellery late at night
were probably known to British Intelligence. Such information would
have reached the Defence Security Executive; and how were they to
know that what was talked about was no more than charming gossip
about the state of the world? Or rather – what more evidence might
such men as those who worked on the Executive require, when it was
probably in their minds to find reasons to imprison my father anyway?
My father, by entering himself so deeply and yet apparently so carelessly
into the world of secrecy and cover-ups, laid himself open to the
revenges of those who played such games professionally.

My father's amazing *insouciance* about all this was in keeping with
his image of himself as a gambler going for very high stakes: he took
risks about money for the sake of what he believed about the fate of
Britain and of Europe; he had always known he might lose; of course,
he would have had no problems if he had won. As things were, he
prepared his defences for the Advisory Committee; but he did not

complain much when he was imprisoned, nor did he complain very much afterwards. It was not in his nature to complain; but his continued denials make it seem as if he knew of the dangers he had run with the Mussolini payments. Curiously, in later life he did not seem to see the risks that had been attendant on the radio deal involving Hitler. But there would have been no personal disaster if there had not been war; and were not risks worth running to prevent the huge disaster of war? With regard to his imprisonment he must have felt that he had struggled to the best of his ability to prevent a war that he considered catastrophic: perhaps it even seemed fitting to him that he should be imprisoned by men who he thought were dragging the country to perdition.

When Diana came up in front of the Advisory Committee in the autumn of 1940 she made no pretence of being anything other than contemptuous. She said in her autobiography that later she regretted that she had not prepared 'a devastating indictment of the unprincipled politicians and their disgraceful behaviour': but she felt herself helpless in the face of the 'triumph of rumour, gossip, spite, and lying tongues'. She found Norman Birkett's questions simply silly: 'Why had we been married in Berlin?' 'Because we wished to keep the marriage secret for a while.' 'Why had Hitler arranged this for us?' 'Because I asked him to.' Then★ –

Birkett pounced: 'This friend of yours is now bombing London!' I said that since Britain had declared war on Germany and we had bombed Berlin it was rather obvious that the Germans would bomb London. Birkett asked me when I had last seen Hitler. In Bayreuth in 1939, I replied. And what had I said to him about Britain? Had I said that Britain would not fight? I replied that Hitler had told me he was certain Britain would declare war; he was convinced of it.

Diana recognised on the committee an old acquaintance, Sir George Clerk, who had been Ambassador in Istanbul in 1931, when Diana had had lunch with him (my mother Cimmie had stayed with him the year before when she had paid her visit to Trotsky). The Committee was holding court in a requisitioned hotel in Ascot: one of the members sent Diana a bottle of claret for lunch: she shared this with her wardress in the stables.

★ *A Life of Contrasts.*

In July it had seemed to my father that once the panic about invasion had died down, reason would prevail and he would be released; after all, many people in government knew him; whatever risks he had taken, they would know his true character. But such people did not have the effective power in the matter of letting him out; he was in the hands of people for whom there was probably little meaning in truth of character.

To myself it is inconceivable that my father would in any way have aided the Germans in 1940. He would have fought the Germans if they had invaded Britain and he had a chance to fight – this was in keeping with his whole character and tradition. It also seems inconceivable that in the event of a German victory in 1940 he would have played a part as a national leader installed by the Germans: this would not have been in keeping with his hope and determination to lead Britain back to a position of national and imperial 'greatness'. Whether or not, or in what way, he might have accepted any turning of British people to him as someone who, after a period of German domination, might restore national honour – this would have depended on the circumstances at the time. There would have been nothing dishonourable in his holding himself ready to try to retrieve something from a disaster to his country which he had always said others would cause.

It remains a fact that in 1940 the majority of people in the country seemed to want him locked up: evidence for this can be seen in the violent reactions of people when the news broke three and a half years later that he was to be released – and this was when the winning of the war was in sight. In 1940 Hitler had gained such an easy victory in France that people were confused and afraid: when people are afraid they need scapegoats on which to vent in simple form their rages: members of British Union, and especially my father, had set themselves up as obvious Hitler substitutes. My father seemed to accept responsibility for the risks he ran; but of course he had been gambling with lives other than his own. As Henry Williamson had written – 'If such funds had been received, [from a foreign country] then I and thousands like me were gulled fools and deserved imprisonment at once'. The cost to others was sometimes great.

Over 700 British Union sympathisers were arrested and thrown into jail: some were taken on the mere gossip of neighbours; their families were persecuted and their homes sometimes pillaged; they lost their jobs and the businesses they had built up; they were spat on and reviled. In jail they had to suffer sometimes from solitary confinement and from hunger. They had genuinely seen themselves as patriots banding together to defend the honour of their country: they were suddenly branded as traitors in a way that seemed likely to scar the rest of their lives. Such a gigantic disparity of vision implies a terrifying naivety on both sides: it was not only the fascists who, in Jung's phrase, failed 'to see their own shadow, their own worst danger'.

My father's one-time henchman William Joyce was someone who did in fact act according to the popular view of fascists: he had gone to Germany just before the war and he now became involved in the broadcasting of German propaganda in English. After the war he was captured and executed as a traitor to England – on doubtful legal grounds, since he was an Irish-American. But in the meantime he had become known to the English jokingly – in keeping with the style of the British in wartime – as Lord Haw-Haw. One evening in the winter of 1939/40 our family was listening to him on the radio at Savehay Farm, and my Aunt Irene recorded: 'I told Nick that for weeks now it has been known that it was Tom's man Joyce: the War Office knew it and Mrs Joyce had written it to the papers.' Irene added, 'Curiously the children, perhaps feeling ashamed, always seem angrily to stand up for these awful statements; and to argue violently with me on the defensive.'

CHAPTER 19

Parental Attitudes

During the winter of 1939/40 my father, who had seemed close at least to me of his children at Wootton, had increasingly moved out of sight; he was in London intent on his drive for peace. We would visit him sometimes in his house in Grosvenor Road which had once been (and was to be again) a night club – it had a huge pale-blue sitting room with mock marble pillars and a dark purple bedroom like a stage set. Here he would be preoccupied, stride about, make up his speeches; shout at his large gloomy manservant who was called Littleberry, and was like Don Giovanni's Leporello.

Shortly after the outbreak of war and the summer holidays in which members of the family, some reluctantly, had been inveigled up to Wootton, there was a big family uproar because my Aunt Irene, who said she would continue to put up money for the children's expenses even when they were based at Wootton, now rebelled – perhaps because there was no need to stay at Wootton because there was no bombing of the home counties; perhaps because of the photographs of Goebbels and Hitler on Diana's tables. Irene told my father she would put up no money except for the old family home at Denham; whereupon in Grosvenor Road my father (Irene recorded) –

was so wild with rage he tore up and down the room in a filthy blasphemous state with dear Ma trying to calm him. I gave out some pretty stiff heated rejoinders while Diana never uttered. The arguments were that it was due to me that the children must live like workmen, Wootton was lost, Eton might go, and Micky thanks to me must go to Baba and in the spring must go to school. I repeated my Denham offer, which was actually listened to politely, but he continued to say he was through with me. The real truth is I have

crashed their castle and brought Wootton to ruins and the funds
they wanted to give to fascism cannot now be safe unless they live
in a cottage.

My father, it was true, was now giving all his income to British Union.
It seemed to me, aged sixteen, that his commitment to the cause of
peace was admirable. I wrote from Eton:

> Darling Daddy,
> I have just heard about the bust-up with Aunty Nina. Of course
> it is a pity we will have to give up Wootton after all, but I am
> sure it will make no difference to Viv or I if we have to live in
> a much smaller house. I do hope you manage to let Denham, as
> the money from that will make all the difference.
>   I am in all the top divisions as usual and doing much the same.
> Eton is incredibly dull in war time. The people are so terribly stupid
> here. They think the Germans will revolt at any moment, and that
> everything is going to be perfectly easy for us. I must say that from
> reading the papers you find it hard to believe that the French troops
> are not on the outskirts of Berlin. Of course all the boys believe
> every word the papers say, and worship that fool Mr Churchill.
> I have found it does not pay to try and tell them how wrong they
> are. The sensible ones, including me, are just waiting for Eton to
> be bombed so we can all go home.

I had developed a sort of patter by which I could defend my father's
points of view: I had also developed an arrogance which was at least
in part, I suppose, a mechanism by which to protect myself and show
sympathy with my father. I had for some time been echoing his arguments – what is the point of a Parliamentary system that pays a Prime
Minister £10,000 a year to run the country and a Leader of the Opposition £2,000 to stop him?; and now I would say – why should not
the Germans march East and then they and the Russians can just bash
one another? People seemed able to give me no reasonable answers
to such questions. I did not, of course, expect people at Eton to be
reasonable.
   I followed my father's analyses of strategy in *Action* during the period
of the Phoney War. These explained how we could not win the war,
how we could prevent the Germans from winning, how with such
a stalemate it was only reasonable to make peace. I could not imagine
how people did not accept this: even people who did not agree with

my father, such as my aunts, continued to say he had the most marvellous brain. My aunts insisted – What a tragedy, and especially in wartime, that England was not getting the benefit of such a brain!

At Eton there were supposed to be masters with good brains, but what was striking was that no one discussed the war with us; no one seemed to wonder why we were fighting or what we were hoping for; why it was that we did not, for instance, just let the Germans and Russians bash one another up. Certainly no one seemed any longer to be under the illusion that we could help Poland. There were certain 'War Aims' officially published, but these did not seem to make much sense beyond the impression of vague sentiments. My Aunt Baba's friend Lord Halifax, for instance, announced – 'We want, I suppose, that every man and woman in Europe should have a chance of leading a decent and orderly life and of developing his or her personality according to opportunity.' This was all very well – but how was it thought that this might be achieved through a European war? (I learned likely answers to such questions so many years, and so many travails, later.) In the meantime it appeared absurd that our teachers at Eton just accepted the occurrence of a European war in the same style that they accepted, and so unquestioningly taught us, the history of the Trojan or the Peloponnesian Wars; or indeed the story of Medea so beautifully murdering her children.

There was a time early in 1940 when my father had wanted to take me away from Eton; he had a plan whereby I should study science under Diana's brother-in-law Derek Jackson, who was a physicist. I wrote to my father: 'If you have been able to arrange anything definite with Derek Jackson I still think it would be best to leave at the end of the summer but if nothing satisfactory can be fixed perhaps it is not worth it.' Part of my protection was nonchalance. In the same letter I described how: 'We had the house sports the other day and amidst great excitement I proceeded to win the Senior High Jump and come second in the Half Mile: I jumped 4ft 10ins in an enormous pair of walking shoes as I had lost my running shoes as usual.' At the end of the letter I put a PS. 'I was so sorry about the Silvertown election [in which there had been a BU candidate] but I think very few people would have got even 150 votes in such a short time.'

When my father was imprisoned there was the business again of running the gauntlet of people's polite, not-quite-observing eyes: more painful this time than that of the publicity concerning my father's and Diana's secret marriage eighteen months earlier, but still not the sort of occasion at which Etonians showed any venom. Eton is good about this sort of thing: it is almost the one place on earth, I suppose, that has such a built-in confidence in itself – in the virtue just of Etonians being Etonians – that this is stronger than any stray occurrence such as that of some Etonian's father being locked up in jail. For this I was, and still am, very grateful. There was no more talk of my leaving Eton.

My Aunt Irene visited me during this summer; she wrote:

I heard Mr Elliott [the headmaster] preach and he gave an admirable sermon on the burden of being an Etonian because those boys had wealth and privilege and theirs must be the future to lead and be worthy of it. Nicky all the time held his head and I felt he was not happy. Later walking me to the station he said he thought Mr Elliott was right but they were all bored with him.

The problem for me was – however much I might be grateful to Eton with its crazy self-confidence, what on earth had this got to do with what was happening in the world outside? School work went on with its strange intensities like the learning of tribal dialects in New Guinea. I continued to be good at passing exams: I worked at night when necessary: I won prizes. The only sport I was good at was athletics: I had given up trying at cricket. On summer afternoons I would wander off to the cinema at Slough: this, of course, was strictly against the rules. I became fascinated by sophisticated, witty comedies such as those of Lubitsch and Preston Sturges. Was this the 'decent and orderly life' that the grown-up world was aiming at? But why was such honour given to the people in the *Iliad*?

For the summer holidays of 1940 myself and my sister Vivien and my brother Micky and almost everyone in the family who were not in jail went to Loch Awe, in Scotland. I wrote to my father in a style that I must have thought was sophisticated:

I wish I had known earlier that we are allowed to write as many letters to you as we like. We all thought for some unknown reason that you were only allowed to have two a week and therefore our letters would never reach you. But Granny says that all our letters will reach you after censorship, so I can write often now.

We are having great fun up in Scotland. Viv and I with Andrée and Aunty N live in the hotel, while Nanny and Mick live in a cottage three miles off with Aunty B and family. It has never stopped raining for a minute since we got here. The hotel has not a person under 42 in the place. I have been salmon fishing once or twice in the river Awe but I never catch a thing. The shooting is really pathetic. There are supposed to be hundreds of rabbits round about and David [Metcalfe] and I walk for miles every evening only seeing one or two. David has got a retriever which he and Aunty B are very proud of: they have sent him to all the best trainers and he is supposed to be the world's best shooting dog. But because he is a very stupid animal to begin with and because the Metcalfe nursery world is enough to drive any dog dippy he runs about in every direction, never comes when he is called, and has to be lifted over every fence.

Thank you so much for your letters. I want to come and see you very badly, but I don't think I am going to be in London at the moment.

We shall all be together again some day, but in the meantime don't worry about us, we will be all right.

Concerning this letter my father wrote to Diana who was in Holloway Jail – 'A long letter came from Nicky – wonderfully catty about his stay in Scotland with his relations.'

I have only one clear memory of visiting my father during his year-and-a-half in Brixton, though it is evident from my Aunt Irene's diaries that I visited him at least four times. I suppose the visit that has stuck in my mind is the first: they were probably all somewhat traumatic. I remember the prison visiting room like something in a railway station: Vivien and I were like displaced persons. When my father bounded in he was, as he always was, full of energy and ebullience and light. He wore something like a boiler suit and had grown a reddish beard. He carried the whole social occasion splendidly. What do children say to a father in jail?

After one of Vivien's and my visits, he wrote to Diana:

Viv and Nick came to see me on Monday – very much themselves, Nick had won the High Jump at Eton – isn't it extraordinary. Only other news of note is that Micky had fallen off a tree and broken his wrist. The luckless Nick seems doomed apparently to stay at Eton in perpetuity. However one can do no more, and I imagine his particular gift has already and finally been destroyed.

Before this – not long after my father had been imprisoned – things had come to a head in the dispute he had been having with the Courts about his children's money. He had been brought from jail to appear before the Chancery Court to be questioned about what arrangements should be made concerning the children's livelihood: the lease of Wootton had been given up and, at the same time as Diana's arrest in June 1940, Savehay Farm had been requisitioned by the Ministry of Supply (it became a centre of research into Chemical Warfare). In anger against what my father saw as the Judge's right to question his authority in any matters concerning his children – and after questions concerning the role played in all this by Aunt Irene Ravensdale – my father renounced all further responsibility for his three children by his first marriage. His account of this in a letter to Diana was –

> The children today were duly removed – the Judge took the line that I should remain guardian in name, but as it was clear that I should have no direction in their education or anything else, I declined responsibility without authority and Lady R was made guardian. I informed the Official Solicitor that this was finality as far as I was concerned. It was suggested that Micky should go with Abinger School to Canada where his cousins were also going: I stoutly opposed this on the grounds that it was disgraceful for well-to-do children to run away to Canada leaving nearly all the rest of the nation's children to whatever is coming. The Judge warmly agreed with this and decided in my favour. So that is something. I am afraid they will keep Nicky at Eton till he is 18 and try to make him as big an ass as most of that class: however I think he will survive it.

My Aunt Irene's version of this story was that since the children's money had anyway been for years under the jurisdiction of the Court, and since she recently and with my father's blessing had been responsible for a large part of the day-to-day planning for the children as well as for the financial loans which kept our old home going, the Court had suggested to her and my father that now he was in jail they might share some joint form of guardianship: they had both said, however, that they thought this would be unworkable. Then when my father was brought from prison to appear before the Court (this is still Irene's version),

> he inferred he never knew the judges had any control over his children. The judge was willing to waive all questions of guardianship

and cooperate with him on important issues but he flatly refused
and wanted entire control for the boys – he was not interested in
the girl. After discussion and deliberation the Judge could only ask
for outside guardianship as he had refused to have any assistance.
My name was put up. He [my father] sent me a lamentable message
saying that I must understand he would never later have anything
to do with the care or guardianship of any of his children, he was
through with them. God in his inimitable way has handed me Cim's
children.

When the Official Solicitor, Mr Gilchrist, came to Irene's house to
break the news to the two older children that their father was no longer
their guardian Irene recorded:

> Viv seemed very unmoved and unsurprised, and said Daddy had
> always disliked butting in on Gilchrist. Nick seemed a bit silent and
> sad, so I left him and Viv to talk and when I got back Viv reported
> Nick was not so upset as his father even at Xmas had said – Things
> may happen to me, and with those judges I will not work, I would
> rather resign.

When Irene told Nanny that she, Irene, was now the children's guardian,
Nanny said – with perhaps one of her startling shafts of wisdom if
not tact – 'The judges might have suggested some man to look after
Micky instead of all this petticoat government.' Irene commented, 'This
was not very helpful for me.'

At Eton I moved with as much detachment as I could up the rungs
of destined ladders: I became myself a member of the Library; eventually
Captain of my House. I never became a member of Pop – that self-
electing society dependent upon fashion. But I was now myself one
of the lugubrious, cumbersome boys who moved round small boys'
bedrooms after supper; sat in wicker chairs impassive and observant;
occasionally played chess. Once or twice after some offence it was
mandatory that as Captain of the House I should beat someone; I
wondered if, after all the talk, I might enjoy this. I found I did not.
I wrote cryptically to my sister – 'What would you do if you had
to beat two boys for throwing mud at a policeman? Split your sides – so
I am all right, as I balance out.' During my last year at Eton I used
to go up once a week to London to see a stammer specialist: he was
a new one but he practised the same techniques; I learned to swoop

and throb like a public speaker. I could still do this quite easily; but it still seemed to me afterwards that I would rather stammer. On my way back from Harley Street to Paddington Station I would sometimes call in on the pornographic bookshops which were at that time concentrated in Praed Street: I might thus fill up one or two gaps in the Library shelves. Or I would make a detour to the non-stop revue at the Windmill Theatre and join the rows of men ready to steeplechase over the backs of chairs when seats became vacant closer to the stage where girls stood from time to time absolutely motionless with no clothes on. I loved the girls: I thought the steeplechasing not quite part of the game.

There was only one local girl at Eton whom I remember anyone ever showing any interest in: she was called, literally, Nina Birch. She would ride past our house each day at the same time on her bicycle: we would all rush to our windows like American sailors are supposed to do in films about the Pacific. Once a boy was caught with her in a pub in Windsor and was duly expelled.

In 1941 older boys had to partake in Air Raid Precautions during term time and in Home Guard duties during the holidays. When incendiary bombs were dropped we had 'terrific sport' (I wrote to my sister) putting them out with stirrup pumps. When a large bomb dropped on one of the main school buildings I and others were having a tutorial next door: what was interesting was to see who dived, and how far, to get underneath furniture.

I described the atmosphere:

> The siren still goes continually: we pile down into the shelter and play endless games of Vingt-et-un at a *penny a counter* which as you know means you can lose ten bob in five minutes. I am terrified all the time, but so far have lost nothing greater than five bob.

The style of most of us at Eton was, of course, to be nonchalant about practical matters concerning the war: I approved of this: it was the sensible counterpart to the lack of speculation about what the war was actually for. It was taken for granted that all of us when we were eighteen were going to train to fight with a likelihood of being killed: this was just one of the 'privileges' (as the headmaster had seemed to suggest) that Etonians had to be 'worthy of'.

In the meantime this gave one a sense of freedom from constraint; but also the arrogance that I suppose is a characteristic of soldiers in wartime. I wrote to my sister –

The Home Guard fortnight was good stuff – two cinemas a day, all quite illegal; bicycling into Bray and Maidenhead to booze and rolling home at night; climbing in through bedroom windows, etc. Many a practical joke. Have you ever realised that you can loosen the springs of a bed so that it collapses when lain on? Good thing to know.

But then when during my last year at Eton I went up to Oxford to try for a history scholarship at Balliol for which I had done hardly any work, I wrote to my father:

The history scholarship was not a success, as I expected, but it was interesting to have tried. I spent 4 days in Oxford while I was doing the exam, and that short time was sufficient to convince me that I was right in choosing to stay on at Eton. The people, especially at Balliol, are ghastly; stiff with Jews. I never saw one person who could have been considered respectable. The atmosphere was rather like that of a girl's school. So I came away with a profound horror of Oxford. I don't think I shall be able to face going back there after the war.

My letters of this time sometimes make painful reading. I have tried in this book to quote what seems representative of other people; I shall try to quote what seems to have been representative, even if unpleasantly, of myself. I suppose at this time I was trying to make myself acceptable to my father. With him in jail, I must have thought one of the ways to do this was to show contempt for the outside world.

Sixth-formers at Eton had to partake of a ritual each 'half' in which they stood on a platform in front of an assembly of boys and parents and declaimed a piece of poetry or prose of their choice. I had the chance of getting out of this because of my stammer: but I wanted to do it: – was not the piece I wished to choose to do with heroics? It was a chorus from Swinburne's *Atalanta in Calydon* which had been one of my father's favourite pieces; he used to recite it to us as children. But how would I fare as I climbed up on to my platform? For a time nothing came out. But then fluently, as if with flags and banners –

> Before the beginning of years
> There came to the making of man
> Time with a gift of tears
> Grief with a glass that ran

Pleasure with pain for leaven
Summer with flowers that fell
Remembrance fallen from heaven
And madness risen from hell

And so on. I think stammering is something to do with one's realisation that what is likely to come out, for all its lovely cadences (perhaps because of them?) has little after all to do with what is going on in one's head. This knowledge is like that of someone standing at the top of the Tower of Babel and being struck by the thought – what must things have been like before?

On my last day at Eton I walked round the playing fields where I and my friends had been happy: there were the hedgerows where we had reclined and talked: the cricket pavilion with its sloping roof against which we played a game of our own invention like real tennis. I felt that Eton had been good to me because it had taught me to be both part of and yet not part of its odd, self-confident world: some such balancing act seemed to be necessary if life was not to become too savage or too blind. But as I walked round the playing fields I swore that I would never send any of my own children to Eton: I would hope for somewhere more steady than the tightrope between rebelliousness and charm. Eton had been good to me because it had oiled wheels with regard to my father; but perhaps the same oil might be making smooth the slope down which indeed we seemed to be sliding to perdition. I had written to my sister about my last year at Eton – 'Vice, sordidity and sloth have come into their proper place at the head of things': this was a joke, of course, but then – what was not a joke? What had happened, what would happen, to the things that my friends and I had tried to talk about as we hid away in our by-ways and hedgerows – God, truth, love?

One of the last essays I wrote at Eton was on the subject of *Words Words Words*. A stammerer is someone who is cryptic perhaps in some effort to get back to that state before the confusion of languages.

Perhaps the world would be a happier place today if God had gone further when he decided to destroy the Tower of Babel. By making men of the world speak different languages, he was only putting a temporary obstacle in their way. But even if he had destroyed their power of speech, they would soon have learned to make their pompous speeches and spread their scandals in another way.

CHAPTER 20

Love Letters

It had seemed to both Diana and my father that they would be let out of prison once the immediate invasion scare was over; there might have had to be some temporary concessions to public panic, but now that their premises had been searched and nothing incriminating had been found – what on earth would be the point of keeping them in? Diana wrote later, 'I imagined there would be a rule against free speech for the rest of the war.' As months went on in fact a great many of the 700 British Union members detained under Regulation 18B were released on the advice of the Advisory Committee; but there was always the Security Executive to have the last word about those whom they did not want to let out.

When my father was locked up in Brixton he was at first put into a cell with a black man; he wrote later – 'some whimsical jackass in office probably thought this would annoy me, but on the contrary, I found him a charming and cultured man: I understand that he was alleged to have played in the Berlin Philharmonic Orchestra before the war, and was arrested on account of the peculiarity of that occupation at that time for a coloured man'.

The detainees were locked in their cells from 4 pm to 7 am; at first they were let out for exercise for only two one-hour periods each day to walk in pairs round the yard. One of the chief afflictions was that of bed-bugs. An ex-BUF inmate wrote:

We used to have bug-hunts every night. They would lodge in the cracks in the bed-boards and tables. Night after night one could hear hammering from cells all over the hall. This was caused by the bed-boards being knocked against the floor to dislodge the inhabitants, which could then be dealt with.

This inmate had a memory of my father:

> I went into O.M.'s cell one morning just after he had finished wash-
> ing. I happened to catch sight of his arms as he was in the act of
> rolling up his sleeves. His arms were covered in bites, by far the
> worst I had seen. I asked him if he had made any complaint about
> it. Not he! He would have let himself be eaten alive before complain-
> ing. 'If the boys can take it so can I' was his answer.

Diana wrote later of the time she was locked up in Holloway —*

> The cells were six feet by nine; each contained a hard bed, a hard
> chair, and a small heavy table. Under the bed was a chipped enamel
> chamber pot with a lid upon which in dark blue was a crown and
> the royal cipher. There was a battered jug and basin and a small
> three-cornered shelf. The sheets were made of canvas, painful if it
> touched one's chin.

> The cold weather came and the prison was icier than ever. A wardress
> appeared with a convict carrying a pile of blankets. I went to get
> one. Never have I seen a more disgusting sight than these old hard
> blankets; every variety of human filth had left its unmistakable marks
> upon them.

> One night a bomb fell near the prison. It broke the water mains.
> In the dark early morning there was the sound of lavatory plugs
> being pulled in vain. The lavatories, always foul, became frightful
> – floors awash with urine, everything choked, an appalling smell.
> We were all grey with grime because the bomb had shaken the
> old prison and a thick layer of dust and soot covered everything.
> We were given half a pint of water each. I drank a sip and tried
> to wash in the remainder.

Diana spent much of the time reading. The wardress told her that most
of the women chose books with red covers from the tray that came
round because they could then lick their fingers and get a bit of red
dye to put on their lips.

My father said that it suited him when the prisoners were locked
up for 'twenty one hours out of twenty four'; he too could get on

* *A Life of Contrasts.*

with reading. But it was misery to other prisoners, especially to the Italians who had been indiscriminately thrown in jail. So my father headed a deputation of protest to the governor, and after this cell doors were kept unlocked during the day. But then, my father wrote – 'the echoing sea-shell of the building resounded to the music of ping-pong and Latin laughter: the subsequent discomfort of being in locked cells when bombs were falling was nothing to it'. He told a story of how a group of warders used to congregate in a cell directly underneath his when bombs were falling, on the grounds that they thought Hitler could pin-point his bombs with great accuracy and he would be sure to spare my father.

Diana found she could not eat the prison food except 'the delicious bully beef' and the prison bread; she lived on these and Stilton cheese which was ordered and sent in for her by my father. Parcels of food were allowed; but it was expected they would be shared amongst fellow prisoners. Half a bottle of wine was permitted; Diana ordered port: 'a glass of grocer's port and a bit of Stilton cheese helped me through many a sad evening'.

The *Daily Mirror* and the *Sunday Pictorial* ran stories about how she and my father were enjoying luxury in prison (my father had in fact given up alcohol) –

Every morning his paid batman delivers three newspapers at the door of his master's cell. Breakfast, dinner and tea arrive by car. After his mid-day meal Mosley fortifies himself with alternative bottles of red and white wine daily. He occasionally asks for a bottle of champagne. He still takes great pride in his appearance. He selects a different smartly cut lounge suit every week. His shirts and silk underwear are laundered in Mayfair....

My father and Diana brought a libel action against the *Mirror* and *Pictorial*: they were awarded damages with costs. The papers admitted they had invented these stories. Diana used her share of the damages to buy a 'huge fur coat' in which she said she looked like 'Fafner and Fasolt rolled into one'.

I wrote to my father from Eton: 'We thought the stories of you playing bridge the whole time were very funny: you know how you used to grunt when anyone played at Denham. Also the champagne.'

They were each allowed one visit a week: my father saw his mother and sometimes his ex-sister-in-law Baba. He told his mother that he would not ask to see his children, they could ask to see him if they

wished. Diana was visited by her mother who brought her two older
children up from the country – 'I shall never forget their dear anxious
faces as they stared at me, and the relief when they saw I had not
much changed and that I laughed as usual' – also her babies Alexander
and Max. 'Alexander looked beautiful beyond words with huge dark
eyes. Max was completely changed from the little baby I had left, he
sat up and gazed about him with a solemn expression.'

My father and Diana were at first allowed to receive only two letters
a week; they each wrote once a week to the other. Then, when these
regulations were relaxed, they each wrote to the other twice a week.
My father's letters to Diana have survived. They are written on the
small four-page lined prison writing paper and are like the letters that
men write from the front in war. They bear the marks of the censors
at both Brixton and Holloway. He had been told not to write about
anything political. In prison, his life in ruins, separated from Diana
whom he loved, there was still an ebullience such as there usually was
about my father. But now – how gentle he was, when he could not
be concerned with anything about politics!

Extracts from these letters can show, better than anything else can,
the side of my father that was caring and enduring. The first letter
was written on the day after Diana's arrest.

July 1st 1940
My Beloved Darling,
I have just seen the news, and you know what I feel about it. I
write this quickly to say that I am worried about the milk condition
and that something must be done at once. If you are at all ill you
are to telegraph for Dr Gilliatt – in any case you are to see him
as soon as possible. If it is better for you to have the baby in do
get him in at once – I will not have any chances taken with you
in a delicate condition. All my fondest love my darling.
Telegraph Gilliatt. X K.

July 8th
The Official Solicitor had the impudence to write and enquire in
what manner I would like to pay the school fees of the two boys
he had just removed – the answer was a raspberry the results of
which I have not yet heard ... Nearly a year since the Earl's Court
meeting – Do you remember it? What a lot has happened since
... Darling Percher, I do miss you so – you are such a brave and
wonderful Percher – I do hope you are not too depressed. Above all do

not worry – take things as easily as you possibly can and do not notice the unpleasant. Make the latest affectation – Gaol's the place! We live in a great and changeful age. The present hysteria must pass quite quickly, and we might soon be together again. Poor Percher will have a job not to see the moon through glass!

July 12th
What a gay life the girls have with a gas cooker – you are lucky! – when I talk about cooking here they all 'simply shriek' and obviously do not believe I can really do it. Is £2 a week arriving for you from Barclay's Bank? ... She must keep herself fit. I do P.T. twice a day morning and evening in my cell and it makes a very great difference. Start by touching the toes a lot – a very good chop exercise ... I am re-reading Anatole France's Penguin Island....

July 25th
Am now resuming my language studies after an interval of five weeks – Wie war das Percheron? Is it correct that all virgins are neuter? Isn't it? Silly Mr Kit!

July 27th
I have started growing a beard. It is to be the Old Brixtonian tie. And guess what colour it is – red!! At least quite a lot of it – silver threads among the gold ... Darling one, I must stop now, it is this incessant social round, quite like you before the shadow fell.

August 18th
Here I am outside, still reflecting with bewilderment that eating is the difficulty with this beard business; it is even more liable than eyebrows to get blown into the soup. What a difference sun does make in this place – it makes me almost feel as if we were again on the magic road just beyond Lyons – we must do that as soon as ever we can when all this is over ...

August 28th
My Darling Beloved,
I hope you are not kept awake all night nowadays by having to go to a cell lower down; but at the same time I would rather you went down than stayed upstairs. Personally I sleep blissfully through them all [the bombs] – retiring to bed soon after the first sirens usually around 9 p.m. and not waking up till next morning. Today seems to have been the liveliest so far ...

December 8th
The noise about prison is certainly much the worst thing ... My
precious one I do so long to be with you and hope so much it may
soon be arranged – it would be such a joy to me, and I think she
would 'do' better. She must not have bad dreams – that one was
due to your feeling you were wasting your youth in prison, probably
coupled with old memories of the motor smash: but she must always
say to herself it is not for long.

December 16th
Always remember that nothing great is ever done without the most
agonising experiences: it is sad, but it always seems to be one of
the invariable rules of this world. I know no single case without
it. Our capacity to endure is the passport without which all our
other qualities take us nowhere: courage, constancy, character. In
the last is comprised the power to endure. I am immersed in *Wahlverwandtschaften* – to spend this time in the company of Goethe is in
a sense 'such a tease' on everything as a Percher would say. But
I do so miss my Darlingest one, and long again to be with her
so.

December 19th
I have read 100 pages of the Goethe and much of it does remind
me all so much of Wootton – I like reading it so much that I cannot
bear to stop and look up words – does the title mean 'by choice'
or 'alternative relationships'? *Wahl* can mean either ... It is a curious
reflection of his genius that, if I did not know the age at which
both books were written, I should say *Werther* was the more mature
book of the two: he certainly fulfils the definition – outside time,
outside class – the Eternal Contemporary. He could never have had
any 'age' – although he is supposed to sense this when Faust goes
blind: 'Thou shalt know care at last!'

December 27th
It was a sad Christmas without my darling one – I thought so much
of her last year in lovely Wootton looking so beautiful when she
was doing the tree ... I feel in a grey mood, but I truly do not
believe our present circumstances will last much longer and my mind
is full of so many things for the future.... Have sent you a copy
of *Zarathustra*: the 3 metamorphoses are at the very beginning; and
the Night Song, even translated, is one of the loveliest things in
all literature.

January 3rd 1941
I am glad A.F. has written to that man: [A.F. stood for Arabia Felix which was my father's and Diana's name for her mother Lady Redesdale: 'that man' was probably Walter Monckton]; he is a good man, and could help a lot to get us together if he tried. With so few couples left [many of the original 700 BUF detainees had by now been released] it is perfectly easy for them to arrange if they liked – and I think it could be done if enough pressed for it in the H of C ... I have been lazy and have hardly read at all for a day or two – reflecting much on the coming year and the future – how interesting everything is! This time certainly gives an opportunity to think things out. That precious one must not go and alter herself too much and lose her pretty ways and paces – he would hate that – he would like just his same darling Percher – not all hogged and pulled to look quite different.

January 9th
I shall see Vivien on Monday and will tell her myself ... control of them [the children] now is absolutely nothing to do with me – I am not even nominally their guardian – I think, in the circumstances, it is a good thing for that to be made quite clear to everyone. As you know I would not be associated in any way with the handling of Vivien before the war and I could not more disapprove of the way they are now being handled – Nick was left at that idiot school by order of the court against my express wishes. I feel very strongly about the whole thing. Miss Ottolie [a character in Goethe's novel *Die Wahlverwandtschaften*] in poignant contrast, goes from strength to strength, her tagebuch yielding a rich store of accumulated wisdom. Some of his remarks have an amazingly modern application: I have just got to the part where the English Lord decides to cheer the party up with the result that everyone is in tears ...

January 17th
The children came and were very much themselves. Nick was pro beard and Viv said it was not nearly so bad as she had expected – ecstatic for her! It is twice the beard since you saw it ... Nick has been studying German at Eton for exactly the same time as I have been studying it at Brixton – but a brief examination revealed that he knew little or nothing of it. So I am telling Miss M to send him my books with the remark that I regret to observe that six months study of a subject in Brixton Prison yields such much greater result than a study of the same subject over a corresponding period at

Eton College. . . . I hear Schiller always entirely re-writes history, and never permitted Mary Queen of Scots to be beheaded – I always feel, too, that so many things could have been much better arranged . . . This has been a long and dreary time and such a waste of life. But I feel now things are beginning to move a bit and much of the long and dreary time may be behind us.

January 30th
Wonderful news appears in answer to a parliamentary question that we are to see each other once a fortnight . . . In the same answer it was said that it had not been found possible to put us in the same establishment; but again, a good many other enquiries are likely to be made about why it is possible to clear out a whole village to make room for the purpose of having alien husbands and wives to-gether in the Isle of Man but not possible to put us together in one house in England which is all that is necessary and is offered free – the disparity in treatment is becoming grotesque.

February 8th
Bores are the affliction – we have a few – I fear I have been rather rough with them. My latest device is to put a notice 'Busy' on my door: try it, and say I do it: then I don't think it could offend any of our friends. When the notice is down anyone can come in – it is really the only way to have any peace for thought or reading. I find the poetic form of Schiller a little difficult . . .

February 10th
My Darlingest Beloved,
I am writing this on getting back to Brixton [he had been driven to Holloway briefly] to say how wonderful it was to see my most precious one in all the world today and what a relief it was to find her the same darlingest one – if possible more beautiful and sweet than ever – but it made me long more than ever to be with you. The time was so short and I had so much that I wanted to say and especially how much I love you . . . I think so much of Wootton and all her loveliness and sweetness there – we will do beautiful things again.

February 24th
I have started on Egmont and find it much easier than Schiller; though the latter I was reading quite easily towards the end. I gather from the notes in this volume that the conversation of the locals with which they always appear to prelude their plays consists largely of

obsolete slang – so no wonder I find it rather heavy going. But I also always found the corresponding parts of Shakespeare a trifle tedious. But directly they introduce the great characters they are superb. So far I prefer Goethe on the whole to Schiller ... Now it is only four days before I see my own Beloved Sonnenpferd again; I just live now from fortnight to fortnight ...

March 8th
It is such good news that Weedoms [Max aged 11 months] is coming up next week, I will leave a V O [Visiting Order] for Pam [his sister-in-law Mrs Derek Jackson] as I did when Stodge [Alexander aged 2 years] came. I am so excited to see him and do hope he will be wearing his well-brought-up face as in the photograph. From his demeanour there I feel I should at once discuss with him the word-meanings of Goethe and Schiller, but expect it will turn out a little different ... By the way, why have *I* got a well-brought-up face? Because I am listening to Chamber Music!! There is a man here who is a distinguished musician – English or rather Welsh – and he plays for me in the chapel – a new treat. Have you ever heard our Elizabethan music? I never had – it is terrific – explains them – gay and heroic.

March 9th
I have just finished the last of the wonderful food you have done for me – the salad dressing was a poem – she is the cleverest of Perchers and a reine de Gastronome! It really was so good and I was enthused by the sauce – how does she do it with scanty material ... I have also been reading Nietzsche's Zarathustra: the great passage which I love so much – anyone if interested can find it on page 35 of the Zarathustra in my cell. It describes the 'child' in the third of the metamorphoses which you have often heard me discuss: you remember – Camel, Lion, Child. It is good enough in English but in the original is colossal and really untranslatable without losing much: for instance how can one do justice in English to the tremendous 'bedarf es eines heiligen Ja-sagens'? 'We require a Holy Yes' isn't quite the same thing!

March 16th
Have not yet been all through Zarathustra in the original, but I think it is in this book that occur the great lines I like so much on the relationship of cynicism and idealism that you mentioned in your last letter – 'Man is the rope over the abyss that divides

the animal from the superman.' He is referring to the incompleteness
of contemporary humanity that must 'go beyond' itself. And, again,
one of his greatest and most misunderstood lines – 'I love the great
Despisers, for their souls are the arrows that are yearning for the
farther shore.' He means that if man is really an idealist he cannot
be content with 'contemporary' humanity; this must 'surpass' itself...
It is indeed difficult to believe in the 'essential goodness' of contemporary mankind; but it is not too difficult to believe in the Purpose
which works through present humanity to the attainment of something higher. Without the Purpose it is all just nonsense – merely
silly – an accident – too complex to be easily believed an accident
– a confusion made up of a myriad of seemingly related chances.
With the Purpose it has sense only if it works through the present
to something beyond. The complete realist, therefore, will combine
complete cynicism toward contemporary humanity with complete
idealism towards posterity. But to be the entire idealist would be
a little tedious – so it is possible to embrace a compassion for con-
temporaries with a thorough understanding of our undeveloped
state ... Too often in recent philosophy you see the idealist turned
cynic – he begins by swallowing the goodness of everything and
ends by vomiting the badness of everything ... in fact typically un-
balanced and hysterical and lacking in all historical and biological
perspective. The child is father to the man – but not yet the man – so
watch out while it is near to the fire, while you work for its future.

March 24th
How I hope to be on the long road to Arles with stops at Pyramides
[a restaurant at Vienne] and Avignon – what beautiful times we
have had and how I long for them with you again. How quickly
we could recover from all this with such a little sun and life. I would
like to sit with you on that fallen log among the bluebells till we
felt better – my memories of you at Wootton are so beautiful and
my hopes for the future with you – how the wheel swings! This
is not an age built for happiness – it is too great. But we have had
some. We have not suffered entirely from the Siegmund compulsion
– 'to whom the gods gave but one gift – the art of loving without
happiness'. We have known a little of Siegfried and the hours where
ends the 'aus sich rollendes Rad' [self-rolling wheel] of which element
we too have a little ...

April 4th
I have sent many quotations because I felt in too savage a temper

really to write – no particular reason at all – just internal combustion. But whatever my mood or humour I always love that Darlingest Percher just the same ...

April 18th
I cannot tell you how precious Stodge [Alexander] was. He sat on my knee as good as gold the whole time and talked – in a proud Oxfordshire accent I thought. When he first came in he stroked my beard and said 'Funny Man'. Finally when they had reached the main gate and I was a long way off I waved to him and he broke loose from trainer and ran all the way over to me – so I was very proud! ... She is such a Beloved one to have given me two such precious sons.... I expect you know that Egmont was really married and had 11 children – Goethe kept it dark for romantic reasons – I take rather hard the view that a man becomes less romantic because he has a lot of children.

April 21st
Am mad about Stravinsky – shrieks or not? – it is my latest affectation ... I thought always he was just a Ballet Boy tho' a very good one – but of course he is much more – has the future within him. He seems to me strangely related to Wagner; this comment I made with trepidation – but was assured it was perspicacious – so was fortified in my well-brought-up face ...

April 27th
My phlebitis so far does not appear to have spread – I expect it is bound to appear in other places as it always does once it starts – but that is nothing to worry about as I can always get the specialist to bind it up as before if it goes much higher up the leg. After all I am an old boy at that business, and know it is all right if it is carefully handled.

May 17th
For me it is a year in prison next week and for you so very soon after. We were trying to think of any examples in which what are called civilized countries had kept political prisoners in gaol for a year under an order of this kind and we could think of none. Plenty of examples of course of keeping political prisoners in other places but not in prison. Furthermore the keeping the woman in prison for such a period finds no precedent or parallel anywhere.... Rather a good aphorism in relation to the present world someone has sent in to a competition in 'Cissy's Weekly' [*The New Statesman and*

Nation] – 'Progress is a convenient term for describing our journey from the golden ages' ...

May 19th

You too might study the subject on which I am thinking of embarking – the study of all societies which have attained or striven to attain strength and beauty in union with – or even through – simplicity of life: eg Sparta, the whole great Hellenic Epic, the Christian attempts – Knightly and Monastic Templars etc – mostly flops in the end, being set up in opposition to instead of in unison with women; the latter necessity being understood by the Samurai who probably created the most enduring and influential aristocracy in the world. As you know, these ideas have always fascinated me.

June 2nd

Curious that in this strange place I am still always short of time – the sole occupation of course is in the mind – that is why, no doubt, some inmates can find nothing at all to do ... The things to which you object in current art are plutocratic values and the demand they create: whatever the character of the labour it merely supplies the demand – to some extent this is true even of genius in art. Have first in all things the transformation of values. When the market is the 'appreciative' artist – whether it be Lorenzo de Medici or a modern world of different values – instead of a successful speculation, the 'creative' artist has his opportunity.

June 30th

I have had a letter from Nick; he is going in for a Balliol history scholarship but does not think he will get it. His letters have suddenly become strangely adult – rather affected. He has evidently benefited from his last visits to the 'great school' – not Eton of course: the real one! [a reference to a visit to Brixton]

July 6th

Lately I have been reading so little that it is really terrible. Sometimes I feel that reading is only useful to start up one's own mind – it is like putting a little petrol in the carburettor of an engine – one just reads a few pages and then starts thinking – it is really the answer to the question one asks so often – what did that book give me for the trouble of reading it? Such however is never true of the immortals – Faust, and Plato. How beautiful is the answer of Achilles when told by the gods that if he avenges Patroclus he too must die – the words of the eternal hero. They were the most exquisite people, those Hellenes ... I was thinking the other day of how modest I am in comparison with most in this establishment in that their idea is always to collect a small circle of others whom they can instruct, while my one idea in conversation with anyone is not to tell him anything but to ask him questions in order to acquire from him any knowledge he possesses – if, by any strange chance, that amounts to anything at all. Flattering myself therefore on this relative simplicity and humility of spirit, I suddenly realised it was really exactly the opposite – for the habit of interrogating rather than informing really arises from my almost sub-conscious feeling that a new fact reposed in my head is so much more important – as it becomes so much more useful – than any new fact lodged in his!

July 17th

The other day I heard the second American joke in my life that made me laugh: 'Do you know where bugs go in winter time?' 'Search me.' The other I think you know – 'How are you feeling this morning?' 'Not quite myself.' 'Congratulations.' Simple, aren't they?

August 4th

I suspected that Nick was reaching a precious stage but did not know it had developed so far as a book by Gerald [Lord Berners' novel *The Girls of Radcliffe Hall*]: he has come on so much that I would quite like you to see him – quite grown up – 6ft 3″ – he is in their top division now with 20 oppidans and 20 scholars. They asked a lot about you and sent love.

August 25th

My Darlingest Beloved,

Oh the Foals! [Alexander and Max] – they are such heaven. They arrived in state escorted by kind Tom [Diana's brother] and the proudest of trainers – they could not be more fascinating and made me long more than ever to be with you and them. Stodge [Alexander] was enchanting and asked repeatedly to be thrown up in the air which was greeted with delighted shrieks – not so the Entschlossener [Max: 'the determined one'] who shouted Go away! when approached and reared back fiercely striking out with both forefeet. However, great was the triumph when the clever finger of the experienced stud-groom melted him to the most charming plump chuckles by the simple expedient of tickling him in the ribs ...

August 28th

She is so clever with her cooking now – what fun we could have

with it if we were together – you doing it and me admiring – so
lovely to do all those things in a leisurely way when there would
be no time pressure. I have lost the latter sense now – it stayed with
me for some months after I had got here – it was such a busy time
before – always with too much to do and too little time. I think
that sense is the greatest disadvantage of the kind of life I used to
lead – it takes away too much from life. The dullness of most people's
lives which you mention is of course entirely due to themselves:
as I always used to say to my revered relation – He suffered under
a terrible life sentence – his own company.

September 25th
On Saturday B [Baba] came with Nick ... no real news yet of the
matter in hand but I am hopeful [Baba was putting pressure on her
political friends to try to get my father and Diana imprisoned to-
gether]. More than anything in the black existence I long to be with
my Darlingest which would turn everything into gold ...

September 26th
That awful Mr Fowler [author of *Modern English Usage*] in a dis-
quisition on the use of French words in English sentences said it
was intolerably affected for English people to use such expressions
as 'A merveille'. The beast! ... I remember reading Quintillian when
very young and coming to the conclusion that it was obviously impossible ever to make a speech: years later I read him again and
realised that every night I was using the methods which he described
so tediously and with such unnecessary complication: which proves
again the truth of my ancient adage – 'Tell me where is knowledge
bred, Twixt the chops or in the head?' Emphatically the former,
as my Percher has always maintained with her usual insight. My
darlingest one has a great natural gift for style and should develop
it in all languages. I am indescribably sloppy and bad except when
performing; but that is always so with me – the engines are either
switched on or off. I flatter myself that they are too big to warm
up except for an ocean voyage – really of course it is just lazy –
but perhaps on the way energy is conserved.

October 25th
I can see no harm in Tom [Diana's brother] writing a letter on the
following lines which were the same as those given to Baba –
'Whether it is the final decision of the government that they should
be imprisoned separately, if it is determined to keep them in prison

at all. They have now been in separate prisons for nearly 18 months despite repeated requests that they be imprisoned together. There are several prisons outside London which are used for both men and women and could in part be used for this purpose by a slight rearrangement of prisoners. I will not raise the question of the justice of the detention nor the conditions of their imprisonments as, apart from recording their strong protest, they have throughout refused to make any personal appeal for consideration. But the decision to treat some 25 married couples of British nationality so very differently from alien internees who are detained together, appears so remarkable a principle that it may be legitimate for me to enquire whether this is the deliberate and final decision of the government.'

November 7th
My Darlingest Beloved
No Monday letter again today ... It annoys me so much because they are the only things I look forward to in this hole ... If again it has gone to Liverpool I shall put in a formal complaint. Today is cold but I have been playing my heavy ball game and feel warmer – most of the best players have gone, and I am trying to teach it to new boys. If we are together I will hardly ever play my silly games and not be so ernst over languages but just concentrate on that Darling Percheron ... Do tell if the tone of the gram is all right, and please do change it if not; because what is a gram without *tone* – in fact what is life without *tone* – what is it without a Percheron – all grey and dull and sad.

December 7th
I have really no news at all – so sorry to hear of Decca's sorrow [Diana's sister Jessica's husband Esmond Romilly had been killed in the RAF] – this age is very sad – there is nothing one can say. We heard more from another expert about the world destruction of the soil – soil erosion – I have studied it lately – it is appalling – I feel all those things so much nowadays – more even than in the past. The old tree throwing out roots, and becoming dull – but still beautiful! Today, Monday [December 8th] I have had a communication which, it said, was also to go to you – made me very happy! I am saying nothing about it to anyone else at present – the rest when I see you. Would not do *too* much about *meubles* at first, because I know what Perchers are when they start galloping. The air anyhow will be pink and blue and gold!

There is just one letter from Diana amongst all the ones from my father. This says:

17th December 1941 Letter 145
My Precious Darling, I got your sweet letter and now I am writing to you for the LAST TIME – imagine it, next time I would have written I shall have the exquisite joy of your beloved self near me with all that means in happiness and bliss ... Today Muv came and the two boys [Jonathan and Desmond] straight from school. They were very sweet and excited but a little bit sad to go off to yet another Christmas without me. I do hope it will be the last. I felt very selfish because my Xmas will be so happy especially compared with last. Muv looked sad I am afraid but was delighted of course we are to be together at long last ... These last days seem more like weeks to me. There is no need for you to bring anything but your eider-down and the little brown Marmite (which is my favourite cooking pot) because I have everything for you even a hot water bottle. I am so longing for you that I walk about in a dream and am not good company at the many farewell parties I spend my time going to. Goodbye my precious beloved for a little while. I will make it rush over – the time that remains to separate us. Come quickly because I love you so much more than all the world. From your very own Percher. X

In early December Diana's brother Tom had been to visit my father in Brixton and then he had gone to Diana in Holloway: he was in the army, on leave, before being sent to the Middle East. He had told Diana that he was having dinner that night in Downing Street with their cousin-by-marriage Winston Churchill; that he would try again to bring the subject up about my father and Diana being imprisoned together. Other friends including Walter Monckton and above all Baba had been working for months to achieve this. That night Tom Mitford managed to get Churchill into a corner: this, in addition to the pressure built up by Baba, resulted in what had previously been called 'an administrative impossibility' being put into effect almost immediately. My father was transferred to Holloway Prison where he and Diana had two rooms in what was called The Preventive Detention Block. My father could now make jokes about being the patriarch of a women's prison: Diana could write that when he arrived their joy was such that 'one of the happiest days of my life was spent in Holloway Prison!'

CHAPTER 21

One Kind of War

The focus of the last third of this book has necessarily to emanate from a somewhat different direction: my father is locked up: he is out of politics for seven years. He was in Brixton Prison from May 1940 to December 1941; he was with Diana in Holloway till November 1943; he was then under house arrest until the end of the war in Europe in May 1945. Then for two and a half years he lived the life of a gentleman farmer in Wiltshire, and wrote two books. He was drawn back into politics at the end of 1947. From then on his life was some repetition of the 1930s, but (or so it seems to me) on a circuit of the spiral that was only like an echo.

He himself saw the seven years of political inactivity at the very centre of his life – from the age of forty-three to fifty – as providing him with an opportunity for reflection and reappraisal. He was grateful for the chance to learn. He wrote in his autobiography: 'Plato's requirement of withdrawal from life for a considerable period of study and reflection before entering on the final phase of action was fulfilled in my case, though not by my own volition.'

During the 1930s he had not only created his own political movement but had demonstrated his peculiar conception of what a political movement might be: he had formed a fascist movement dedicated to peace, a revolutionary movement whose members were instructed at all times to obey the law. This meant that in practical politics he had often seemed to get the worst of both worlds; he was reviled by those who feared a fascist revolution; he was treated with no great seriousness by those fascists who saw revolution in terms of the manipulation of violence. But none of this sort of criticism seemed to him to be of much importance. What mattered to him was not so much that a political movement should succeed as that any success should be on his own

terms, and these included at least the intention of orderliness and
rationality. If, in the hard light of what human beings were actually
like, this attempt failed, then he did not seem to mind too much if
the rest of his activity failed. His business was to promulgate his ideas –
and then people could either follow him or try to destroy him as they
liked.

There is a sense in which – for all the hardship and frustration which
eventually made him ill – he did not feel imprisonment as a disaster:
he had done his best to prevent a European war – to argue rationally
against what he saw as the real disaster. If other people chose to defeat
him, at least, there was beginning to be the evidence of the appalling
cost of any victory. His imprisonment would be evidence of how
strongly he had fought in the cause of peace.

The first world war had been a decisive experience for my father: he
had come to see his subsequent political movement as an army that
would march to prevent further wars. In this the direction of his aim
had been the opposite of Hitler's (how much simpler to follow was
Hitler's!) but how did my father come to hold such paradoxical
ideas?

A largely unknown part of my father's life is that to do with
his experiences in the first world war: it is upon this that light
would presumably have been shed by his mother's diaries – which
he himself in later life went to such lengths to destroy. During the
first world war it seems there must have formed in him the patterns
of mind that later tried to impose themselves on politics: in his autobiography he gives the impression that he emerged on the social and
political scene after the war almost as if he had discovered he were
a changeling: he felt free from conventions of his past: a controlling
pattern was simply his horror of war. And yet he wished to continue
to act in the manner of a soldier.

My father, as with most of his generation, had been starry-eyed in
1914: he had been anxious to get into the fighting before it might
be over. He had left the Cavalry when it seemed that there was no
prospect of its being used and had joined the Royal Flying Corps as
an observer: he had been flying over the enemy lines in flimsy machines
at a time where there was a high likelihood of their being shot down
by machine guns. He had trained for his pilot's licence, but then during
training he had crashed. As a result of injuries sustained in the crash,
and after a winter with his regiment acting as infantry in the trenches
defending Ypres, he had been invalided out of active service in March
1916. It was perhaps his initial enthusiasm for war that made his sub-

sequent horror of it so profound: he was also perhaps influenced by the fact that the considerable courage he had originally shown and had hoped to continue to show had been thwarted by injuries sustained as a result of misfortune or misjudgment. From his own descriptions of war he seems to have played peculiarly passive roles: he does not seem to have found himself involved in circumstances calling for the sort of responsibility and dash – even the jokes – that in later life he saw as being characteristic of soldiers and which he said he so much admired.

It so happens that just at the time when my father was forcibly removed from the political arena as a result of his efforts to stop war – and was given a chance to reflect upon both his own failure and what he saw as other people's ruinous stupidity – at just this time I, his eldest son, was preparing to go off to war: I joined the army a few months after my father and Diana were reunited in Holloway. My attitude was almost the opposite of what my father's had been in 1914: I was, after all, the child of what he had learned and what he had become. In 1942 I saw the war as something of an absurdity; but nevertheless I accepted it was something that had to be undergone; there did not seem to me, as there did not seem to my father, any contradiction in the idea that one could properly both fight for one's country and yet be outraged that there was not peace. In some sense in 1942 I was behaving with regard to the war as my father said he would have behaved if he had not been imprisoned. Such paradoxical attitudes did indeed, for myself too, result in some hostility to conventional passions: it was perhaps the defence of myself against the inroads of these that resulted in my sometimes unpleasant intellectual arrogance.

The years when my father was in prison and I was going and had gone off to war were the years of my closest relationship with him. He looked from a distance on, and wrote his instructive letters to, someone who might have been, who might be, something like himself. To me, and in my correspondence with him, he seemed the person from whom I could learn. In writing about myself in war I have felt I might in some sense still be giving information about my father: there were multiple reflections here: for both of us there was the question of what we had learned and might still learn.

I have tried to write of myself, as I have said, in something of the same style in which I have written of other people: this is not easy: admissions about oneself are apt to move, if not towards self-defence, towards self-flagellation. But one of the points of these books – biography or autobiography – has been the attempt to create an attitude by which the darkness in people (there is always darkness) might be made to seem not so much evil as somewhat ridiculous: evil may thus be exorcised: ridiculousness becomes life-giving.

This sort of attitude, I think, was representative of some characteristic of my father's: he could go roaring off; but then he could sometimes laugh at himself. At the end of his life he could even be kindly about what previously he would have railed against in others. Of course he continued to let himself be surrounded by people who could not.

In 1942 what I had in common with my father was this contempt for people who so senselessly and trivially seemed to glory in war: who seemed so complacent about the holocaust they were accepting if not causing. This contempt was I suppose one of the things that my father had learned from war: this is what I, his son, felt even before I went into it.

From then on, it seems to me, the way one goes is partly luck; partly a matter of everything one has ever learned from oneself and from those close to one.

Both in war, and in the battles one has with what one is and what one becomes, the questions are – how does one survive? but also and perhaps more practically – what are the parts of one that one comes to feel are worthy of survival?

It was taken for granted, as I have said, that from Eton one went as reasonably quickly as one could into some front line in war; this was one of the duties, or privileges, of being an Etonian. One usually joined the army: there was likely to be some family reason for joining the navy, and the air force was definitely *outré*. In the army one went into either the Guards or a Cavalry regiment; or – if one wished to be slightly dashing but still well within the pale – one joined the Rifle Brigade or the King's Royal Rifle Corps. These regiments had the reputation of being more intellectual and even artistic than the more solidly snobbish Guards. For this sort of reason – and because I think my Aunt Irene was on good terms with one of the senior colonels – I decided to let myself be put forward as a potential officer in the Rifle Brigade.

There were questions, of course, about whether or not I would be accepted. There was my stammer: there was the more ominous question of my father. In 1940 there had been doubts about whether or not my brother Micky would even be accepted into a prep school; there had been an occasion when my Aunt Irene, applying for a job in the Women's Voluntary Service, had herself apparently been the subject of a security check on account of her being related to my father. By

1942 it was true that the atmosphere was less conducive to panic. But apart from any of this I still had the confidence generally felt amongst Etonians that the very fact of being an Etonian would be of more weight, even in army terms, than the fact of something like one's father being in gaol. I went for an interview early in 1942. I was accepted – it seemed without too much difficulty. I was to report to the Rifle Brigade depot at Winchester in April.

I went with a group of ex-public schoolboys who were earmarked as potential officers: it had been explained to us that for two months we would be treated no differently from other private soldiers. I wrote to my sister of our arrival at Winchester Station:

> At once of course we split up into our school cliques – Etonians rather aloof and bored and hands in pockets: the rest alternating between Rugby raucosity and grammar-school timidity. We walked crocodile-wise, Etonians drifting at least 100 yards in the rear, until we arrived at a place which reminded one of Brixton ... We were herded to our quarters, the basement of a morgue, with rows of beds constructed of steel bars, many vertical, and a few bent horizontal and arranged neatly so that the bars coincided with one's hips and chest and the gaps with one's head and waist ...

A week or two later I was writing to my father:

> The routine is as intense as expected: non-stop from 6.30 to 6 and very often extra fatigue after that. But there is barely time to stay depressed, and the evenings are made happy by the mere fact that we can get outside the barrack gates. We are all mixed up with the conscripts – men of 35–40 – better than younger ones who would be more aggressively hostile to us future (we hope) officers. But these are bad enough. They fuss around swearing (*always* the same drab monosyllable) spitting and interfering with everyone else with hoarse belches of amusement. The sergeants are wonderful men, who give us hell on the parade ground call us such names that make us laugh and wonder at the power to conceive such obscenities. Off duty they do quite a lot to help us.

What I remember now about the Rifle Brigade Depot at Winchester is the strange mixture of bonhomie and misery – the former mostly to do with the drinking of beer and the bandying of insults; the latter often to do with my stammer. We potential officers would be taken out of our squad one by one on the parade ground and made responsible for the drilling: it sometimes seemed that I, standing with my mouth open like an Aunt Sally at a fairground, might unwittingly become like the Emperor Christophe of Haiti who used for his amusement to march his crack troops over a cliff. However once when my squad was proceeding at the fast trot that was the customary style in the Rifle Brigade straight towards the doorway that led from the parade ground into the NAAFI canteen I thought I might after all take some advantage of my odd situation: I relaxed: my squad were half way in towards cups of tea before the sergeant-instructor beside me started bellowing – About Turn! Left Turn! Right Turn! Knees Up! At The Double! and so on. The insults that the sergeants were so proficient at hurling at us pleased us, I suppose, because as at school we wanted to laugh but ecstatically could not: there was a friend of mine called Pollock who became something of the platoon butt; the sergeant would stand very close to him and yell – 'Pollock! Spell it with a P do you? You sack of shit!'

From Winchester we moved on, in our ex-public school *bloc*, to Tidworth on Salisbury Plain; then on to an Officer Cadet Training Unit in the outskirts of York. At each new place there were forms to be filled up which included questions about 'father' and 'next of kin'. There was the weird feeling of ground being apt to fall away as I wrote 'Oswald Mosley, Holloway Prison, London N7'.

I wrote to Diana:

I do hope that Daddy and you will find life more bearable now that you are together. I am longing to come and see you and will do so at the first opportunity. Are you allowed to cook? I pity any poor third person who has to listen to you talking about food all day like Viv and I had to at Wootton. Although I am actually sympathising more and more with this.

To my father I wrote:

I will visit you as soon as they let us animals out of the zoo. Till then I am sure you are having a much happier and more comfortable time than me, which is peeving. I wonder if I might get arrested?

Into these letters of mine to my father there returned, at intervals, the phrases to do with the rhetoric of contempt. At Winchester there were the men whose 'humour is the humour of the over-sexed schoolgirl

and their habits the habits of verminous bluebottles'. At York – 'It
is unfortunate that even the OCTU is capable of procuring little else
than these baboons, several diseased debauchees, and many pleasant
nonentities.' My letters continued – as the one after my trip to Balliol
the year before – from time to time to sound fearfully like an article
in my father's old newspaper *Blackshirt*: I still hoped, I suppose, thus
to show solidarity with him. I was however (or so I boasted) reported
by those responsible for my training to be 'a popular and successful
leader' and 'an excellent cadet'. It seems to me now that what was
going on was an example of the way in which humans do indeed
get carried away by words in their needs for defence or attack: the
fact that they hardly see themselves doing this (and only with such
difficulty learn!) is one of the tragedies (not excuses) described in this
book.

I wrote to my sister of my 'idle pansy pose' with which I was
apt to 'baffle people' because alongside it I had, for instance, just won
some regimental athletic contest. This attitude was a more conventional
one for ex-public schoolboys to adopt when faced with the problems
of dealing with an alien world. From the OCTU at York I wrote
to my father:

The training thank God has become more interesting, and we play
around with theories of defence and attack for armoured divisions
rather than with our drab rifles and Bren guns. The officer, too,
is charming; and one can afford to be rude to the sergeant, a flea
of a man, with a certain impunity. The physical exertion demanded
is extreme: we frequently do 10 miles across country with packs, rifles,
equipment, etc. in under 2 hrs, which is heavy going.

We have now finished our mechanical course from which I passed
as a 1st class driver mechanic which is really very bogus and was
granted only through systematic flattery of the instructor; also our
wireless course, which was not so successful, as I was rather over-
confident and spent most of the time listening to the BBC and trying
to wreck wireless schemes by sending out false messages which
displeased people and I am afraid I got rather a low mark.

But we are embarking on the most important part of our training
now – endless tactics and toughening courses; horrible 5-day manoeuvres in Northumberland sleeping open-air with one blanket and
being harassed by live ammunition and artillery barrages. Then on
December 18th we pass out, complete with natty suiting and
prominent chest, and are allowed to show off to families for a week

or two. I will come and see you just before Christmas. Love to
Diana.

The world outside went on in what seemed to be its own senseless
way; few of my father's prognostications about the reasonable behaviour of men in war had turned out to be true. Hitler had not tried
to destroy the British army at Dunkirk; he had chosen not to try
to invade England when it was the only country left facing him; then
in 1941 he had turned his back and invaded Russia, thus putting himself
in the one position that he had declared previously would be disastrous –
that of having to fight a war on two fronts. My father's arguments
for not standing out against Hitler in 1938 and 1939 had been based
on the supposition that Hitler was not mad: now Hitler seemed to
be aiming at some grandiose self-destruction. However the British did
not seem to be adopting any very rational attitude to the war themselves:
we were now fighting side by side with Russians with whom we had
considered declaring war on two years before; it did not seem likely
that even after victory the Russians would help us to carry out what
were our stated war aims – to do with the providing of a decent and
independent life for people in Eastern Europe.

During 1941 and 1942 my sister Vivien and I during holidays or
periods of leave (my sister, after a time of working as a nurse and
in a mobile canteen, settled for doing war-work as a machine-tool
operator in a factory making nuts and bolts for armaments just off
Curzon Street) found our lives now revolving around the London world
inhabited by my Aunt Irene. Irene's house on the edge of Regent's
Park had been bombed; she moved in 1941 to the Dorchester Hotel,
where she stayed on and off for the rest of the war. The Dorchester
Hotel had become a rallying-place for many of the influential and once-
beautiful people of the kind who had used to gravitate around my
father and mother; they were now in the entourage of the people who
were running, or were letting run, the war. Irene spent much of her
time doing relief work in the air-raid shelters of London's East End
('under the LMS railway was sheer animal life in all its nakedness and
horror'): then –*

when I went back as I sometimes did to the Dorchester Hotel to
get away from the filth, fear and hideous suffering, and to get a
quiet night and bath, it always seemed a grotesque contrast to see

* *In Many Rhythms.*

a whole roomful of well-known men and women dining and supping in evening dress whilst the nerve-racking detonations went on all the time and the Hyde Park barrage shook our very foundations ... The air-raid shelter in the Dorchester, which Lord and Lady Halifax showed me with Mr and Mrs Maisky [the Russian Ambassador and his wife] with rows of chairs with their occupants' names, made me feel I would be happier with my gallant East Enders.

In London on a weekend leave, I myself was sometimes given what had once been a servant's room at the top and back of the Dorchester Hotel; I would drift between here and where my sister shared rooms at the top of the Park Lane Hotel with two other girls working in her factory. Irene described how the American Presidential Candidate Wendell Wilkie came to dinner at the Dorchester and was 'violently critical' of women 'in furs and jewels': he said he 'could not make them out, as if the war were not on'. Passing through, I did not see anything so very odd in this: was it not what I had always imagined of the grown-up world? And, since it was quite likely that one might soon die, might one not take advantage of whatever the grown-up world had to offer?

One of the only good (but it seems to me truly good) side-effects of war is that it breaks down some of the social conventions which in normal times are to do with the power of money and it gives genuine social prestige to people who are about to go and risk themselves in battle. In London at this time to be in the uniform of a front-line infantry regiment meant that – however young – one got things like – well – the best tables in the best restaurants. Some money of course was needed but not much: there had been imposed, as if miraculously, limits on things like the cost of meals. So when one was not frozen on manoeuvres in Northumberland or beleaguered in raucous barrack-rooms one could be – as soldiers are apt to be – on the town. Even behaviour that is absurd is smiled upon in wartime: society can be generous to its sacrificial victims.

The peculiar circumstances in which my sister Vivien and I found ourselves – with no family home and our parent in jail – meant that we had surrounded ourselves each with a surrogate family-circle of friends; these would come together at moments when I and my friends were on leave (Viv worked a ten-hour day on weekdays and seven hours on Saturdays). We formed a self-professed 'gang' or 'clique': we enjoyed the oddities of what was offered by war-time London. There was a fashionable (but not too fashionable) night-club of the time called The Nut House: here presided the comedian Al Burnett: habitués would squeeze into a cellar and would become stupefied and at home while Al Burnett sang songs like *The Sheik of Araby* (the required response was – 'With no pants on!'); there was a song which began 'Bell bottom trousers coats of navy blue' and we would intone the mysteriously significant antiphon – 'He'll climb the rigging like his father used to do.' There were girls called hostesses who would come and sit at our table when my friends and I were on our own; but they were only there, they would explain laboriously, to encourage us to order champagne. This suited me, who was still obviously, from Eton and after, massively mixed up about sex. The style of going 'on the town' seemed to most of us still to do with elaborations of the games we had learnt in childhood: there were ritualistic drinking games to see who would or who would not pass out; races round Berkeley Square; waltzing on empty bandstands. Once we got hold of a boat on the Serpentine and sank with it gallantly at midnight.

I had one rare Etonian friend however who was normally and aggressively sexual: he was determined – I think this was during our last holiday from Eton – to do what young men sooner or later traditionally are supposed to do – which is to pick up a tart. It was assumed that I was to be his companion in this; I was flattered rather than enthused. I had been somewhat emboldened recently, however, by the proprietress of The Nut House – a middle-aged lady who had told me, inevitably, that she had known my father – asking me also, did I know how like him I was? My friend and I set off once more for The Nut House. The hostesses explained as usual that they could not help us; however the doorman might. While we waited for the doorman to summon a taxi with two tarts in it I remembered how my father had told me many years ago when he had given me his pre-school talk about sex – If you ever want a woman, don't pick up just anyone, come to me. I had thought this uncommonly nice of him – though always unlikely, in the event, to be practical. The taxi arrived. My friend and I piled in. In the black-out, but unerringly, my friend got hold of the one of the tarts who turned out later to be quite pretty: I had got someone who, as we struck matches to light cigarettes, seemed to have the appearance of my grandmother. The taxi took us to one room where there was a bed and a sofa: my friend settled quite at home on the sofa; Granny and I got nowhere on the bed. I remember her playing with me a variation of 'This little piggy went to market': if I had been feeling witty I might have riposted – 'It looks more as if this little piggy's staying at home'. But one of the morals of this story was –

it was my friend, and not I, who had to worry about the clap.

When a year or so later I turned up in the hall of the Dorchester Hotel – 'looking grand' my Aunt Irene said 'in his new officer's uniform' – I was about to be put in charge of men to train them for, and then lead them in, matters of life and death. I was aged nineteen. For Christmas that year the family went off to our Aunt Baba's house in Gloucestershire. There, on the evening of Christmas Day, we were joined by some of our gang of friends and we played our games – word games, acting games, paper games, hiding-and-catching games. Irene reported – 'Viv and Nick were furious because at midnight Baba rushed down and stopped them dancing a ballet to Tannhäuser.'

CHAPTER 22

Conversations in Holloway

Some time after I had joined the army my father seems to have felt that although (or because?) he had no more responsibility for me in matters of guardianship, he might yet become some sort of mentor to me in intellectual affairs: he had few outlets for his restless energy in prison: I think also he liked to feel that he was in some sort of liaison with me as I went off to war.

He wrote to me from Holloway:

11th January 1943
Darling Nick. I am so glad to get your letter: the blankets, I heard, will be being supplied by family. Have you got a 'flea-bag?' – the only comfort in the last war. I nearly got one for prison and will send you one if you like. It is a jumble of blankets stitched together like a sack: once inside – Nirvana! You will anyhow have a chance to read at your new place – would you like me to send you some moderns – simply selected for Prose Style? I have here for instance an odd job lot such as Trevelyan and Heard – former on Hellenism and the latter on what N S & N [*New Statesman and Nation*] calls 'Back to Mumbo-Jumbo' – you should take in the latter journal – 'Cissy's Weekly' as we always call it – to be diverted by a prettily precious intellectualism. It is very well done from its standpoint. Both T and H are good exponents of a limpid modern style. Ditto Ross Williamson in *AD 33* – Christianity extolled and churches assailed: to signalise publication he has just been ordained! He was here the other day and promised to do anything he could to help you in early literary efforts. Then I have the other Williamson, Henry, also a friend of mine as you will see from beginning [Henry Williamson had dedicated his *The Story of a Norfolk Farm* to my

father]. He is much the best seller of the lot. But I do not advise following his style, which is idiosyncratic – something of Lawrence who was his great friend. Have you ever looked at the latter's *Seven Pillars of Wisdom*? Will send you Lytton Strachey's *Books and Characters* if you have not got it; he is really the father of contemporary style – you will enjoy him – also J. B. Stephens' *Crock of Gold* if you have not read it – I guess you would particularly like this from what you said you were reading when here. It made a great impression on me when I first read it and again later. You should of course read the classics, Gibbon and Macaulay – *not* in order to write like them but to absorb a sense of rhythm and thought-sequence – just gymnasium work – one does not do the exercises in the street but walks better down the street for having done them. Liddell Hart and Fuller are both good stylists and write on your job: I can send them also if you like. I love D'Annunzio at your stage – in pessimistic romantic vein – but am not sure he would be good for you! He is translated into beautiful English. My favourite work at *this* stage is Simon's (André, not St) 'Soups, Salads and Sauces' – wartime fare for the fastidious.

My father had said that he had selected these books for their prose style; however nearly all the authors he mentioned were also friends or acquaintances who admired him or who had worked with him at some time; he would not have seen anything odd in this. He did manage to send to me many of these books. I had been posted to the Rifle Brigade's Holding Battalion at Retford, in Nottinghamshire. I wrote to him:

We stay here for three months anyway, and then the first batch are sent abroad. I don't really mind whether I stay or go very much. The great hope is to get out to Africa just as everything is clearing up there. I think I would be good at reorganising Arabs. But I shall want a little fighting to impress my grandchildren if nothing else.

Because I was now an officer and thus considered fit to be responsible for the lives of men in battle, my father asked the authorities if, when I visited Holloway, I might be allowed to spend the whole day with him and Diana in their room in the Preventive Detention Block rather than just the regulation short time in one of the visiting rooms. This application was granted. This was the beginning of my close relationship with my father. The circumstances were propitious: it was as if we were outside normal categories of space and time: we were like revolutionaries meeting to discuss our plans for the world in Siberia.

February 1943, Holloway.

Darling Nick,

The Governor has been so good as to apply for you to lunch over here and now awaits the reply: if affirmative, Sunday would be the perfect day ... Trevelyan book on *Hellenism*, such are the pitfalls of my writing [I had mis-read 'Hellenism' as 'Hitlerism'.] Heard was a very good semi-popular writer of philosophic-scientific stuff and was used for this every week in *Action* when Harold Nicolson was editor. Sachy [Sitwell]'s *All Summer in a Day* I would recommend – one of the best titles I think – next to old Watts Dunton's *Revival of Wonder*. Also of course Sachy on Baroque: he is, perhaps, the most gifted of the S trio; but for purposes of forming style try Osbert – either of them you would find enchanting as guides to literature. I was going to suggest Virginia Woolf, whom you have found already; also, in something of the same category, David Garnett and E. M. Forster. How strange and interesting about *Crock of Gold* [I had known and loved this since childhood] – a great favourite with Mummy too. And what about English poetry? I will try to get together a mixed collection for you. Have you read Shaw's *The Perfect Wagnerite*?

February 10th 1943 Ranby Camp. Retford. Notts.

Darling Daddy,

Wonderful news that I will be able to stay for lunch and sample the choice vegetables and gourmet dishes ... I am beginning to enjoy the duties of officering a little bit more now that I know the men in my platoon and can take an interest in them as human beings rather than as particles of a military machine. I don't think I shall ever like the work – perhaps I am too lazy or perhaps because it seems such an appalling waste of time for everyone; but I get on well enough with the men and we manage to have quite a merry time whenever circumstances permit. Since I last wrote I have sampled E. M. Forster (*A Room with a View*) and found him very entertaining; together with Maurice Baring, Aldous Huxley, and still more Virginia Woolf who never ceases to please. Of poetry I am disgracefully ignorant. I went through the stage of Swinburne-worship while I was at Eton, but I suppose I want something more than that now and the truth is I have found nothing to take its place. Keats, Shelley – the old worthies – mean very little. I think perhaps Milton is the man for me.

I was first allowed to spend the day with my father and Diana in Holloway on February 21st 1943. I got off the bus in the Caledonian

Road and turned up a side road towards the prison: there were huge gates like the porter's lodge of an Oxford college. My credentials were checked; there was a clanking of keys; a slow walk beneath high walls across cobbled courtyards. This first time I did not know what to expect; later, I would prepare for these visits and would smuggle in under my huge army overcoat – worn even at the height of summer – food (one could still buy odd luxuries at Fortnum and Mason), drink (a bottle of brandy or champagne), gramophone records (Kirsten Flagstad singing Isolde), books (the second volume of Spengler's *The Decline of the West* which no one else had been able to find for my father and which with much pride I had hunted down in the Charing Cross Road). The wardress would lead me to a door in a high inner wall; the scene was like an illustration to some fairy story gone damp and burnt at the edges. Beyond the wall my father would be waiting. We went past his kitchen garden of which we had heard so much – on a piece of ground like a railway embankment he was growing aubergines and *fraises-de-bois* as well as cabbages and onions – up an echoing stone staircase in a building like a deserted cotton mill to the room where he and Diana lived. This was high and austere and dingy and yet contained bits of Diana's furniture which gave it an elegance like that of some provincial museum for shells: there was Diana's old gramophone with its enormous horn that had contained tiny sounds like those of the sea. My father and Diana seemed trapped by a sort of ring of dampened fire: within, there was as there usually was with them some demonstration of order and light.

The days that I spent in Holloway were always days of celebration: for my father and Diana, I suppose, they were breaks in the monotony of their lives; for myself they were times cut off from the crazed projections of the outside world. Diana would prepare one of her legendary dishes from, later, my father's legendary vegetables: I would produce my tinned ham or my bottle of champagne; on the gramophone there might be the *Liebestod* or *The Entry of the Gods into Valhalla*. Afterwards my father and I would go out into the garden to talk. Of course I myself may have made something of a legend about all this: but this was what it seemed like – we were conspirators believing that we might alter the world: shadows coming together beneath high walls with spikes on top like crowns of thorns.

March 14th Ranby Camp. Retford. Notts.
Darling Daddy,
I am at the moment most violently in the throes of Ross Williamsonism.

You remember that book of his that you sent me – *A.D. 33*? He answers the perpetual question of how to reconcile God-all-good with God-all-powerful by the simple assumption that God is not good (in our sense of the word) to everyone, which is a far more satisfactory answer than 'God is not all powerful': it is easier to have faith in a capricious God than in a weak god continually harassed by the sharp tail of a powerful Devil. And equally logically he shows that all our worldly conventional standards of good and evil are entirely contradicted by Jesus's (and God's) standards of good and evil (a conclusion to which one might come, I think, merely by a glance at the horrors of worldly conventions). The only thing which leaves me rather doubtful is the way in which he accepts Humility as a cardinal and essential virtue. Perhaps I have the wrong conception of humility but I do not see how he reconciles it with his horror of any signs of passive indifference. Can one be actively, vitally, and effectively humble? Humble towards God, yes: as he says, if you recognise yourself to be one of God's elect your gratitude and devotion to him will take the form of humility; but surely the doctrine of Humility implies it as a general form of behaviour toward one's fellow men; and as one's fellow men are 90% the dull indifferent baboons whom R. W. detests, what place has Humility in his relations with them? But perhaps I have got the wrong end of the stick.

I don't know why I am bubbling on like this; it will do me good to put on paper some of these ideas which seem to me so momentous; I expect they will all seem very commonplace to you.

I am known amongst my men as 'Mad Mr Mosley' which I take to be a well-merited compliment but I feel it would be frowned on by authority. I feel I am a very bad soldier, but I am able by my wits to keep pace with the dimly serious militarists who seem to haunt this morgue. But there are times when circumstances are too much for me, and I weep for the waste of it all.

Give my love to Diana. I sometimes very seriously wish I could be with you in Holloway, to sit and read and listen to Wagner on the gram and sample the excellence of Diana's cooking. I know I should find it more congenial than army life. And I could learn more from you than from all the books I have time to read now.

25th March 1943 Holloway
Darling Nick,

I was so glad to hear that you liked the books. R. W. says he would like to see you some time when you are in London. His theme, which you mention, has something of Spinoza – 'Because you love God, you have no reason to demand that God should love you'. He might have added – 'Particularly when we compare the attributes usually ascribed to God with those which we can observe in mankind'. But the idea of a God who likes and dislikes – however well founded on some cases – does not seem entirely to answer the old 'God-all-good and God-all-powerful dilemma': for clearly the buffets of fate are directed not only at the nasty but also at the very highest types – not only the tragic romantic of Byron vintage but also real and obvious good men – saints and martyrs etc. In fact it may also be said that not only the capacity for suffering but also the experience of suffering often culminate in some of the finest types the world has seen. Unless therefore the God standard deviates entirely from anything we can conceive it would appear that an all-powerful God afflicts these because he capriciously dislikes them. We are therefore driven back towards a conception of suffering – of all the phenomena which are shortly called evil in the experience of man – as fulfilling some creative purpose in the design of existence: back in fact to the Faustian Riddle, usually stated with the utmost complexity but for once with curious crudity in the 'Prologue in Heaven' [in Goethe's *Faust*] when The Lord says to Mephistopheles – 'The activity of man can all too lightly slumber; therefore I give him a companion who stimulates and works and must, as Devil, create'. *Faust* is meant to cover the whole panorama of human experience; but I believe this to be, on the whole the main thesis of all its innumerable profundities. Many commentators would disagree; and, as more books have been written about it than any play in the world except Hamlet, we had better leave it there for the moment!

But Goethe does not attempt to answer, within my knowledge, the still underlying question – 'Why then the agonising process of creation at all?' Why did not perfect and powerful God forthwith create perfect beings without the long process of evolution lashed forward by suffering? To that I know no adequate answer in any of the philosophies or religions of the world: here we approach the mysteries. It is a sobering thought that the foremost minds of mankind have striven with these things for 3,000 years and that the greatest among them have admitted to mysteries which cannot be pierced: many, like the Greeks and German neo-Hellenists, even go so far as to say it is fatal to attempt to do so. Can one say more than that the dominant phenomenon of life as we see it is the organic processes of nature – beginning with such small and crude material and working under the impulse of struggle and suffering to every higher form and beauty – 'recurrently' perhaps but also 'spirally'. Here, as so often, the poets and prophets (I mean the real ones!) serve us better than the philosophers. Can we go much further than Schiller in *Die Künstler* with the lines which he repeated in the moment of his death – 'That which on earth appeared to me as Beauty will meet me on the other side as Truth.' The consideration is also often present in my mind that the purpose of existence might well be frustrated through a complete solution of the mystery of life by mankind: we are plainly here to live this life: how much interest would the purposes of this life retain if we saw the whole purpose? Nietzsche, here at any rate, plays his part in his triumphant affirmation of this life and his furious denunciation of the flight from it.

I am sending you under a separate cover a commentary on his doctrine by a Cambridge don [A. H. J. Knight] who sets out much of it quite well but is so opposed to him that he finally produces a feeble travesty of what N meant which is refuted by quotations kindly supplied in his own book. Oh these dons and commentators! the depths of their intellectual dishonesty are unfathomable! But let them by all means direct you to great subjects with the vast store of their erudition. But then always go to the original – in the end even genius should be allowed to speak for itself! I pondered long before sending you any Nietzsche, but think you now are intellectually strong enough to take it. The real thing is not to swallow him whole but *to see him in relation to the whole*. To be lightly repelled by the unbridled violence of his mind and exposition is as great an error as to become obsessed by the power of it – as many have been.

In Christianity you have the thesis: in Nietzsche the antithesis. There remains synthesis, eternal synthesis, which is the task and hallmark of all supreme minds. I mean not merely the narrower terms of the Hegelian dialectic which you should one day study – thesis, antithesis, synthesis – the statement of the idea, its refutation by its opposite, the synthesis of both which approaches truth – but the wide clashes of the great spiritual movements whose fiery collisions can fuse into a higher unity. You might attempt the Christian – Nietzsche synthesis one day, and would be helped in the attempt by the 'child' of the third metamorphosis – 'Unschuld ist das Kind und Vergessen, ein Neubeginnen, ein Spiel, ein aus sich rollendes Rad, eine erste Bewegung, ein heiliges Ja-sagen. Ja, zum Spiele des

Schaffens, meine Brüder, bedarf es eines heiligen Ja-sagens: *seinen* Willen will nun der Geist, *seine* Welt gewinnt sich der Weltverlorene'. ['The child is innocence and forgetfulness, a new beginning, a sport, a self-propelling wheel, a first motion, a sacred Yes. Yes, a sacred Yes is needed, my brothers, for the sport of creation: the spirit now wills *its own* will, the spirit sundered from the world now wins *its own* world']. Perhaps not so remote as N thought from a conception of Christ which, however, is not quite accepted by the churches! You will find a vehement reflection of some of your feelings on humility in his 'transvaluation of values': pride is among his cardinal virtues: though here again, was Christ humble? Not with the money-changers in the temple at any rate; though the feet-washing etc would seem to indicate the contrary. In genius, or the inspired, or whatever we call it, superficial contradictions however so often cover an underlying unity. Is this seeming contradiction more than an inspired extension of the old Roman 'Parcere subjectis; debellare superbos' [Spare the humbled; make war on the proud] carried to the extent of an overwhelming pity and tenderness towards the poor and afflicted, compared with an arrogant combativeness towards the corruptly affluent? Synthesis, ever synthesis!

There was a day in April when I went to visit my father and I had a bottle of brandy amongst other offerings festooned beneath my greatcoat; we sat late around the table where we had had lunch – talking of Nietzsche, I suppose: about the problem of pity possibly being a mechanism by which nothing might be allowed to change; might not arrogance then in some way be a love because thus humanity might evolve? We were getting no doubt towards the end of the bottle of brandy; there was the sound of footsteps coming up the echoing stairs. We listened; we were in gaol after all; like schoolboys, we hid our glasses and the bottle beneath the table. There was a knock on the door. My father said, 'Who is it?' A voice said, 'The Governor.' My father said, 'Oh, do come in!' The Governor was a pleasant, sandy-haired man: he said that he had come to tell me that I had long over-stayed the time allowed for my visit; but he had not come to complain, he had just come to tell me how now to get out of the prison. My father said, 'I wonder if you would like a glass of brandy?' He produced the bottle from under the table. The Governor said, 'Ah, you don't often see brandy like this nowadays!' And so we all had some celebration – perhaps, as my father might have said, some synthesis; perhaps even a move towards the metamorphosis of the child.

I remember going back after this day in Holloway (I was smuggled out through a side gate by a smiling wardress) all the way on foot through blacked-out streets to the Dorchester Hotel: I had made some plan to meet my sister and a friend there and go to a play. I was hours late: I had missed the play: I did not mind. I was pulled along on some tightrope as if by strings from the sky. I was thinking of all that my father had said – about Nietzsche's theory of Eternal Recurrence, perhaps, by which Nietzsche seemed to be throwing down a challenge to life by saying that one should be brave enough to live every moment as if one knew it might endlessly recur (had my father got this right? might he not think Nietzsche was talking about a fact rather than a state of mind?); or about the way in which Nietzsche distinguished between what he called master-morality and slave-morality – which distinction was not a technique for domination (was it?) but rather a means of assuring that each person could choose only such freedom as he was able to bear. I was thinking also of the jokes, the laughter – the story my father had told in his best Mitford-copying voice about the time when the compost heap that he had so lovingly prepared in his garden had been cleared away and he had overheard Diana crying out to the wardress – 'But it was the *breath of life* to Sir Oswald!' I was being pulled along by all this – and by the question: does not the ridiculousness of things become not ridiculous by the virtue of your knowing it? – so that when eventually I arrived at the Dorchester Hotel and found that my sister and our friend had waited for me and had missed the play (*Hedda Gabler* of all things!) and were understandably annoyed (they had been anxious about me and had even thought of ringing up the police to ask – Is he still in prison?) I remember walking away across Park Lane and sitting on the plinth of the enormous statue of a naked man with a drawn sword and a shield raised to the sky. My Aunt Irene, also at the hotel, recorded – 'I suddenly saw Nick on the edge of tears.' I wondered beneath my statue – What does one do with all these images that come down like bombs, like lightning flashes, like doves or manna from heaven?

May 29th Ranby Camp. Retford. Notts.
Darling Daddy,
I do not see that Eternal Recurrence is incompatible with the Superman theory so long as the circle begins to recur only after the Superman stage has been reached: the Superman stands at the summit of each circle and the Superman himself is endlessly repeated: this has nothing to do with Goethe's spiral, which is altogether a smaller

and more limited thing in time. If one accepts Nietzsche's contention (I don't see why one should) that time is endless and energy is limited, I suppose some theory of Recurrence must follow naturally.

I really have no opinion here. I see everything as a possibility, and have not the conviction to decide what is a Truth and what is Right. I do not see how one can ever have this conviction, and even if one has it, why one should presume that one's convictions are right. My reason tells me what theories are the most possible, the most likely, the most desirable; but it needs more than Reason to put any theory across; it needs a great Faith. And my Reason tells me that it is dangerous to trust in Faith, for how does one know that one's Faith is Right? And so I am stuck; and am likely to remain so, I feel, until I am old and wise enough to have Faith in my Reason.

Nietzsche's contention that the Übermensch [Superman] is 'beyond good and evil' is of far deeper significance than 'above morality'. To be above morality is merely to be sufficiently civilised to be able to do without a conventional code of behaviour to control one's filthy impulses: to be 'beyond good and evil' I think implies that one does not recognise good and evil as such, but one does have values (both ethical and religious) that are based on entirely different standards.

With Nietzsche's values I have very little sympathy: 'Heiterkeit' [serenity] – yes, that is perhaps the most desirable quality that any mortal can possess. But 'Härte' [hardness] – why always the emphasis on domination and power through 'Härte'? With the principles of Herrenmoral [mastermorality] I agree entirely – duties towards one's equals; a belief that 'what is harmful to me is harmful in itself etc' – but is it necessary for the Herrenmoral to take Härte as its primary value? There is no beauty, and I would say very little nobility, in Härte.

I am just back from the most perfect fortnight spent camping out with my platoon in Derbyshire. We wandered through many of the old haunts – the upper reaches of Dovedale and the valley of the Wye; we spent two nights in a lovely valley called Ravensdale, which was fascinating, and once we passed close to Wootton but I was afraid that the sight of it again would make me sad, and so we swept past. Now the boredom of barrack routine has set in again.

I have become involved in a correspondence upon the Church with Aunty Irene. One of her East End priests to whom she sent on my letters wrote me the most half-witted reply; I really do believe that these men do not understand what they say: which perhaps is best, for it is happier for them to be charged with ignorance and stupidity than with gross perversion and distortion.

I wish I could talk with more energy and conviction when I come to visit you. I think you stuff me so heavily with delicious food, and drench me so plentifully with great flagons of Bristol Milk, that it is all I can do to hold myself together. I do enjoy those visits so very much, and I learn more and am more stimulated in those few hours with you than I would ever be in a lifetime with any of my pseudo-intellectual friends. We (my friends and I) do have the most fiercely profound arguments, but I always feel that they are somehow entirely irrelevant. So I yearn for more conversation à la Holloway.

1st June Holloway Prison.
Darling Nick,

I was delighted by your letter – in fact I turned to the Percheron and said 'It is odd, the lad really is brilliant!' She observed that she did not see why it was odd: and there, as Beachcomber says, the matter rests at present. I will write you at greater length later – unless, by any luck, you come here in the interval: but herewith a few preliminary grunts.

I agree that one of the prime needs of the world today is a Faith in the shadowy realms of metaphysics which can be believed by the modern and educated mind: further agree that it is impossible for finite reason to elucidate all the mysteries; but I come more and more to the conclusion that it would be possible to formulate a Faith (now largely felt but inarticulate) which draws the spiritual in life from the best of the thought, creeds and civilisations that the world has so far produced; weaves it into a coherent whole of conduct and attitude to human existence, and attunes it to the main tendencies of modern science which, in turn, can defend its novelties from the usual reception of new ideas by a hard analysis of those motives in human conduct and belief that have preceded it. As I am probably too old, and in these circumstances anyhow in no fit state to undertake anything of the kind, you had better get busy!

Incidentally and disjointedly there is all too much Härte in nature and in all evidential 'Purpose' in life: the problem of the extent to which this 'Härte' can or should be modified or sublimated in higher developments of communal organisation is one of the profoundest of all – we want to fulfil and not to frustrate the Purpose as revealed in nature, but in ever higher forms. I am glad you don't swallow

N whole; but, re Härte, the old boy would probably reply – 'No beauty nor nobility in Härte, agreed: but what have men (majority) done to Beauty and Nobility – destroyed the one and persecuted the other. What then is the answer of the emerging Übermensch to this situation except Härte?'

One must always remember that to the lonely N the higher men appeared almost as a persecuted sect struggling for survival. I always found his attitude to Mitleid [pity] repulsive: but believe that 'compassion' will come again in a higher form one day when the higher men are not underneath but on top. How in fact can they express their destiny except through the constructive equivalent of pity – which is a high design to lift mankind? That is the will to achievement which is as far beyond N's will to power – isolated self-development and self-assertion – as his Will to Power is beyond the Will to Comfort – disguised as self-sacrifice by those who cannot achieve. I sometimes think that my initial error which lasted too long was the belief that reason and goodwill were enough – Love is still the end, I believe, but, in the world as it is, Love is not enough – so perhaps I should say with Swinburne – 'I have lived long enough having seen one thing that love hath an end'. You are right, I think, that N really means 'Beyond Morality' rather than 'Beyond Good and Evil' – eg he would say that Pride as evil and Humility as good should be reversed; but that is really a moral question; he would not say he was in favour of cancer, where we really enter the realm of evil – natural catastrophe which is not man-made. But as you say, in Divine Purpose – what of the phrases Good and Evil? What is the place of the latter in the scheme of things? I should think it can be discerned – Goethe had a glimmer – but it can be taken much further: it is the basic problem before which all churches have relapsed into the childish. The natural non-man-made-horror – that is the fundamental question. Every Greek tragedy was largely man-made for all their passion for life – quarrelling and murdering each other about matters of small consequence in any world ruled by reason and beauty. But when man has done his worst, remain the things that God has done. Why? The riddle of existence. Some reply should be attempted.

Love Daddy.

CHAPTER 23

'Any Relation – ?'

With myself in the army and my father in prison I continued to want to strike some attitudes as if with him against the world. I wrote to him that I had found hitherto 'no true kindred spirit with whom either to disregard or to shock this pallid society'. He seemed to become this kindred spirit.

Surrounding my growing relationship with my father was my day-to-day life in the army. I began to keep a diary of this: in the diary is shown something of the obverse side to what was arrogant – of the language of contempt perhaps being turned back against oneself. I wrote fairly often of my stammer: a stammer is the indeed often ludicrous outward sign of an inward contradiction; it is as if the sufferer were half conscious of having swallowed paradoxes as if they were some snake. I wrote at this time (of course there is nothing less conducive to sympathy than self-pity) – 'How despairing I am become! my thoughts are all of death this week: it is all due to stammer: I cannot remember it so bad. It is obvious I have no idea where it comes from, and no control over it whatsoever.'

I had got fairly used to the yelling out of orders; but as an officer in charge of a platoon I also had now to give lectures – on subjects such as Chemical Warfare or Current Affairs. I would find myself once more on a platform like a scaffold; my sergeant would shout for silence; amongst the thirty or so assembled men there would be an air of appalled expectancy. After a time in which nothing much happened one or two of the more sensitive of my audience began to roll about in the aisles: how well I myself remembered this! – the agonies and ecstasies of half-suppressed laughter. My sergeant would yell – 'Don't laugh at the officer!' There was, I suppose, something healthily inimical to illusions about 'master-morality' in this. Oddly, I think my platoon did get to know quite a lot about Current Affairs and Chemical War-fare: perhaps people learn when there is the opposite of an imposition on them.

I am going on about this because in so far as fascism is a subservience, as I have intimated, to the despotism of words, then the stammerer is an archetype of that within which the battle of the fascist versus the anti-fascist is fought. It is not that he renounces the use of words: he recognises their terrible power by which he himself might be taken over; yet there is a part fluttering inside him that cannot, or will not, have this. Stammering is the protection of oneself both from other people's aggression and from one's own aggression against others; but then the question of interest is – in what ways might this be or not be beneficent? If there is something destructive in the take-over power of words – in the illusion that one can deal with people as if they were words – then might there not be some efficient virtue in the rebellion, however tawdry, against this? At Ranby Camp it was a fact that I did manage to have a good platoon – perhaps simply as a result of some sympathy. I wrote in my diary: 'Maybe it is true to say that lack of means of slick expression has made me rely on "charm" and given me cause to understand – both of which I would not have cultivated were I let loose among the flurry of words.'

Discipline in the army was conventionally maintained by men being shouted at by junior officers and NCOs or, for more serious offences, by these putting a man on what was called 'a charge'. This meant that the offender came up before the Company Commander who was a Major or the Battalion Commander who was a Lieutenant-Colonel; they were empowered to dole out punishments such as loss of pay or confinement to barracks. I found myself with a deep reluctance ever to put anyone 'on a charge': all the time I was in the army I think I did this only once – when I was sharing command of a platoon with another officer and thus had to go along with convention. For the rest – it seemed to me that the point of an officer was that he should be superior to convention – necessarily, perhaps, if he himself from time to time was apt to find himself marooned in front of his men like an Aunt Sally. Of course, in this attitude I was protected by the whole traditional weight of army discipline.

Ranby Camp, Retford, was a lot of huts in flat fields with the officers' quarters on one side of a road and everything else on the other. I wrote to my sister: 'In the ranks one was restricted physically by petty regula-tions and intellectually by the insensitivity of one's comrades; but as an officer one is up against these two body-belts to just the same degree and combined with them is the appalling tyranny of etiquette and good manners.' But it is not of this that I now remember very much. I remember the ways in which we were able to get away from the rituals and rigours of the officers' mess into the training schemes, for instance, in the hills and vales of Derbyshire; into the war-games which were extensions of the games of hide-and-seek and 'lions' which we continued to play as grown-up children. My friend and rival platoon commander in this was often Raleigh Trevelyan – who later wrote *The Fortress*, one of the best books about the Second World War. Raleigh and I would set up camps in the Peak District with our platoons on different hills; we would meet to carouse at night, then separate in order at dawn – surprise surprise! – to attack each other with whoops and blank cartridges and things called thunder-flashes. Then we would drive to picnic at some beauty spot: this was called training in embussing and de-bussing.

With regard to what I described to my sister in my niggardly manner as 'the simpering solemnity of this miserable mess' – what I now remember of life in the officers' quarters was the way in which, when we got drunk at night, some of us would congregate in one of the junior officer's rooms which had been turned into a night-club called *The Juke Box*: here we would indulge in some of the fantasies that seem often to be on the periphery of the consciousness of soldiers – among Greeks and Trojans, Shakespeare seems to suggest; apparently among – ah! – the Nazi SA. We would put music on and dance; one or two of us would dress up; we were Narcissi paddling amongst our own murky reflections. How innocent this was! – or is it innocent if soldiers thus manage the dirty business of war?

As Narcissus I tried to explain myself to myself. I wrote in my diary: 'Theory – damn the world if you feel like it: practice – don't be rude to anybody except those who cannot hurt back'. I became obsessed with the matter of what was and what was not hypocrisy. One had to present some façade to the world to stay alive: when one became conscious of doing this, did this or did it not provide a centre from which one could balance the demands of the outside world with what was going on inside?

It seemed to me the worst danger of all was not to be conscious of the predicament – to be taken over, helplessly, by the demands of one or the other of the outside or the inside world. Everyone was engaged on some wheeler-dealing with those around them; they lashed out in the struggle to be on top; they lay down in surrender in order not to be destroyed. But regarding the inside – how seldom people

Wootton Lodge

Oswald Mosley at Wootton

Diana

Oswald Mosley and Diana at Wootton

Nicholas, Diana, Jonathan Guinness

Right: Oswald Mosley and Diana

Earl's Court meeting – 1939 (*C. A. Daniels*)

Street meeting in Bermondsey – 1938

Oswald Mosley on way to court from Brixton Prison as plaintiff in libel action – 1940
(*S & G Press Agency Ltd*)

The author's platoon in troop carriers – Northern Italy, April 1945

Mervyn Davies and Nicholas

Nicholas

Alexander, Diana, Max, Oswald Mosley – Crowood 1946

Oswald Mosley speaking at inaugural meeting of Union Movement, 1948

Oswald Mosley in pub with followers, 1954 (*BBC Hulton Picture Library*)

Rosemary – North Wales, 1950

Nicholas – 1950

Alexander, Max, Diana, Oswald Mosley – Venice, late fifties

Oswald Mosley in Trafalgar Square – early sixties

saw what puppets they were: how little they knew of the strings! It
was people like this who blindly caused destruction – and were
destroyed. A creative sort of arrogance might be a characteristic of
those who were conscious of their helplessness; who would thus have
a freedom of vision not available to those who were not.

I wrote in my diary – 'I am completely selfish re the myth-picture
I have imagined of me: fortunately, one of the virtues of this picture
is unselfishness'.

One of the ways by which I tried to escape from a self-reflecting
solipsism was through my relationship with my father: he seemed to
me an oracle of which I could ask the answers to things; it was with
him I shared hopes about finding meanings in the world. I could, by
getting drunk with friends, imagine at moments I glimpsed the beatific
vision; I also dreamed of some girl with whom one day, hand in hand,
I might look down on the maze of common myth-making. But my
father seemed to do with what was sober.

Another way of hoping to get some hand-hold on 'reality' was
through religion. I was trying to take Christianity seriously: I carried
on a correspondence with priests through my aunts Irene and Baba.
I could not make any sense of the words of Christianity: it seemed
that they made out God to be some fearful kind of moneylender who
laid out loans of life and then demanded from humans heavy interest;
when humans could not redeem their pledges God then sold his own
son as a sacrifice. The priests who wrote to me insisted this imagery
was a travesty; then they just seemed to repeat it in different words.
So in what manner was it that they heard their words? I began to
make up what I thought was my own hugely original religion – in
fact obviously influenced by my father. I suggested that there were
four stages at which humans could be in their relationship with God
(I assumed the existence of God: so did my father). The lowest stage
was that in which humans were unaware that such a relationship with
God could exist; the next was that in which humans were aware of
being in some relationship with the universe but did not know what
to do about it (I put myself in this category); the next was that of
people who seemed to know what to do even if they could not clearly
put this into words (saints and mystics); and the fourth stage was Christ
or what might indeed be called God himself – God both found, and
made of oneself, as a result of a process. God the Holy Ghost was
demonstrated by the fact that humans were able to glimpse all this;
they could launch themselves on, even be guided in, this process if
they chose. This was some version of what my father came to call

his 'doctrine of higher forms'. But within all this there was a recognition of the limitation of words; words were not ultimate; they were tools that could be used, understood, for good or evil.

Such things went on in my mind as we jogged along the road between Retford and Worksop carrying what seemed like half a hundredweight on our backs; as we drank ourselves at night into the imagined company of Erich von Stroheim or Marlene Dietrich. There were always rumours about when, and where, we might be sent abroad: I wrote to my sister: 'One is being made pretty for the slaughter'. But also – 'I want to go abroad because there at least something definite will happen: here one is entirely negative, everything one does is exactly the opposite of what one feels one should do, and what time one has free is spent bolstering energy for further self-repression. Oh dear!'

By the summer of 1943 the war in North Africa had ended; there was the invasion of Sicily; then the start of the long, slow crawl up Italy. There seemed no doubt that the Allies would win the war: the Russians were advancing from Stalingrad; Hitler was beginning to put into effect his plan of taking transport away from his hard-pressed armies and using it to promote the murder of millions of harmless Jews – thus spurring on his own self-destruction. The Allies had just announced their policy of unconditional surrender – thus making things more difficult for themselves by stiffening the resolve of the forces around Hitler. Things did indeed seem to be happening the opposite of the way people intended. For myself – I felt I had to fight; but what on earth was the style in which to fight sensibly?

Some time in August I was sent on embarkation leave; I visited my Aunt Irene and Micky and Nanny in Cornwall. Irene made three comments about me in her diary: 'Nicky is in a curiously aloof and pondering attitude and was shatteringly crude and offensive about Christ'; 'Nicky told me he and his father were now in perfect accord in their outlook'; and 'Nicky owned that he thought his father had gone so wrong in his views that he had had to be arrested'.

I have a strangely luminous vision of my last visit to Holloway: my father and I had gone as usual into the garden to talk; we were by the cabbage patch once more like conspirators beneath the high walls that might have ears. He said – If anything should happen to you (I do not think I can have dreamed this) anything such as if you got stuck, I mean, in a foreign country – then he gave me some sort of password. I have forgotten exactly what – some code-phrase – something about the poplar trees I think at Denham. I was to re-member and if necessary use this code-phrase, if ever one of us were in a position in which the other wanted to get in touch with him secretly. I thought – But the Germans cannot now win the war: so you mean – I might be taken prisoner? It was true I had sometimes wondered about being taken prisoner: how I might spend the rest of the war sensibly reading Goethe, Nietzsche – as if beneath the high walls of Holloway prison. My father had often had a conspiracy view of history. When I said goodbye to him he looked very thin and ill and tired.

One of the last acts I performed before I went abroad was to go with my grandmother on a deputation to the Home Office in order to put to a high-up official a plea for my father's release. My father was truly ill now, his phlebitis was getting worse, doctors had even said that without freedom to exercise he might die. He had been three and a half years in prison; he had been charged with no offence; it was inconceivable in the present state of the war that he could be any threat to security. We said all this in the Home Office; my grandmother did most of the talking. The high-up official sat behind his desk with the tips of his fingers together: he seemed to be listening and yet not really penetrable; like some sort of portcullis. He said – He would take note of our arguments and would pass them on to the Minister. My grandmother said – This is his son going off to war. I thought – Yes, you bugger, I'm going off to war.

I sailed with one of my old Etonian friends called Anthony on a troopship and we went far out into the Atlantic to pick up a convoy and then turned down through the Bay of Biscay; it became very rough and gradually the officers' dining room emptied and I and one or two others were on our own eating mountains of eggs and steaks and oranges because the ship had stocked up recently in South Africa. We did not know where we were going; we looked out vaguely for the Rock of Gibraltar or the Cape of Good Hope. I had arranged my own code with my sister whereby I should be able to get news of our where-abouts past the censors of our air-mail letters. We landed at Philipville in North Africa not far from Algiers: I wrote to my sister (we were both cinema fans) – 'We might be able to visit Jean Gabin or Charles Boyer'. At Philipville we stayed for two months in a tented camp amongst sand-dunes: we bathed, we drank red wine, we played bridge. I wrote to my sister:

Yesterday we played football in a temperature equivalent to the melting point of flesh: ten effete and flabby young officers beat eleven horny old Scotsmen, who have sulked most ungraciously ever since.

To my father I wrote:

> We went out on a little manoeuvre last week and toured round
> in armoured cars miles into the interior. During one scrimmage with
> the 'enemy' I captured an enormous Captain in some rather hush-
> hush job whose face seemed vaguely familiar. Unfortunately I treated
> him with great respect, for it later turned out to be Randolph
> Churchill. If I had known earlier, I would have hurled him into
> a dungeon full of syphilitic Arabs. I am sure he would have enjoyed
> a taste of the Brixton atmosphere.

The attitude of myself and indeed to some extent of my friends towards
the war continued to be enigmatic. Becoming fed up with the hanging
about in Algeria, I and some others volunteered for the Parachute
Regiment; I was told I was too tall and too myopic. Then I was having
renewed fantasies about being taken prisoner – having made my gesture
to dutiful behaviour, I might thus spend the rest of the war profitably
studying and practising writing in a camp. This was again of course
a joke – yet not quite a joke. The war was as good as won after all:
what was the point of being killed in what seemed to be everyone's
long haul towards self-destruction? And part of me still wondered –
what on earth were we doing in a war in which in practical terms
(as my father had so often said) the only real winners in an allied victory
would be America and Russia? Britain would find herself as a second-
rate power without her Empire. I wrote to my sister, 'The whole
business is so obviously absurd: so tremendously ridiculous.'

On 16th November 1943 I was on a boat again to Taranto in the
heel of Italy (my code-phrase for this to my sister was – 'In whose
beginning is the home of Scarlett O'Hara'). The fighting in Italy had
got stuck in the mud and mountains somewhere half way between
Naples and Rome. My friends and myself had been destined as reinforcements for a Rifle Brigade battalion; when we arrived, there was
no Rifle Brigade battalion left in Italy. We were told we were to be
parcelled out as reinforcements to other regiments which were in need
of officers. One of my friends had a brother who was in Army Group
Headquarters; we went to see him and he arranged that we should
be sent to a battalion of the London Irish Rifles which was a 'black-
button' (rifle) regiment, and thus we would be spared what we made
out we saw as the indignity of having to join a 'brass-button' regiment
of the line. This arrangement was to have important consequences for
me: I remained with the 2nd Battalion of the London Irish Rifles for

the rest of the war: I moved out of the somewhat snobbish confines represented even by the Rifle Brigade, and was from now on – at first by chance but later by determined and happy choice – beyond some sort of pale within which I had been brought up.

On my way up to the front line, in a Transit Camp called 3 C R U, I read in the local army newspaper that my father and Diana had been released on health grounds from Holloway Prison; there were enormous crowds in Parliament Square demanding that they should be put back. Headlines continued for days: there was a photograph of a placard saying 'Hang Mosley!'; a re-print of a *Daily Herald* article which declared, 'Mosley is not merely a man whom the Government considered potentially dangerous and therefore not fit to be left at large, he was a symbol of the evil against which this country is fighting to the death.' I wrote in my diary: 'O frabjous day calloo callay! God am I glad and relieved! It is now imperative to get home as soon as possible.'

In transit camps, and away from my sophisticated friends of the Rifle Brigade, the name of Mosley suddenly became a difficulty such as I had not known it to be before; people to whom I had to introduce myself, perhaps with some newspaper open on their desks, were apt to say – 'Not any relation of that bastard?' – not imagining that the answer could be Yes. When I would say just 'Yes' (what more does one say?) for the most part my questioners would apologise profusely. Sometimes their embarrassment became so drawn-out that I wondered – Might there not be some style, some look in the eye perhaps, by which for the sake of all concerned one could say Yes without the rigmarole attendant on saying it?

I wrote in my diary:

It seems obvious that I am to make my base with Daddy and Diana after the war. I hope to God Daddy never does anything rash politically again. It is terrible to think how he bungled things earlier – how a wee bit of hypocrisy and political licence would have made all the difference ... They are obviously still very frightened of him. But perhaps after all this screaming is preferable to apathy; he is still a force to be reckoned with in the political world. With a little shrewd propaganda I have no doubt he would be most urgently reckonable. But where is the propaganda to come from? If only he had friends worth tuppence! ... Me?

CHAPTER 24

Another Kind of War

On the 1st of October 1943 my father, from prison, had written to his mother:

> My darling mother,
> You asked me to write to you my views on my physical condition which has worried you and other relations. I need not enlarge on the medical reports which you have in your possession. The condition is ascribed to confinement; and freedom, fresh air and contact with friends is prescribed. On the other hand I understand that the Home Office medical opinion ascribes my state of health more to psychological circumstance than to the physical conditions of my confinement. How phlebitis in the thigh is psychologically produced the text books do not describe. In short, I believe the Home Office views to be not only nonsense but dishonest nonsense. The purpose is perfectly clear and is two-fold: 1. to suggest that nobody could become so ill in their pretty prisons for physical reasons; 2. to suggest that, the condition being psychological rather than physical, it does not matter so much whether I am in prison or outside – in fact, that release is not essential to recovery.
> I have some little advantage in this matter having read at least as much psychology as most practitioners in the subject. But in this case, no very specialised knowledge is required to psycho-analyse the psycho-analysts! The medical facts seem to be perfectly plain: 1. I come of country stock which is naturally and severely afflicted by close confinement; 2. I was warned years ago, and correctly, that I had a physique well constituted to endure exceptional strain and fatigue but, conversely, particularly and adversely affected by inactivity. The outward symptoms were slow pulse and the necessity

to take violent exercise such as fencing to ward off diseases of a sluggish bloodstream such as phlebitis. On the other hand, as all my intimates know, psychological matters do not and never have affected me one jot. It is suggested that I feel a great sense of injustice at my imprisonment, and that the necessity to repress this feeling has psychologically and therefore physically affected me. It is true that I think our treatment is a disgraceful and disgusting business but I never worry about something that I can do nothing about. It is further suggested to me that I am oppressed for the time being by the thought of one day having a great public struggle to justify myself, etc. It is incredible that anyone should think I could be worried by anything so remote. Such a struggle cannot, anyhow, arise till after the war. My organisation is banned; I cannot speak as a member of British Union. Therefore, in or out of prison, I will not speak at all. It is further suggested that I may be worried by public opinion concerning me. When have I ever been? Twenty years ago I joined the Labour Party. Since that moment I have never lived a day when some section of the public did not think me a double-dyed villain; sometimes more, sometimes less; all depends on circumstances! No one has ever been more abused than I have been throughout my political life. The only difference is that now I cannot reply. But my reply can keep till after the war: like whisky, it will improve with keeping! I withdraw not a word I have ever uttered, nor ever will, whether I live or die in prison or outside. But I remain silent so long as British Union is banned. That is all the law requires of me, or can require. Let me sum up this pyschological nonsense with a little analogy. If you put a wild animal in a cage of course it affects his health and, before very long, probably kills him. Furthermore, it probably annoys him if people rattle their sticks along the bars of the cage. Once back in his natural jungle, every mandarin in Fleet Street can rattle a bit of iron or a bit of wood till he is blue in the face without that animal suffering any pyschological disturbance whatever.

People closest to my father at this time thought that psychologically he probably did encourage the worsening of his phlebitis – and why should he not? – there was little chance of his being released except on health grounds from the imprisonment in which he was now being kept largely for reasons of spite. He passionately wanted to get out; he really did become ill: he would have to protest in words that this was nothing to do with his own volition.

He was examined by three prison doctors and two eminent consultants brought in by the family – Lord Dawson of Penn and Dr Geoffrey Evans. In the opinion of all five (in the words of the Home Secretary when reporting to Parliament) – 'If the patient remained under conditions that were inseparable from detention there would be substantial risk of the thrombo-phlebitis from which he is suffering extending and producing permanent danger to health and even to life.' This weight of doctors' opinions was added to the efforts of people who had been working for his release behind the scenes: my Aunt Baba had unceasingly been getting her friends Lord Halifax and Walter Monckton to put pressure on the Home Secretary; Diana's mother Lady Redesdale had gone to Winston Churchill's wife Clementine, who had been a bridesmaid at her wedding forty years before, and had asked her to ensure at least that the facts of my father's illness were known to her husband. (Diana wrote that Clementine Churchill had 'infuriated' her mother by remarking – 'Winston has always been so fond of Diana'; also for suggesting that prison was at least protecting my father and Diana from the fury of mobs outside.) The Home Secretary Herbert Morrison took the decision to release my father and Diana in November 1943; there was immediate uproar from the press and from Labour MPs and trades unions.

Herbert Morrison explained to Parliament that he had chosen not to run the risk of 'making martyrs of persons undeserving of the honour' and so had 'substituted for detention some system of control approximating to house arrest'. He had done this because 'at this stage of the war.... I was satisfied that no undue risk to national security would be incurred'; also 'on the general principle that the extraordinary powers of detention without trial must not be used except in so far as they are essential for national security'. None of this meant much to some Labour MPs: one insisted that 'Mosley had been let out because of his social position'; another that 'this man used to go to Bethnal Green in an armoured car with a chauffeur ready to hit anybody on the head with a steel bar'. Ellen Wilkinson, loyally defending Herbert Morrison against what she called such 'mob-hysteria', was herself accused by the Distributive and Allied Workers' Union of being thus responsible for 'one of the greatest crimes ever perpetrated by an individual against the working class'. The *Daily Mail* commented that the Labour Party seemed to be 'struggling with its own confused complexes'. Arthur Greenwood was one critic of Herbert Morrison who made partial sense even if it was irrelevant: he said – 'Mosley has tried to destroy every kind of democratic institution.... and has made no public statement saying he has renounced his views'.

When my father and Diana were released they had to be smuggled out of the 'murderer's gate' of Holloway because press photographers had constructed a sort of grandstand outside the front gate. They went to stay in Oxfordshire at the house of Diana's sister and brother-in-law Pamela and Derek Jackson. The house was besieged by reporters: in London booths were set up on street corners in order to obtain thousands of signatures to advocate the Mosleys' reimprisonment. Various eminent people were lobbied for their opinions: Bernard Shaw was asked – 'Do you think it is too strong to say that the Home Secretary's decision is calculated to cause alarm and despondency among the masses?' He replied – 'I do not think your proposition is strong at all, it makes me suspect you are mentally defective.' Diana's sister Nancy wrote that she had only been able to squeeze through the crowds and get into her local underground station by joining a column of demonstrators chanting 'Put him back!' Diana's sister Decca, who was a communist, wrote an 'open letter' from America to their cousin-by-marriage Winston Churchill demanding that 'they should be kept in jail where they belong'.

The Home Office realised suddenly that Derek Jackson was a notable physicist as well as having been an RAF rear-gunner; he was at the moment doing secret research work for the Air Ministry. It was decided that thus he was not a suitable host for my father and Diana; they had to move; they went to a half-deserted pub in the Cotswolds, *The Shaven Crown* at Shipton-under-Wychwood. Here the siege by the press went on. It was reported that the Mosleys could not find domestic help because of the hostility of local people towards them; offers of help then poured in, causing my father to remark that they had been given '£50,000 worth of free advertising'. After a month or two my father bought a house at Crux Easton, near Newbury (Savehay Farm was still requisitioned). At Crux Easton the conditions of house arrest were quite stringent: my father and Diana could not move more than seven miles from the house, every month they had to report to the police in person, they were not allowed to communicate with any former member of the British Union, and all speeches, publications and indeed any form of political activity was banned. These restrictions remained in force until the end of the war in Europe in May 1945.

I wrote to my father:

November 22nd.   3CRU CMF
What exultation there was this morning when I read in an old news bulletin 'Sir O.M. was to be released for reasons of health'. I have

gone about ever since with grapes and vine-leaves in my hair ...

What are your plans? I long to know everything. I do so wish
I could be with you to enjoy the first fruits. We have been deprived
of so much time together, and it seems it will be further ages now
before we can finally escape the evils of this bloody war.

I have been plunging here and there into Plato with whom I am
very disappointed. He seems to spend his time in arguments to prove
that the Good is not the same as the Bad, and that the immortal
differs in many respects from the mortal ...

Meanwhile my programme is Rome by Christmas and Venice
by the Spring, where you must join me and we will revive the glories
of the Renaissance.

December 5th
The news out here arrives in the most unsatisfactory and unreliable
gusts so I am in ignorance about the latest developments in the great
public squealing-match. Yesterday I was visiting a friend in Army
Group HQ and thank God he had a very recent Hansard: but since
then there has been uncomfortable silence punctuated by rude letters
in the local papers from repressed corporals ...

In the meantime I am most fiercely engaged in a prolonged discussion upon eternal verities and practical politics with two refresh-
ingly intelligent people who, although they were inclined once to
think of you as the most horrible of ogres, and even now fight most
stubbornly against the penetration of my logic, have yielded enough
to give one hope that there are still sane people in the world. The
trouble is that they would really prefer absurd chaos in government
to organised system because they consider the one 'english' and the
other 'unenglish'. At which I give up. What is the answer?

I have read most of Zarathustra. There are bits of it that might
have come straight out of the New Testament ...

My father's release meant that now more than ever I wished to get
home: the reaction of people to his release had been so venomous that
it suddenly seemed difficult – with the war largely won – to put one's
heart into the triumph of this society. I continued my spasmodic journey
towards the front line: I reached the 2nd Battalion of the London Irish
Rifles just before Christmas: their headquarters were in a village called
Pietra Montecorvino at the foot of some of the highest mountains
in central Italy. While I was reporting to the battalion orderly room
my kitbag with all my clothes and bits and pieces was stolen, presumably

by villagers: I had left it in the street outside. This was a disaster of unimaginable proportions! we were already high up in snow and ice: now – good heavens – I would have no more comforts than anyone else! I joked to my sister: 'Oh would that we could take 50 hostages from the village and shoot them if the kitbag was not produced in 5 minutes!' My tin box full of books had survived. Literature suddenly seemed of less importance than clothes.

On my way up through southern Italy I had depended on books: I had been reading T. S. Eliot: I wrote in my diary: 'He casts spells with words but with meanings as well as with sounds.' I had found a few people with whom to discuss such things; but for the most part I had been on my own. Then suddenly with the London Irish Rifles I was writing – 'My Company Commander has actually read *The Mill on the Floss*!' and a day or two later – 'He began to quote "Footfalls echo in the memory ..." and with what delight did I carry on (not without error) towards "the door we never opened into the rose-garden"!' My Company Commander was a calm, authoritative Welshman called Mervyn Davies. He was some five years older than I. He became my friend, and in many ways my new mentor, until the end of the fighting in Italy. I wrote then of my relationship with the 2nd Battalion of the London Irish Rifles – 'My posting to this Bn in 1943 was a true miracle.'

With the London Irish Rifles I was with men who had fought in North Africa, Sicily, up through the calf of Italy: many of them were exhausted: I knew nothing about war. In front of us there were mountains nine thousand feet high; the Germans were entrenched some-where on the range in front; the immediate enemy seemed to be the weather. Our own front-line companies had been withdrawn because of snowdrifts and bitter cold; supplies had not got through, and men were suffering from frostbite. They for the most part had no special winter clothing – and I now had none either, with the loss of my kitbag. But, as is the way with armies, it was thought that morale could best be kept up by the sending out of patrols. Early in 1944 I wrote in my diary:

Jan 2: Big moment when I take out my first patrol; sweat up a snow-laden hill in the most brazen manner and slither down again à la Duke of York. Jan 3: Bigger moment when given baptism of fire by desultory shells and mortar bombs not close but a horrible whine as they drop overhead. Jan 4: Hellish day standing on top of a frozen hill covering G Coy while they dilly-dally with mules and two buriable bodies. Jan 5: Platoon and I on our own gibber in the face of blizzard for 4 hrs and I have seldom been in such desperate straits – except perhaps on Jan 6; which was a repetition of the day before, from 8–2.30.

There is a break in my diary for a fortnight. Then there is an entry – 'It is difficult to write retrospectively of an experience so horrifying and unreal and yet every minute of which I suppose I shall never forget.'

Some events do take on a portentous significance. For months now I had made my jokes – or were they jokes? – that the most sensible thing at this stage in the war would be to get myself taken prisoner: I felt this partly presumably because of what were obviously my split attitudes about my father (and my father's own complex attitudes to the war) but I had myself felt some despair at the people who seemed to get excitement out of war without being involved in the fighting – and indeed without stopping much to enquire what on earth the war was for. And so – why should one die for their stimulation and enjoyment? But as I got nearer to the front line it did seem that people had perhaps here some feel of what war was actually about: this was nothing to do with what was put out by politicians: in fact front-line soldiers seemed to have a contempt for nearly all politicians, and indeed for all those at any base who talked in bellicose terms. Front-line soldiers showed very little approval of the killing of the enemy: the front-line enemy in fact were held to be in much the same sort of predicament as they: what war was about to these people seemed to be some almost personal even if appalling test of endurance put upon all front-line soldiers just by the near-lunatics at home and at the base. This test had to be undergone, and some sort of personal victory achieved – why? but of course, this could not be put into words. If one began to try, then one would end up sounding like people at the base. Among the London Irish Rifles within a few days I got some feel of this: of course the war was bloody ridiculous! Who ever thought it wasn't! And of course all politicians and base-wallahs were power-maniacs and parasites – so what? There was some revelation to me in this 'so what!' If war was really an endurance test for some people to undergo and learn from with bravery and cunning and honour – indeed, yes, so what?

The platoon I had taken over was composed of Irishmen and English-men and Welshmen: many of them had been fighting for a year: they had been told repeatedly they might be going home; they found them-selves in arctic conditions among some of the highest mountains of

Italy. I was ten years younger than most of them; I was recently out from England and was not even from their regiment; there had been no time for them to get to know me nor I to know them. When we got back from our patrols to the village the officers retired to an upstairs room. There was too much tiredness for any effort that did not seem essential.

Then there was a day when the blizzard lifted and we were told we were to return to the positions in the hills. There was a two-hour trudge through snow-drifts: then the ruins of a dug-in tent with some shallow slit-trenches on a wooded slope. This was the foremost platoon position of the Company and indeed of the Battalion. The Germans were said to be across a valley half a mile or so away. We settled in – two men to a trench – the trenches three foot by six foot and about three foot deep; the ground was too hard to make them deeper. We could not move much by day or the Germans saw us and started shelling; mule-trains came up with provisions at night; food was carried to and fro in containers. Within the eight-foot-by-six dug-in tent which was platoon headquarters there lived and slept, as if in an igloo, myself, my sergeant, a wireless operator and a runner.

Every morning the section-leader corporals would come in from their outlying trenches for their orders. There was not much to say – Watch out for German patrols, keep your heads down, do not let your weapons freeze, do not let yourselves freeze, this cannot go on for ever. One or two men went back with frostbite. One wondered – would anyone be able to fire his rifle? But then – would the Germans be able to fire theirs?

One morning I was giving out orders to my three corporals and my sergeant all squeezed into the tent when the air went in and out suddenly as if an enormous noise had gone off in the sound-box of my head: it became apparent at once that almost everyone in the tent was wounded; I myself was covered with blood; I found out later that this blood was from my sergeant. It appeared that a German mortar-bomb had gone off either in or just outside the tent; there were other bombs going off; there were the sounds of machine-guns through the pine-trees. We knew the drill for this: we scrambled – we found we could move – to our action trenches; my sergeant tumbled into our trench in front of me; he crouched in the bottom face down, clutching his chest, saying over and over 'God have mercy!' There were noises, now, of men coming down through the trees on the left; more rifle and machine-gun fire; then a strange howling like that of wolves. White shapes flitted on the slope like ghosts. We knew the drill for this: I

yelled – 'Enemy through the trees, one hundred yards, open fire!'
Nothing happened. There had been no drill for this. I thought – Of
course, we have been taught how to give orders; we have never been
taught what to do when orders are not obeyed; such an event could
not be thought of; yet it is the one that most matters. More mortar
bombs and grenades were landing: I had a machine-gunner out at the
front and on the left. I yelled my orders again; my sergeant, beneath
me in the trench, said – 'Don't tell them to shoot, sir, or we'll all
be killed!' I thought – Well, that's what we're here for, isn't it? Then –
But this is ridiculous! I began to crawl out of my trench towards the
machine-gunner on the left; there had not been much room in the
trench anyway with my sergeant; I thought I might get the machine-gun
firing. I myself carried only a pistol: this again was what we had been
taught – officers only carry pistols, because it is their job to give orders
to men who have rifles and machine-guns and will fire them. I thought –
But did not the people who taught us this at the base in fact know
that it is ridiculous?

I had got about half way towards the machine-gunner on the left;
I was on my hands and knees like a St Bernard, my pistol hanging
from its lanyard round my neck. Then a grenade landed on the snow
somewhere beside me: it seemed to smoke: I went head first into a
snow drift. There was the air going in and out again; the ringing
of the bells in the head and in the heart. I used in later life to try to
think I fired at least one shot from my pistol: I do not think I did.
It was true, probably, that if I had, quite a few of us might have been
killed. As it was I found myself being yanked out of my snowdrift
by the lanyard of my pistol; there was a German in a white camouflage-
smock above me; I helped him to pull the cord of the pistol over
my head. I thought – This is really very shaming. Then – But all
this that is happening is just what I wanted to happen, isn't it? I am
being taken prisoner: I am apparently not wounded: I can spend
the rest of the war in a prison camp thinking about Goethe and
Nietzsche. Then – But of course I know, don't I, that I must try to
escape.

The Germans were huge red-faced men in white uniforms some
of them wearing snow-shoes and carrying snow-sticks. They were still
making their strange wolf-like noises – I remember wondering afterwards if they had been drugged. They were prodding at us with
bayonets; we were being herded into a column to be marched off over
the hill. There were five or six of us wounded; most of these could
walk. I began to complain to my men about why they had not fired

a shot. The Germans told me to shut up. I said, as if to no one in particular – Well, we must get away.

I had had the idea that I wanted to be taken prisoner because this made sense if the war made no sense: but what was happening now was deeper than any sense: there was some impossibility in the soul. I had always known, hadn't I, that if one could bring oneself to look, there were forces deeper than sense.

We were being led off in a long line over the snow-covered hills. If I did not quite know why I had to escape, certainly I did not know how. The Germans were these authoritative men like ski-instructors. There was still quite a lot of firing going on – from our own people somewhere back on the right; from the Germans giving covering fire from the left and front. But this was quite like one of the adolescent games I still liked to play; shouldn't I be quite good at it? I thought my best chance might be to wait till there were bullets or a bomb going off quite close, and then I would pretend I had been hit and roll dramatically down the hill. I lurked at the back of the column making out I was seeing to the wounded; then I put a hand to my heart, and fell. A German almost immediately came up and prodded me hard with a bayonet; I got up quickly. But I was still very ashamed: what had I been doing all this time thinking such things were a matter of words – war, and being taken prisoner?

I determined to make one more effort – to improve, perhaps, on my performance. I should hurl myself into my part like Macbeth; like Hamlet. When the next mortar-bomb landed close I took off, rolled over and over, I came to rest at the side of a rock some distance down the hill. I determined to try to stay there whatever happened. There were snowflakes in front of my eyes; their formations were so beautiful! There were the clear-cut mountains beyond. Some way ahead of me was one of our men who had in fact just been wounded: he was calling to me for help; I wanted to tell him – You fool, can't you see I'm dead? The German with the bayonet was coming down towards me: I thought – This time of course he will shoot me: it was good of him not to have done so the first time. There were lines from T. S. Eliot going through my head – 'And I have seen the eternal Footman hold my coat, and snicker, and in short, I was afraid.' Then the German was close to me and had the muzzle of his rifle pointing at me – he was this large, ruddy-faced man like a gamekeeper – and there was a thump – this was the first time I heard this thump – and the German put an arm out as if he were holding a flag and went down on his knees on the snow. What had happened, I learned later, was that my friend Mervyn Davies had been coming up in a counter-attack on the hills behind and he had shot the German at long range – an extra-ordinary shot, some two hundred yards. The German died a few feet away from me: he groaned, and then stopped. After a time I stood up. Most of my platoon and the Germans had gone over the hill: there were three or four wounded left behind. I saw Mervyn Davies in the trees: I waved at him: the mountains were very beautiful. Mervyn told me later that he had nearly shot me too, thinking I was a German. He had refrained from doing so only because he had not wanted to be involved in any more killing.

Some stage of my life ended here. Up till now there had been all the words – the idea that if human beings were ridiculous, oneself might not be. Now – what was more ridiculous than this idea! But some got away.

I greeted Mervyn: I helped with the wounded: I prepared my report for the Commanding Officer. Of course it was a bad performance that a young officer had lost the best part of his platoon at his first sight of the enemy: thirteen had been taken prisoner; three or four had not been rounded up at the beginning of the action. But still – I had been with them for only a few days; I had not trained with them; and I had myself got away. Beyond this – What I had felt, what had happened to me, how could this be put into words?

Some five years later when I came to write my first novel I tried to put something of it into words – in quite a different story, but trying to describe the same sort of thing. And of course the words are ridiculous! but what is it that happens when you know this?

War is too big a thing to think about from the outside when you are in it – you have got to accept it on its own terms, like the world, and not attempt to value it by some personal idea. To us it was a killing dying silliness but then the world was silly too; and we were part of it, the silly world, the dying people of Europe killing themselves and us killing them too – and we accepted it, the whole of it, and what thereby it entailed – you've got to fight so you might as well fight prettily, you've go to die so you might as well die prettily, you've only got yourselves to think about because the thing beyond you is entirely unthinkable so you might as well think yourselves pretty: that was all it was, and pride of course too; pride of the right kind, pride in pity, pride in pretty things.

CHAPTER 25

What Do We Learn?

I got a letter from my father written at the end of 1943:

> The Shaven Crown, Shipton-under-Wychwood.
> It is Christmas Day, and how I wish you were here – nothing was
> sadder than your absence on the first Christmas for 4 years. I have
> made a beginning with getting better, it will be a long job, wonderful
> the difference it makes getting out of that place. I hope soon to resume
> reading and thought with more capacity ...

> Darlingest Nick, I can never tell you what a joy to me it was to
> know you as an adult and to find what a perfect community of
> mind and spirit we had – to search together through all the higher
> and lovelier things of life – may the time come soon when we may
> be together again – in some happiness.

I wrote to my father (these letters were subject to military censorship):

> January 27th
> Your letters did much to save my life in the past month which has
> been something of a nightmare. The frightened 'porker' nearly fell
> a victim to the butcher's relentless axe; was actually being led away
> to cold storage when with many a grunt and shrill squeal he tucked
> his tail between his legs and ran. This is horribly obscure I'm afraid,
> but Viv may have been able to elucidate ...

> Ever since I began to live – since I surmounted the adolescent stage
> – I have been wandering like Shaw's Caesar 'seeking the lost regions
> from which my birth into this world exiled me'. I have found many

islands ... but was always without a home, until one day I went
to Holloway to visit a stranger and then I knew that I had found
the 'lost region' – and now I do not believe I can ever be entirely
unhappy again.

My father, it seemed, had exemplified to me (as he perhaps had to himself?) the feeling that war was a senseless game in which it might have
been rational for me to have been taken prisoner; but now – arising
perhaps from the ashes of this recognition – there was also a knowledge that there had to be an effort at commitment to deeper rules
if one was not to be trapped.

Some time during the winter my battalion left the mountains and
moved down towards Naples and the plain. I had been given a new
platoon largely of reinforcements like myself: I trained with them; began
to know them. I wrote to my father, 'I even have a corporal who
lends me his complete Shakespeare!' At first we were not allowed much
beyond the limits of the camp: there were rumours of the big push
towards Rome in the early spring. Then –

March 13th 1944
The other day I managed to wangle a trip into the city of the
'Vivien'. Having slipped away from my fellow visitors whose one
desire it was to drink the greatest possible amount of synthetic spirits
in the shortest possible time I wandered down upon the front below
the hotel in which we used to stay and on to the quay from which
we used to board the Vivien and sail happily across the sea-blue waters
of the bay. It was all much the same: Capri arose dreamily out of
the mist: I thought I could make out the cliff of Sorrento on the
opposite shore. The little restaurant on the quay where we used to
eat those delicious fish dishes was sadly battered, and there was none
of the old noise and gaiety; but I felt very sentimental and rose-
blown as I ruminated on the absurdity of our position in such serene
surroundings, and the futility of all worldly things.

This was the first of my sorties on leave or from hospital which were
the counterparts of the rigours of war. If wars had to be fought, Italy
seemed the place to fight in: there were enchanted gardens just beyond
the act-drops of squalor and fear.

The big push in the spring was held up because of bad weather:
at the end of March our battalion took up defensive positions on top

of Monte Castellone to the north of Monte Cassino. We climbed at
night in violent rain up a narrow rocky track that seemed at an angle
of 45 degrees; mule-trains both came down against us and tried to over-
take us from behind; war seemed, as so often, not against a human
enemy but against forces of nature. At the summit we took over from
Frenchmen who had constructed small stone shelters like hollow cairns;
they shook hands quickly and disappeared. When the light came up
there was the enormous and beautiful 14th-century monastery of Monte
Cassino on top of its mountain below: it was like some half-squashed
slug. It had already suffered the most destructive of the bombing attacks
made on it: every now and then as we watched more bombers would
float over: they dived down like seagulls above flotsam.

There had been the arguments – should it or should it not have
been bombed: what did one think about the bombing of any of the
marvellous buildings of Italy? Monte Cassino dominated the road to
Rome: Germans were said to be inside; later, there were said to have
been none. But there were Germans dug into the slope of the mountain
so what did it matter if there were none at the top? The point at issue
was – what did a regard for one of the great art-monuments of history
matter when put in the balance against the risk to even a single human
life? From our stone igloos on our mountain it did not seem to us,
looking down, that there was anything much to be discussed: of course
to us and to those like us our lives seemed more important; of course
to others, and in the future, they would not. Politicians and generals
would, as always, fit their arguments to suit their own fears and
ambitions.

Shells whizzed over the top of our mountain from the German guns
in the valley beyond; sometimes they landed just short of the crest;
sometimes they skimmed just over and down to the valley behind.
Once there was the sudden collapse of air again as if in a soundbox,
and it seemed that a shell had hit the stone roof of my igloo and had
bounced off and on like a flat stone on water. My sergeant and I sat
facing each other in our rocky hole with our knees almost touching;
we scooped cold stew out of tins and used the empty tins to shit in;
there were the jokes – could you tell the difference? At night we sometimes had to go out on patrol: there was this terrible army fantasy
about the moral virtue of patrols: we would go just over the crest
of our mountain and squat among the dead bodies and tins of shit;
we could go no further because of a precipice. We were like targets
for the shells that failed to go over towards the valley.

Then I was writing to my father:

April 17th

I am at this moment sitting on the beach 4 miles east of Amalfi
trying to decide whether or not to bathe. I think perhaps I shall
'milk it' for in April the sea-blue stream does not look too inviting
... I have been for the past 3 weeks on a bleak mountain until
yesterday when I tottered down in the small hours of the morning
and was the same day having lunch in Naples en route for four days
at this lovely village [Maori]. We stayed last night to hear the opera
in Naples – Bohème – which was on a grander scale than one would
find almost anywhere else in Europe. The transition from my bare
mountain to the bedside of the dying Mimi was almost too sudden
and I was near to tears with the poor Rodolfo.

I thought Ravello extraordinarily beautiful. Unfortunately we
were not allowed into the Rufolo Gardens – Wagner's enchanted
gardens in Parsifal.

Tomorrow I want to try to get to Paestum. Isn't it there that
there are the loveliest Greek temples outside Greece?

Then we were back training for the big push in the spring. Throughout the winter, troops had been slaughtered half-way up Monte
Cassino: there had been the landing behind the German lines at Anzio,
but this had been contained. It was decided now to try to block out
Monte Cassino with smoke and to attack straight up the valley underneath towards Rome. Why had this not been thought of before? My
father's old friend General Fuller wrote later that the winter battle for
Monte Cassino was 'tactically the most absurd and strategically the
most senseless campaign of the whole war'.

We were doing our training (I wrote to my father) 'in a beautiful
valley full of fruit trees in full blossom and lovely winding streams';
we were billeted on a farmer 'who was obviously a one-time gourmet
and he feeds us with eggs and bottles of red wine which we drink
solemnly from morn to night'. In training there was the problem which
had confronted me earlier so startlingly and which could now be studied
– that not of just how to give orders, but of how to ensure that they
would be obeyed. This seemed to be in the area of what could not
easily be put into words; it was to do with camaraderie; perhaps with
something like love. I now lived with my men in the stables of the
farmhouse: my officerly status was indicated by my sleeping-bag being
elevated to a manger. We went out on mountain-climbing schemes,
river-crossing schemes; we turned these into competitions with other
platoons like children's games. I taught them the actual children's games

I had played and we played these in the evenings – 'Lions in the Dark' was good training for night patrols. We spurred ourselves on in the river races by bellowing Paul Robeson's song from *Sanders of the River*: we made up a battle cry which was – for no known reason – Woo hoo Mahommet! We even evolved some private language by which, as at prep-school, our solidarity might be shown: in place of the ubiquitous word 'fuck' (I once questioned the driver of a broken-down truck, and he informed me 'The fucking fucker's fucked') we substituted the word 'waggle', with what seemed to be the appropriate attendant style – 'I say, just waggle over that hill, will you, and see if there are any wagglers on the other side.' We became a good platoon. I wrote to my father:

> The other day I heard two riflemen in my platoon bellowing at the tops of their voices the tune of the *'Horst Wessel'* with all the old words in English including the line – 'We'll fight for Mosley!' I was covered with confusion and have not yet dared ask them where they learned the words. They are very probably old members of the B.U., being extraordinarily pleasant and sensible men.

When the push began in May the 2nd Battalion of the London Irish Rifles were to be in the second wave as it was called to cross the River Rapido and to move up the Liri Valley. On the roads there were tanks with giant flails on cylinders at the front for exploding mines; iron rolls like bandages for laying across ditches. We were pushed off the road, we lay in fields, we waded across the Rapido River hanging on to ropes. There were shells whooshing overhead and a terrible sound we had not heard before – a vast moaning and shrieking in the sky as if from witches. This was caused by a multi-barrelled mortar said to have been invented by the Germans specifically to instil ghostly terror. We waited, as one so often waits in war, in hedgerows, in hollows; while people went to and fro trying to find out what was happening. I began to compose a poem. Was not this what people did in time of war? manipulating words, to try to make things orderly, to bring down witches.

> The cornfields wave towards the sky
> And from above the clouds reply
> With smiles of gentle sleepiness.
> Below the summer sun's caress
> Lies softly on the silent plains

> And deep within the sunken lanes
> The trailing thorns hang down to dream
> And slowly in the silver stream
> The leaves of weary willows drift
> And sway to lazy winds that lift
> The heavy heads of drooping trees ...

And so on. Casualties were coming back from the battalions in front. We heard that our Colonel had been killed, when he had gone forward on reconnaissance. The Monastery on top of its hill, on our right, suddenly loomed up out of the smoke: it hung over us, decomposed, a dead genie out of its bottle. Mortar bombs came down. There was machine-gun fire. Nothing much seemed to be happening.

> But Stranger, Stranger, don't you see
> Behind each crimson-tinted tree
> Within these hollow haunted walls
> And torn upon each thorn that falls
> So gently, gently, groping down;
> Beside the shining fields that crown
> The sleeping summer's brittle glare
> With ripples in the sun-swept air ...

I didn't like that line. I crossed it out. You could do this with poetry. Somewhere close to me there was a wounded German shouting – he had been hit in one of the first attacks – I was supposed to be able to speak some German, so I went to him in his ruined dug-out and held his hand. He poured out words to me; he was terribly anxious about 'das Brief'; I looked around and found what seemed to be a letter to his wife or sweetheart. I did not know what to do with this, he seemed to want me to read it to him. I tried to, but before long he died.

> That here one summer long ago
> The silent lanes did slowly flow
> With drops of dying hearts that bled
> And drained the dying to the dead.
> That here vain tears of frozen grief
> Once trembled on each withered leaf
> And hung from every tearing thorn;
> And out amongst the golden corn

Blind eyes did strain in vain to see
The light that mocked their agony.

Words, damned words: what were people doing with their poetry, their fine rhetoric? Did one think one could make war pretty? Would it not be better to shit on war?

During the night there were thousands of fireflies that got mixed with tracer bullets so that there were patterns in the sky like atoms and shooting stars: the mortars groaned as if the sky were protesting at having to receive back so many dead.

At dawn the next morning I was doling out food from a huge cauldron that had been carried to the edge of my hastily-dug trench; there were still stray bullets and bits of bombs dropping like dead flies; then as I stretched out my hand to take a second helping of food – I had apportioned it out to my platoon: there was a small amount left over: I thought, why not? – something struck me, very hard, on the wrist. I wondered – a bullet? shrapnel? nanny? I had in fact been wounded, it appeared, quite deeply in the wrist. It did not hurt much. I thought – I cannot be so lucky! Then – But is it quite bad enough? People gathered round to give an opinion. A bandage was put on; taken off; it was decided that I should go back and at least show my wound to someone at Company Headquarters. I found Mervyn Davies: I said to him – Do you think I should be one of those legendary heroes who are wounded but who carry on in war? He said – I don't know, should you? The doctor saw me and placed me, rather ostentatiously, on a stretcher. I was carried back to hospital.

On the afternoon of that day when our battalion at last made the attack for which we had prepared a German shell made a direct hit on the headquarters of my platoon where I would presumably have been had I not been wounded; the sergeant who had taken over from me and most of those with him were killed.

In hospital I thought – But one day I should try to put into words what cannot be put into words: what is chance, all right, you can look at it; but what is it that makes it work for you (is it just this looking?) or not?

Some three weeks later I was writing to my father –

June 9th
My wanderings have taken me into what I think is the most ex-hilaratingly beautiful place I have ever seen. You remember Ischia? – the lovely island opposite Capri which we visited in the 'Vivien'

and where the peasants welcomed us on the beach with smiles and
bottles of sweet white wine. How I got here I hardly know. Sufficient to say that my way from the hospital back to the battalion
seemed about to be so tedious that faced with a delay of ten days
at some dreary reinforcement centre I stormed up to the C.O. and
demanded leave. He complied with surprising readiness, only
stipulating that I would have to find my own accommodation. From
then on fate took charge. I arrived here yesterday evening from the
preposterous barrel of a steamer ... I was met by a smiling old man
who took me to a clean white room with a balcony that looks over
the sea ... the dinner I ate that night was such as I have not dreamed
of for years except perhaps in the noble precincts of Holloway. Today
I strode over the high hills that run along the centre of this island;
in Forio a crowd of children and old men gathered round me at
the café begging for cigarettes and hoping to humour me by saying
how wonderful they thought the English were and how they hated
Mussolini. I told them that I was a fanatical admirer of Mussolini
and a hundred per cent fascist, at which they at least stopped plaguing
me for money. One little boy broke into the lusty strains of *Giovinezza* until he was hustled away by an outraged policeman. I wish
you were here to enjoy it with me.

In Naples I met up with some old Rifle Brigade friends and there were,
I rhapsodized to my sister – 'exotic bathing parties in the gardens of
the Winter Palace of the Kings of Naples at Caserta; parties in limpid
rock-bound pools surrounded by classical statues and pink champagne'.
We went sailing from the harbour at Posillipo; each night there was
the Opera. For my twenty-first birthday on June 25th we planned 'the
Borgia of all orgies'. Then as it turned out I spent the day in a train
in a railway siding on my way back to my battalion. I wrote to my
father – 'But I am not sorry ... I need a little quiet rest at the front
after the bewildering hilarity of transit life.'
     I told him how the day before I had at last managed to get to
Paestum.

I determined to make the pilgrimage thither from Naples, some 60
miles hitch-hiking over comparatively unfrequented roads, which
meant that I arrived on the scene having walked the last 3 miles
in the heat of the day. I came across the first temple quite unexpectedly rising rather bleakly from the bushes and long grass by
the side of the road. In the suddenness of the discovery I think I

was a little disappointed: it was such a cold and desolate ruin; the pillars looking rather thin and forlorn under the golden heat of an Italian midday sun. But then as I wandered up beneath the grey portico I caught a glimpse of the second temple – the only temple that really matters at Paestum – a glimpse of gold more golden than the corn which shone about it, more serene and beautiful than any concentration of Italian sun. I rushed towards it in an ecstasy of wonder.

I had expected to rejoin my battalion somewhere near Lake Trasimene and to continue with them fighting up through Italy. Instead, in my railway siding, I heard rumours that they were on their way back and I was advised to wait for them in Rome. Rome had been taken by the Allies some three weeks before: there was still an air of celebration. Myself and a South African officer who was also waiting for my battalion went sightseeing. I thought – All this haphazardness goes on like particles in the brain: they rush hither and thither: then suddenly the shape, the thing, is there; you know it exactly. My friend and I managed to attach ourselves to a party of American Roman Catholic padres who were on their way into the Vatican to have an audience with the Pope: we veered off down a side passage before our credentials could be checked; we found our way to the Sistine Chapel. There we had been lying on our backs looking at Michelangelo's ceiling for some time before the Swiss Guards came to chuck us out.

CHAPTER 26

A Fairly Ordinary Kind of War

The letters that my father wrote to me during 1944 have become lost: I carried them with me all through Italy; after the war he asked me if he could have them back because he wanted to use them as material for the philosophical chapters of the book he was then writing – *The Alternative*. He said he would return them to me later: he never did. The relevant chapters in *The Alternative* however give some distillation of these letters.

The questions left somewhat up in the air after our talks in Holloway were – can one look upon life as something that humans can push into shape by efforts of will, or does life in fact very largely go its own way and efforts to push it are counter-productive? And if this is the case, is not the best a human being can do to try to understand it and only by this (but in no certain way) influence it?

In one of his last letters to me of 1943 my father had quoted the passage in Eckermann's *Conversations with Goethe* in which Goethe is recorded as saying – 'It would have been a poor joke for God to have brought together this coarse world from simple elements and to have launched it rolling through the sun-rays of the centuries if he had not had the plan to found on this material basis a plant-school for spirits.' This, in later life, became something of a motto for my father: it was a basis for what he referred to as his 'doctrine of higher forms'.

At the very end of his life (1979) my father said in a letter to his biographer Robert Skidelsky that he had 'come more and more to believe that my main contribution to thought will be the "doctrine of higher forms". In *The Alternative* (as in the lost letter of 1944) he wrote of this doctrine and of what he saw as man's function as a result of it:

We believe that it is now possible to derive from the actual evidence available in the world some idea of the pattern of God. It is possible not only to discern his presence in the elaborate laws which govern the mechanistic universe, but also to perceive something of his purpose and method in the assisted evolution of striving man against that causal background. The very factors which appeared in earlier knowledge to deny that purpose, now confirm design and reveal method. The brutal ways of nature 'red in tooth and claw' are, in fact, necessary to stimulate into activity any elementary form of existence; and they persist, in some degree, in the great catastrophes of humanity which is not yet ready to advance in harmony with the natural purpose by strength of the spirit . . .

To what end is the whole great purpose directed? *Ex hypothesi* it must be impossible for finite mind to comprehend the infinite: it is enough to discern sufficient of the purpose of God on earth to be able to place ourselves at the service of that aim. It is certainly clear that the purpose, and the proved achievement, of this will on earth is a progressive movement from lower to higher forms. When we assist that process we serve the process of God; when we oppose it, or seek to reverse it, we deny the purpose of God . . .

We must deliberately accelerate evolution: it is no longer a matter of volition but of necessity. Is it a sin to strive in union with the revealed purpose of God? Is it a crime to hasten the coming in time of the force which in the long, slow term of unassisted nature may come too late? We go with nature: but we aid her: is not that nearer the purpose of God than the instinct to frustrate?

My own letters of this time left philosophy somewhat in abeyance: there were too many impressions coming in; of terror, wonder, uproariousness: whether or not one stayed alive – what luck! In order to put oneself in the way of luck, was there anything better that one could do than to be receptive to impressions through one's eyes, ears, mind; to impose plans, would be a distortion of reality.

When eventually I joined up with my 2nd Battalion of the London Irish Rifles I found that they were on their way back to Taranto in order to embark for the Middle East for a period of re-equipment and – for them – well-earned rest. It seemed to me that I was indeed having a miraculous war. I wrote in code to my sister about our probable destination – 'I have got Gippy Tummy'; or, more obscurely – 'Do you know a woman called Maugham?' (see page 241 of *Rules of the Game*).

We landed in Egypt and went to a camp between Cairo and Ismailia on the Suez Canal. Here a life of sailing, sightseeing and cricket continued. I wrote to my sister: 'The Sphinx has a pile of sandbags under her chin which gives her the appearance of suffering from tooth-ache.' To my father:

> There is an interesting officer in my company who before the war was an active communist. He is intelligent and very reasonable, and when we feel earnest enough we talk of this and that, and the more we talk the less is the difference that I can see between the con-ceptions of the communist and the fascist corporate states. But then the only training I have had in the theory of fascism has been the pamphlets that you sent me when I was to debate upon the subject at Abinger Hill.

Also:

> I think the Hellenists of the 18th and 19th centuries shrank from the acceptance of 'horror' in nature because they did not realise what far greater potentialities for horror there are in the *un*natural man. To a sensitive spirit of this generation the ruthless sense of doom in nature is not a quarter so horrifying as the miserable sense of futility when in contact with the 'unnatural' man of the present day. Anyone who has fought in the last 2 wars must realise this. It is incredible that there are sane men who believe that by renouncing natural life they can alter it or be immune from it.

When front-line troops were 'resting' it was the custom that they should be given a certain amount of licence: this was their recompense for having been in, and being about to return to, active war. During the summer several of my Rifle Brigade friends had been killed: survivors felt their turn might soon come; junior officers were especially vulner-able in a comparatively small-scale war like that in Italy. What I remember about our six weeks' rest in Egypt were dinners under fairy lights in the garden of Shepheard's Hotel; a nightclub on the Cairo race course round and round which I walked holding hands with a girl called Kitty and talking, I suppose, about the metamorphosis of the natural man from the camel to the child. In Alexandria one was apt to come across King Farouk in a nightclub and one would sing in chorus 'King Farouk King Farouk hang your bollocks on a hook' until there was trouble with either the Egyptian or the military police.

Towards the end of our stay tempers between soldiers and the local populace became so inflamed that there was a small riot in Cairo in which windows were broken and trams were overturned. It was said that men of the 78th Division (of which the London Irish Rifles were part) were to be sent back to Italy as some sort of punishment; but there are always such conspiracy theories in war.

I had been kept in touch by my sister with events at home: Vivien and Micky had been to stay with my father and Diana at Crux Easton: 'we all went for a vast picnicking bicycling expedition: Daddy looks quite wonderful with a pair of clips on his trousers and an ancient degraded cap turned back to front like a butcher boy'. The feud rumbled on between my father and my Aunt Irene – 'Daddy is terribly bitter about Aunty Ni ... he says he offered to have her as joint guardian but her reply was she could not be joint guardian with a person whose political views she so heartily disapproves of and for this he will never forgive her ... I think Daddy is a trifle unfair because I do happen to know for a fact that it was the Wards in Chancery people who approached her first with the project though she as usual did not do things too tactfully.' There was a weekend at which Vivien took down to Crux Easton my two great Eton friends who were both back in England with wounds: 'We all sat around till 3.30 a.m. listening to Poppa discoursing fascinatingly upon the theme of Wills to (a) Comfort (b) Power (c) Achievement – Superman to the Child and so on – with a spot of Democracy v. Fascism thrown in.'

When I landed at Taranto again at the end of September I wrote to my father: 'I am not really sorry to be back ... I hope soon to be able to visit Florence and Pisa and Siena and perhaps in a little while there will be Venice or Nice.'

There were now Rifle Brigade battalions in Italy and there was some demand that I should return to them: I made a formal request to stay with the London Irish Rifles, which was granted.

The front line had got stuck in almost as high mountains as those of the previous winter, this time between Florence and the northern plain. We were once more in trenches three-foot by six with rain filling them up and the sides falling in and ourselves not being able to move out of them by day: by night we slid about on patrols and sheltered behind haystacks and the rotting bodies of cattle. There were outbreaks of dysentery and malaria: this was a time when both men and officers were apt to go to their superiors and say that they could not go on. There was not much anyone could do about this; we were in the last winter of the war; such people were just sent back to some job or

other with which they felt they could deal. There was no evidence
that if some people were allowed to do this, everyone would: front-line
war was a battle with personal pride anyway. Every two weeks or
so we went back for a few days rest in a camp of tiny bivouac-tents
in the valley. I wrote to my father:

I have been reading with a certain amount of concentration lately
– quite a lot of Shakespeare and Ibsen – it seems to me that their
greatness as artists depends upon the fact that they were neither of
them ardent philosophers, thus they produce art for art's sake, even
Ibsen, who is careful in his plays never to solve the problems he
creates – or if he does, to contradict his first solution in a later play
– using social and moral-spiritual problems merely as a framework
for his art. This leads me to wonder if philosophy and art can ever
be reconciled – in Goethe, perhaps, you would say? But I've also
read Shaw's *Back to Methuselah* and his theory of creative evolution
fascinates me: he proposes that man can surpass himself when once
his desire and his will are strong enough ... but this is really too
facile a proposition ... man will need vast painfully-acquired wisdom
before the 'transvaluation of all values' can be achieved.

The situation in the mountains was that the allied armies had nearly
broken through to the northern plain before the onset of the autumn
rains; but now, largely because of the diversion of forces to the rather
unnecessary landing in the South of France, we were suspended once
more in country where armoured vehicles were unusable and even
infantry could move up and down the precipitous escarpments only
with the greatest difficulty and at night. Sometimes on a fine day we
got a glimpse through to the flat ground somewhere around Imola:
this was our promised land: when we got there, we felt, the war would
be over.

There was a day in October when the army commander thought
that a last effort should be made to get through to the plain before
the onset of total winter: following the belief that no one could move
by day, a divisional attack was planned for night. For two nights the
London Irish Rifles were part of a diversion within this attack; we
slid down chasms in driving rain and could not get up the other side;
we were shot at by machine-guns firing on fixed lines from the flanks.
We did not know where the enemy were, we did not know where
we were ourselves, we did not know who was being shot at by whom.
Several of our officers were killed; one, the South African with whom

I had gone sight seeing in Rome. When we retired we learned that the larger attack had failed because there was a ruined farmhouse on the spur of a hill occupied by the Germans from which with their machine-guns they could dominate two or three valleys.

It seemed that either this plan to break through to the plain had to be abandoned or there had to be a change from the convention that one could not move by day: in darkness, people simply gave up. There were conferences at Brigade and Divisional level: it was seen that in any case nothing further could be done until the ruined farmhouse, which was called Casa Spinello, was taken. The Brigadier sent for the Colonel commanding the London Irish Rifles: the Colonel sent for Mervyn Davies. In a letter that I wrote shortly afterwards to my sister I said – 'They conferred: and Mervyn, to his everlasting credit, declared that he would take Spinello with his company alone, that he could do it in daylight, and that moreover he could do it that very afternoon.'

That day the rain had stopped. We had moved to trenches slightly on the reverse slope of our hill. We were standing up and trying to clean our weapons when Mervyn came along with a look both grim and apologetic and said to me, 'I've got an MC job for you.' This was a phrase used to describe a task for which, if it succeeded, one would probably be decorated; and if it failed, one would probably be dead.

The plan was that first my communist friend who was called Desmond Fay should go out on a patrol with just his sergeant and try to capture a prisoner at Casa Spinello in order to find out how many Germans were there: then my platoon would attack and try to take the farmhouse at 4 o'clock in the afternoon. Then the rest of the company would come up and consolidate.

Desmond carried out his part of the plan brilliantly: he got to the outbuildings of the farmhouse without being seen, grabbed a sleeping German out of a trench, and ran back before anyone knew much what was happening. The captured German said that by day the farmhouse was held by about thirty men.

My platoon was now down to about fifteen men; the rest were sick. When I gave out orders the plan did seem crazy: we were to try to do on our own by day what a whole division had failed to do by night; we were just to walk out, and then run, and hope – what? – that the Germans would not believe that anyone would do anything so crazy? It was true that many of them would be sleeping by day; but after Desmond's patrol, would not they be alerted?

Some time before the attack one of my corporals began to cry in the bottom of his trench and said he could not go on: I was put out by this for a time: then I said it did not matter.

When four o'clock came Desmond Fay led us out along the route he had reconnoitred that would enable us to get to within about a hundred yards of Spinello without being seen from the farmhouse: we could, of course, be seen by the Germans on the hills beyond. Desmond was a short sturdy man with close-cropped hair who usually had a cigarette dangling from his mouth; he led us along the side of a steep slope of shale; one walked by putting one foot in front of the other; one kept going. We knew there were also our own people watching from a hill behind – the Brigadier and the Colonel, like Napoleon with his marshals. I suppose I had worked out that something like this sooner or later had to happen: I had been very lucky so far in war: perhaps I was lucky even now (I was becoming expert in working out how all was for the best in the best of all possible worlds) to have this chance to balance the rather inglorious events of my being captured at my first sight of a German and then being wounded just before the big attack in the spring. After a few hundred yards Desmond indicated the brow of the hill on the left beyond which was Casa Spinello. I crawled with my men to just beneath the top. So far, no one had reacted to us.

I remember fear quite well: it is quite different from pain, which one cannot remember. Fear is the feeling that there is something that may not be able to be borne.

When I gave the order to start running – I had been a good quarter miler at school – it was obviously in my interest to get across the open ground as quickly as possible. I was pleased to see how close the farm buildings were – not more than a hundred yards – they were mostly rubble; there were holes in this into what might be dugouts. I was carrying a Thompson sub-machine-gun (the days were long past when I felt properly armed with an officer's pistol); I could not see any Germans; when I looked back my platoon seemed unnervingly far behind. I yelled to one of my corporals, 'Come on, McClarnon!' He – a short-legged man – yelled back, 'I'm coming as fast as I can!' I reached the rubble of some farm buildings. The main farmhouse seemed to be one of those constructions on a slope where the ground floor at the back turns out to be the first floor on the far side. I was moving towards this first floor rubble when grenades started landing all around; a German popped out of one of the holes; I shot and missed; my other corporal, Corporal Tomkinson, shot and hit him. There was a voice which started shouting, 'Don't shoot Johnny! Play the game Johnny!' I called to McClarnon to look after the people in the farm buildings: Tomkinson and I ran on. We arrived at the first floor of the farmhouse and now there did begin something indeed like one of the catching games I had played as a child; the Germans were apparently on the ground floor below us with their entrance on the far side; when Tomkinson and I tried to get round on the right we were shot at; but if we did not get round, they could throw grenades at us continually from the far side. We tried to get round to the left where there was a hole through to the ground floor; when I peered down this there were three Germans peering up at me. I was very frightened and fired first and wounded one or two but then I ran out of ammunition (afterwards I was glad) and I watched them run or crawl slowly out of an opening at the far side while I changed my magazine. Tomkinson and I tried to get round on the right again and we threw one or two grenades at what seemed to be the entrance to the main dug-out on the ground floor; but there were bullets flying off the stonework from the hills behind and my magazine was once more empty; and then a German came out of the dug-out and fired at me at what seemed to be point-blank range; I disappeared round the corner of the house with a leap, as I described it in a letter to my sister later, 'like that of Nijinsky in *Le Spectre de la Rose*'. Tomkinson stayed for a while shooting back; then I gave orders that there were to be no more sorties to the far side.

We stayed on our first floor, crouched behind the skeletons of walls, and wondered what the Germans would do in their ground floor below. Once they started firing up through floorboards and we were all leaping about like people in the red-hot bull of Phalaris: then we fired back and there were cries again of – 'Don't shoot Johnny!' I tried to explain in my bad German (why does one insist on trying to use one's foreign languages?) that we would not shoot at them if they did not shoot at us (what were the conditional or subjunctive tenses?).

By this time Mervyn had arrived with the rest of the company; he tried to get round to the far side; he was wounded; he lay on the rubble. I tried to get him on to a stretcher; he said he would go back on his own. It was vital that he should arrange for reinforcements. I watched him hop away on one leg like a bird – straight through what later turned out to be a minefield. Reinforcements coming up later walked into it, and did not get through.

There was one German who from the beginning had been trying to get himself taken prisoner: he was going round smiling and nodding to everyone and people were telling him for goodness sake to shut up.

It was now becoming dark. We had settled down on our first floor; we suddenly felt confidence, even exhilaration. During the night I think two or three counter-attacks came in: once the Germans crept right up to the walls of the farmhouse and shot one of our men through a window: then grenades were flying about like crockery again and everyone was firing – I now had ten machine-guns in the small building and it seemed there was no question of anyone finding enough room to break in – one man had lost his spectacles and was firing straight up into the air with his machine gun – we were all yelling our war-cry – Woo hoo Mahommet! After a time, everything became quiet again. I counted our men. Out of the whole company we seemed to have only twenty fit men and ten wounded who could not be moved. But no one seemed to have been killed. There was some exhilaration in this.

The question remained about what would we find on the hills beyond in the morning. If we were successful in our attack, another large-scale divisional night attack was supposed to have gone in which, it was hoped, could now succeed because there would be no cross-fire from Spinello. But if this large-scale attack had not succeeded, we would ourselves of course be hopelessly exposed to counter-attacks in the morning. During the night we heard noises – comings and goings – but we did not know of whom. When light came up we were standing at our windows like lonely pioneers in Western films waiting for the view of Indians – or cavalry. As our paper-white faces became visible there were, yes, figures on the hills beyond: they were moving too openly, surely, for them to be enemy: we were confident enough to try a small cheer. And then we stepped out into the thin morning air. Around the right side of the house where so many of our men had been wounded there was the entrance to the main German dug-out; the body of the German who had shot at me at point-blank range was lying blocking it; we pulled him clear. I called to anyone left in the ground floor to come out. There emerged twelve men one by one like wasps out of their hole; they were most of them wounded. We sent them back with our own wounded. Then we stood about, not really doing much, in the cold bright air. We were told to dig trenches, to consolidate the attack which had so well succeeded; but we could not be bothered to do much about this. That evening we did the long march back to the valley where there were our bivouac tents. I remember resting half way with my seven or eight remaining

men and being told by some senior officer to get up and get on. I
told him to fuck off. There was this sort of aloofness now from both
fear and exhilaration; but what had been the style of our achievement?
In my account of this battle to my sister a month or so later I wrote:
'I find it hard to believe it was I who did all these peculiar things ...
I have yet to meet a man who fought well because he believed in the
cause for which he was fighting ... it is always pride that incites and
succeeds in war.'

CHAPTER 27

Peace

The war in Europe lasted another seven months: I did not get home
for nearly another year. After the battle of Casa Spinello the war became
a matter of endurance – could one or not, and in what way, hold on.
Nothing much in terms of the war was achieved by the battle of
Spinello; we took one more ridge; we did not get through to the plain.

The Battalion stayed in the mountains until the new year: we were
sometimes in tents; sometimes in the trenches filling with water and
surrounded by the rotting bodies of cattle. I had one four-day leave
in Florence when I bribed my way into the barred and bolted Museo
Nazionale and stood gazing at the outside of the crates which contained,
I was told, sculptures by Donatello. I wrote to my father: 'My Rifle
Brigade friends live in a lovely villa on the outskirts of the town whither
they invite the decaying remnants of the Italian nobility who are
amusing for a while but eventually become horribly tedious.' Then
I was in the mountains again where I 'constructed for myself a pleasantly
secluded little dungeon about 7ft by 5ft and 3ft high where I hibernate
for 24 hrs a day communing with the muses and concocting grotesque
dishes of tinned food over a tiny petrol fire and beating off the savage
assaults of rats'. What was terrible about this time were the continuing
night patrols: a game was played with the higher levels of command
about these: absurd orders were given – that one should penetrate miles
behind the enemy lines over ravines and rivers and so on – what one
in fact did was to tip-toe down paths which were likely to be mined
and festooned with trip-wires just as far as where one might reasonably
say one had been 'held-up' – 'reasonably' being what one knew would
seem acceptable to higher command. I remember one flat stretch of
road in a mountain valley where there was a bridge over a stream
almost exactly half way between the German positions and ours:

typically, each side was convinced that this bridge had to be in its hands by nightfall though it was abandoned by day; so when evening came each side would prepare a patrol for a complex sort of race to the bridge: if you started too early it was still light and you got shot up; if you started too late the other side would be there first and you got shot up. I remember becoming increasingly demented about this bridge: when the nights came round for it to be my turn to do the race I began to think again – For God's sake, is it not possible to find some way by which to give up?

There was an interval just before Christmas when we were in another part of the mountains and the days became clear and bright and in the valley in front, somewhere in no-man's-land, there was a farmhouse apparently deserted by human beings but which seemed to teem with turkeys and chickens and pigs: they could be watched through binoculars; we were hungry. There was a man in my platoon who claimed to be a butcher; he suggested – why not take down a small patrol – he would do the job quite silently – and there was our Christmas dinner! After a time (such is gluttony) I agreed to this: myself and five or six volunteers set off with the self-professed butcher; we arrived at the farm; our expert crept into the turkey house; after a time the turkey house exploded as if with shrapnel: birds came out in every direction pursued by the butcher with a bayonet: someone suggested – Shoot them! I yelled – No! Eventually we got two or three birds with rugby tackles. They were enough for a Christmas dinner.

There was one man in my platoon who was an ex-jail-bird from Belfast whom I had thought it best to try to keep under some slight supervision by making him my personal runner: we got on well together: he would procure for me mysterious perks. Once when we were about to move off from our tented camp to the front line and we were being inspected by the Brigadier he, the Brigadier, stopped in front of my runner and said, 'And what's wrong with you my good man?' and my runner said simply, 'I'm drunk!' Another time in the front line and in a fairly perilous predicament I told him to take some message and he refused: I said, 'Obey my orders or I shall shoot you!' – He tore open the front of his battledress and said, 'Shoot me sir!' I said, 'Oh, all right!'

Then there was a day when we were on our mountain and I watched our Colonel coming slowly up the path with his adjutant behind him and they were like some religious procession and I thought – Oh well, I think this is all right. The Colonel told me I had got the Military Cross for the battle of Casa Spinello, and so had Mervyn Davies and

Desmond Fay had got a bar to the M C he already had, and Corporal
Tomkinson had got the Military Medal and Corporal McClarnon had
been specially mentioned. I thought – Now, will it not be easier to
give that shutting-up look to people who inadvertently make remarks
about my father?

Then in the new year we were back at our road with the bridge
in the middle and I was thinking – This is all very well, but what
does happen if one cannot bear it? There was a hayloft in which I
sometimes slept and I remember wondering if I could fall from this
with one leg carefully placed under the other so that it would break:
this would be more aesthetic than the traditional shooting off of a
toe or a finger. Then one morning I found I was shaking; this seemed
too pleasurable to be with fear; I thought – Can I again be so lucky?
I went to the Medical Officer and he said I had either malaria, or
jaundice, or both. So I was in a luxurious ambulance once more,
bouncing back over mountain roads with a temperature of a hundred
and three, and so happy to be off again on one of my Grand Tours.

From a convalescent home at Sorrento which was in the very hotel
where I had stayed with my father and Diana and my sister in 1936
I wrote a 21-page letter to my sister on what I thought or hoped
I had learned from the war:

> I went into it with certain pompous opinions about my virtues and
> capabilities but amongst them were absolutely no pretensions that
> I would make a good soldier. I thought that all business-minded
> men would be 100 times better at organisation than myself, and I
> thought that all the eager hearties who seriously believed in the
> righteousness of this war would be 100 times more brave. After
> twelve months in Italy I realised that I was wrong: I did not under-
> estimate my own abilities, I overestimated everyone else's. And this
> startles me considerably; for I, as you know, consider this war a
> blasphemous stupidity, and yet in a spirit of unwilling desperation
> I have put more into the winning of it than most of those who
> say they consider it a holy crusade against the powers of the Devil.
>   I still do not think I have any pretensions about myself as a soldier.
> When things are not dangerously active I am intensely and professedly
> idle. Every minute I have to give to this war I grudge angrily. Even
> when things are dangerously active I go about my business in a spirit
> of complete misery. And yet I have the reputation of being in action
> a model subaltern . . .
>   It is interesting to note that after 12 months of fighting I will

forgive anyone the old failings, the boorishness, the stupidity, the dullness, if he does not possess the failings of a bad soldier. That boils down to the realisation that out here the only thing that matters tuppence in a man is his ability to be brave. That is the only standard by which one judges anyone. For if they are not brave, it is 10 to 1 that they are miserably hypocritical as well.

Now there are incredibly few people who do possess this virtue. Those who possess it least are those who preach most lustily about the holiness of the war crusade. Fortunately in my Battalion nearly all the officers do possess it: they do not remain long if they don't; and that is why I am able to get along very well with them whereas before I would have been driven into my frenzy of petulance by their shortcomings. But this breeds tolerance for people who are fundamentally worthy: the war is a great head-sweller to the few who fight it but it produces a lofty, cynical, benign swollen head – which does not rant or strut and still maintains an almost reverent humility towards anyone who knows why and whereof it is swollen. So although you may find me complacent I hope it does not take too odious a form. On the whole I think the tolerance and humility with those who understand will be far more prominent than the other feelings. But you will find out!

After Sorrento, I found myself once more in what I described to my sister as 'the full gaiety of the Naples winter season'. The Transit Camp seemed to have lost my papers; I came across my friend Anthony who was back in Italy after a time in England recovering from his wound; I rented a flat in Naples where we stayed high up in one of the tall narrow streets with the washing festooned across it like flags. There were expeditions to Pompeii and Herculaneum by day; Gigli and Caniglia were said to be coming to the Opera at night: if there were no seats one could usually squeeze into the orchestra pit or the Royal Box. My old friend from Retford days, Raleigh Trevelyan, also recovering from wounds, wrote from Rome that now there was even better social life there: 'I exchange pleasantries with Marchesas and dance on polished floors to the gramophone with Ambassadors' daughters: every Friday I partake of tea and scones with the Princess Doria ... The Vestal Virgins are preparing a new bullock, snow-white, to sacrifice in your honour; the priests of Dionysus are already weaving garlands to adorn the pillars of the temple.' He added – 'How unfashionable you are supporting Gigli: you'll be a social failure in Rome.'

In Rome I missed Raleigh who had moved on to Florence. I caught

up with the London Irish Rifles on the eastern edge of the northern
plain at Forli. It was by now the end of March 1945. My return coincided
with a delayed St Patrick's Day celebration and everyone got very drunk.
I wrote to my father:

> I still wonder at my good fortune at finding my way into this
> Battalion ... The Rifle Brigade was all very jolly in the insouciant
> days of Winchester and York, but out here I think I would have
> been stifled by their so carefully posed artificiality of decency. Here
> the atmosphere is almost Dionysian ...
>
> When I went away in January I left behind my little translation
> of Zarathustra with earnest instructions to one and all that they should
> read it before I came back. To my surprise I find that they have
> followed my instructions to such good effect that the talk which
> floats around the Mess at dinner time is no longer of the obscenities
> or military pomposities to which one had become resigned, but is
> full of erudite allusions to Will and Power, Superman, Feasts of the
> Ass, etc; which, although no one knows very well what he is talking
> about, I find most comforting. It is surely unique to find the Mess
> of an Infantry Battalion that discusses Zarathustra?

From Forli we set off to play our part in the big last offensive of the
war in Italy. A toe-hold had been established on the east of the plain:
the London Irish Rifles were to work with a regiment of tanks and
push west through something called the Argenta Gap. The people we
were to work with were the fashionable 9th Lancers; in them were
some old Etonians I knew; we eyed each other warily. The infantry
were to be carried in armoured personnel carriers – a platoon of infantry
to each troop of tanks. When the going was straightforward the tanks
were to be in charge and go ahead, and then when they came up against
anti-tank opposition they were to stop and give covering fire while
the infantry took over and went round a flank and wiped out the opposition. This was my one experience of comparatively large-scale war
such as it must have been in France or Russia; tanks drove fast over
flat ground with dive-bombers overhead; these latter could be called
up on the radio and would swoop down like hawks on recalcitrant
opposition. It was not all easy: once one of the neighbouring troop-
carriers was hit by an anti-tank shell and there was a sort of thin shower
of flesh and bone: there were the times when we were out on foot
again and stumbling along ditches with the vision of trip-wires and
mines. But what I remember best is the awful, heroic feeling of being

a conqueror – the Italians coming out from their farmhouses cheering and with bottles of wine; the Germans in columns with their hands up. Of course, there must be some reason why young men have so often liked going off to war.

The business of prisoners became difficult: the advance was often held up by the problem of finding anyone to escort them back. On the second or third day the Tank Major who was in command of our Infantry Company at the time told us that we were taking too many prisoners: did we understand? this was an order – we were taking too many prisoners. I think one of us – probably Desmond Fay – quietly spat. And of course, we went on taking too many prisoners.

I wrote to my father:

It is a happier form of warfare than any we have done before but I find it exhibits the most unfortunate characteristics of one's nature. I actually find this conquest and pursuit faintly enjoyable – and at last understand the fatal temptation of aggression. But nevertheless it is for the most part tedious, and I am irked by the feeling that the end ever remains the same distance from us even as we advance.

There was a day, however, on the edge of Ferrara when more than ever there were crowds coming out with garlands of flowers; bombers remained circling overhead as if satiated: the German dug-outs were empty except for the litter of old love-letters and the smell of stale bread. And on the wireless from Germany there was perpetual music by Wagner. The war was over.

I wrote to my sister:

Kennen Sie what victory means? It means at the moment I am the tempestuous possessor of three cars – a Mercedes which goes at such horrific speed that I am terrified to take it beyond second gear, an Adler saloon that cruises at 60 without the slightest indication it is moving, an open Opel which streaks hither and thither to the desperate confusion of all stray pedestrians. It means that we dine on champagne each night except when we feel leerish enough to start on the brandy with the soup. It means – oh well, so much really beyond cars and wine that I suppose that they are of an infinitesimal insignificance.

But then almost immediately it seemed that another war might break out; we suddenly journeyed (with our fleet of cars) to Udine, Tarvisio,

Villach – to the borders of Italy and Austria and Yugoslavia where
there were Italian partisans fighting Yugoslavian partisans, Tito partisans
fighting Mihailovic partisans, and the vast Russian army looming somewhere in the background and rumoured to be considering – dear God!
– continuing its march westward. There was a night when we drove
for miles to somewhere I think near Graz and came face to face with
some Russians; they were solid-faced men in uniforms that seemed
always a size too small for them; they had the ability to show absolutely
no emotion whatsoever. Then we were removed from Graz as suddenly
as we had come. We came to rest by a beautiful lake in Austria called
the Ossiachersee. One of the buildings in our occupation was a ware-
house full of the liqueur called Schnapps: a neighbouring battalion was
rumoured to have captured a mobile mint which printed money. I
wrote to my father:

> The end of the war seems to have been the occasion for Chaos to
> reign ... We are in Austria – in some of the most beautiful country
> I have ever seen (and with some of the most beautiful inhabitants)
> and although we have little or no trouble with the local people who
> receive us with bountiful grace and charm, we continually find our-
> selves surrounded by such a rabble of Serbs, Slavs, Croats, Creoles,
> Czechs, Chetniks, Chindits etc. as resembles the Tower of Babel on
> a sweaty afternoon. It has been a situation of extraordinary interest;
> too complex to allow me to scribble down my impression of it in
> this hasty fashion; but some day I might be able to tell in suitable
> words of the consummation of the great Tragedy.

We were close, in fact, to the area where there were being rounded
up those Russians and their dependants who had fought on the side
of the Germans and who became known in later years as the Victims
of Yalta: they were to be returned to Russia according to an agreement
at the Yalta Conference; in Russia, there was the likelihood that they
would be shot. The London Irish Rifles were not involved directly
in any of this; some neighbouring battalions were: soldiers were ordered
to push protesting women and children into cattle trucks – some did;
some simply did not. There was at least one commanding officer in
the 6th Armoured Division who went up to his assembled prisoners
and told them for goodness sake to bugger off. The orders from the
top were terrible and daft; but then so many orders from the top in
wartime are terrible and daft, and it is up to people on the spot to pay
such attention to them as they think proper. This principle was
established later at the trials at Nuremberg. The situation in Austria

at this time was not easy for people at the top; some efforts presumably had to be made on paper to sort out chaos. The London Irish Rifles were engaged in trying to dig out high-up Nazi officials and members of the S S. I wrote to my father:

> I am acting second-in-command of the Company which entails endless flap and fuss and as I am the only officer who can speak a smattering of German I am continually handed out to be jabbered at by some miserable suspect. We have had some quite melodramatic scenes in the rounding up of such political and military personnel as are wanted by the authorities. Also much amusement. The local chawbacons are amazed at the way in which the British Soldier tends to dissolve in laughter during situations of the utmost gravity.

There was something life-giving in this laughter: there was also the memory of my father's prophecy that even if we won the war there would occur precisely what we said we had begun the war to prevent – the overrunning of Eastern Europe by a potentially hostile and an aggressive power. This prophecy was now coming true: so was this an occasion for laughter? I sometimes began to think it was. Human beings seemed to involve themselves almost inevitably with catastrophe: there was still the question of in what ways catastrophes must be learned from – even in what particularly profitable ways, just by their being catastrophes.

I wrote to my father:

> My admiration for the German forbids me to believe that they will ever rest so long as we are in their midst. Will we then have to resort to such savagery as they were driven to in the countries they occupied? The folly of it all! Are not pride and honour the Dionysian curses on mankind?

But I was wrong: out of the catastrophe something in fact had been, could be, learned.

All through this time my father had written to me his encouraging, discursive letters: he had followed my fortunes in the war: he had been pleased at my MC. I had few doubts that when I got home I would feel myself still close to him. I had felt myself changed by the war of course: there was something that I had learned about the life-giving qualities of ordinary virtues. But then – would not he too have been changed? He had said he had wanted to have a period of learning.

CHAPTER 28

Homecoming

House arrest ended for my father with the end of the war in Europe: my sister wrote to me: 'I arrived home from work one day to find Daddy squatting in the sitting-room – his first visit as a free citizen to London for 5 years! It was a lovely surprise.'

In a letter to me of 11th May 1945 (the first one preserved after the batch that has been lost) my father said, 'I have been suffering early stirrings of a book: what are the pains of women in childbirth compared to such a moment! I thought of including in it some of our themes, which might indeed be a book in themselves.' He added, 'It is my silver wedding day today – 25 years from first marriage. I thought so much of you all.'

The first book that my father wrote at the end of the war was called *My Answer*: its purpose was 'to justify our position in the past', not to 'provide a policy for the present or the future'. It consisted of a 20,000-word *Essay in Foreword* and then a reprint of the 1938 *Tomorrow We Live*. His aim was to show that he did not need to retract anything he had said before the war (he was reported in the press as saying somewhat cryptically, 'My opinions have not changed: indeed, they have developed'): he claimed that what he had written in 1938 had been justified by events. And indeed a year after the end of the war in Europe Winston Churchill was saying, 'This is certainly not the liberated Europe we fought to build up,' and my father was commenting that to such remarks he 'should merely write Q.E.D.' In *My Answer* he went back over other old ground: he quoted a speech by Lloyd George in 1900 – 'Is every politician who opposed a war during its progress necessarily a traitor? If so, Chatham was a traitor, and Burke and Fox especially; and in later times Cobden and Bright and even Mr (Joseph) Chamberlain.' My father described the activities of himself and other members of British Union at the time of the outbreak of war as those of a man 'whose old mother expresses her firm intention to go down in a fighting mood to the "local" where a number of tough characters are wont to assemble: he will be alarmed ... his disquiet will in no way be lessened by the fact that his old mother has seen fit to arm herself for the occasion with nothing more formidable than an umbrella and a shrill tongue. He will do his utmost to dissuade her ...(but) when the inevitable row begins he will do his utmost 1. to protect her; 2. to extricate her as soon as possible with the minimum possible hurt ... What an appalling conception that the son should be the first, when trouble begins, to stab his old mother in the back!'

My father suggested, following on from the study of psychoanalysis that he said he had been able to make in prison, that the reason why the charge of treachery was foisted on the British Union was because the Labour Party suffered guilt from the early days of their own movement – this guilt was to do with their 'early associations with Russian interests'. What had been objected to about British Union was not so much its attitude to the war, as its National Socialism. This★ –

could be suppressed, and its protagonists silenced in prison, by the whispered suggestion that they must be traitors to their country because they thought the war was unnecessary. We were at war and this was the excuse for everything. Any little man who had ever failed to answer our argument and never dared to meet us in public debate could stand with 'security' the other side of prison bars grimacing his defiance and jabbering his insults. Every little man with a 'hush-hush' job could flatulate his innuendos over the cocktails which he could never afford in such inspiring quantities when his own abilities in business had to pay for them instead of a salary provided by the tax-payer. What a chance for every mediocrity and dunce on the fringe of politics; for every little 'Tadpole' and 'Taper' to strut his little hour! ... Fine was that evening and deep the heady draughts of 'democratic' wine – when Stalin was so matey and the supplies were getting through to Archangel!

This was the style of my father's feelings; it represented something of what I had felt myself about people who flourished in the politics of war. But there was something numbing in the idea that he might have nothing to retract. In Italy and then in Austria I had continued

★ *My Answer.*

to write my letters to my father about the things which, when he was in a benign and non-political mood, he would say mattered to him more than anything else in the world.

I am vastly interested in this physicist/philosopher controversy ... I agree with you that surely there can be no reason to suppose that human will is subject to physical laws; but do the physicists allow such a thing as luck? I feel one can bait a physical determinist by such a homely example as the toss of a coin – many vital decisions have been made through the toss of a coin: can the force of a thumb-flick be foretold by the knowledge of the background of the flicker?

It appears that the physicists have indeed done away with the old theories of matter and energy and have arrived by scientific means at much the same conclusions as Berkeley and Co hazarded in the 18th century ... The point I find fascinating is that the universe as we know it cannot be composed of ultimate matter and energy but only as the reflections of ultimate reality in some Universal Mind; and that we are only able to see these reflections as reflections again in our own minds. Now this is a very acceptable conclusion ... it does at least suggest that the Universal Mind has some affinity to our own feeble minds; thus giving us an enormous significance in the universe, when before it seemed as if we were of no account.

I think that if I get out of the army before I am 23 I shall go to a university and read philosophy for a year or so. I think it will be necessary to study quietly in some erudite backwater in order to reorganise one's thoughts after the chaos that war has produced. Or do you think the process of reorganisation could be more profitably performed in the octagonal room at Crux Easton?

In Austria we lived on the fringes of our beautiful tree-encircled lake: we had had to give up our cars but – 'riding is now the thing: I love galloping feverishly along straight tracks in woods'. I continued my conversations with my communist friend Desmond Fay. When he had entered Austria he had expected to find a people brutalised by Nazism; what in fact was there was an atmosphere like that of an idealised socialist state. We were billeted next door to an orphanage: the children were the most beautiful anyone had seen; the place was run by women of such calm, clear-eyed dignity that we, the conquerors, found ourselves behaving as if bowing and clicking our heels. Desmond Fay of course knew I was the son of Oswald Mosley; we had not talked of this directly until we reached Austria: then Desmond said – 'Ah yes, but Mosley, he was after all a serious politician!' Some time later I let slip the news that I was an Old Etonian: I don't think Desmond ever quite forgave me for this. To him a fascist, however much an enemy, was still within some recognised pale: but an Old Etonian!

From the Ossiachersee I went on leave to Venice; I stayed on the Lido where we had been as children in 1930 – in the summer holidays with Bob Boothby and Randolph Churchill and Mrs Guinness. I found it suddenly impossible, I wrote to my father, to do any more sightseeing: all I wanted was to come home.

I wonder if Nietzsche's final madness was really the decadent desperation that people suppose – if it was not perhaps 'tragic' in the ultimate sense – the culmination of a tragedy in the true Greek style – and therefore something to be greeted and accepted with a 'holy yea-saying'? Is anything much known of Nietzsche's final madness? It is a theory that entrances me – that perhaps it is the ultimate culmination of all 'great spirits' that they should appear to be what the rest of the world calls 'mad': that perhaps this one form of madness – the Dionysian madness – is really an escape into the 'eternity behind reality': neither an advance nor a regression in life but just a side-step into something that is always beside life. Or am I slightly mad?

It seems to me that the physicists have argued themselves out of their original premises and are floating blindly ... If all our sense-perceptions, measures, observations etc are unreliable, indeed misleading, when it comes to interpreting the 'real' world, why do they presume that any experiment they make has any bearing on reality at all? The only thing they can be certain about is that they can never be certain of anything ...

It seems that the Infinite only makes itself known to the finite by means of selected symbols or 'emotions' (which are really perhaps only the result of symbol-action): it is beyond the comprehension of the finite (human?) mind to understand the reality behind these symbols. But this does not exclude the possibility of creating – through a fuller understanding of the symbols – a higher form of consciousness which might ultimately glimpse the reality that lay behind.

At Ossiachersee there were rules about non-fraternisation. There was one very pretty Austrian girl who used these rules to play an expert fraternisation/non-fraternisation game: most of the young officers were a bit in love with her. Perhaps I was myself: but there were the hang-ups from Eton, from the tart who had been like my grandmother, even perhaps from the travelling exhibition about the dangers of venereal disease which followed us up through Italy with huge warning photographs like the Eumenides. There was a night in Naples when a friend and I went with two nurses on to the beach; but I still did not seem to have a proper hold on this game: did or did not No No really mean Yes Yes? Life was more simple as Narcissus.

I became Battalion Sports Officer, which meant that I could pick myself for any team: I could open the bowling at cricket and go in second wicket down: I could make out I was at home in basket-ball and hockey. The one game in which I could get away with none of this was soccer, which was taken seriously; I picked myself for the opening match and had to substitute myself after ten minutes. I was still able to justify myself in the job occasionally by my prowess at athletics; but then I entered myself for the 440 yards at Army Games at Klagenfurt; I was in a heat with the champion of the Jewish Brigade who had once run at the White City; I kept up with him for about three hundred yards, then retired from athletics altogether.

During the spring I was in correspondence with my father and sister about what would happen to the family after the war – where would we live, who would live with whom according to who were and who were not speaking to one another. My sister now had a flat in London; my brother Micky was at prep school and spent the holidays with Aunt Baba or in houses rented by Aunt Irene; my father said he did not want to go back to Savehay Farm, he wanted to buy a proper working farm and had his eye on one at Crowood near Ramsbury in Wiltshire. But he was adamant (my sister wrote) that he would not take up again any responsibility for my brother Micky. This was a mystery: did Micky remind him of my mother? or was it just that responsibilities for children, as opposed to dreams of being responsible for the world, were for him too close to reality's blood and bone? This seemed more likely as time went on and his attitude to his children became clearer: it was a measure of the peculiarity perhaps of his children's vision of him that they took it for granted he was too removed from mundane matters to take much responsibility for them. And so – was it not up to my sister and myself to make some sort of home with Micky, together with Nanny and my mother's old lady's maid Andrée who had been waiting loyally in the wings during the war and who previously had done so much to make life bearable for us? But it seemed vital to me that I should be with my father. In the spring of 1945 he bought the

1,000 acre farm at Crowood and planned to manage it temporarily at least by coming over each day from Crux Easton: it was arranged that for that summer Vivien and Micky and Nanny and Andrée would all move into a part of the house at Crowood that was empty and thus would have some contact with my father. On the periphery of all this were my Aunt Irene, still not on speaking terms with my father, and my grandmother 'Ma', as usual brought in to try to keep the peace. But there was some story now about Aunt Irene and Aunt Baba not being on speaking terms: I could not make out much of this from my lakes and woods in Austria: there apparently had been some dramatic confrontation in the corridors of the Dorchester Hotel, and my Aunt Irene had gone to recuperate with the wife of the Dean of St Paul's. My sister Vivien and I were apt now to see ourselves as arbiters amongst people who seemed sometimes slightly possessed: she wrote to me, 'You and I are what might be deemed the body of the octopus with all these tentacles stretching out'. I wrote to my father, 'I wish furiously that I could be home to organise the various family divergencies.'

Then on July 24th –

I shall after all see Crux Easton before you go. I leave the Battalion on July 30th en route for home and 4–6 weeks leave in England; after which I shall, unhappily, have to go to the Far East; but that at the moment seems such a remote contingency that it does not worry me a jot. The authorities declared that I was eligible for Burma – just, by three weeks – having been slightly under the prescribed limit of two years abroad; and as such I have to go, and nothing that any kindly C O., Brigadier etc. out here can do can stop me.

As it happened I received the news with something like relief and would not now alter the arrangement even if it were possible. I have been growing moribund in Austria, with the harassing job of organising sports from the confines of a stuffy office. Leave I am sure will miraculously revive me.

So fatten the calf and assemble the chawbacons in preparation. I certainly could have been given no better time for leave. I should arrive about the middle of August and will have all the end of the summer holidays to play with. And with Nursery World settled at Crowood, the family can be combined without the tiresome need of splitting the leave between two camps. It will indeed be a heroic month.

The idea of seeing you all once again is really too great for me yet to assimilate.

I am saddest about leaving the Battalion, which is unique, and had for me achieved the almost impossible of making war tolerable in any circumstances.

I set out on the long and now familiar road through Florence and Rome to Naples: at Naples I and my companions waited for a ship. We were sitting one day on a terrace overlooking the bay when we read in the local army paper that a bomb had gone off in Japan which was a new sort of bomb – something to do with what goes on in the heart of matter. It might indeed be so fearful that future wars would be impossible. The Japanese were already talking of surrender: so millions of lives, including our own, might be saved. Of course, the cost was the tens of thousands dead at Hiroshima. But was it not about just this sort of thing that it was impossible to talk?

We sailed for home on August 22nd and arrived at the end of the month. I caught a train from Liverpool and arrived at my sister's flat in the evening. There was a message for me to come on to Crux Easton – 'The room over the octagonal awaits you.'

I do not remember much about the first few days of my homecoming: perhaps, as I had said, there was something too great for me to assimilate. I arrived in the middle of the night: I have a memory of everyone – my sister was there too – in the kitchen in their dressing-gowns giving me eggs and coffee. My father and Diana looked absurdly young: they were in their pretty, rather bourgeois house: we were behaving as a family! Everything was so correct: I hardly knew how to deal with this. I could not talk about anything much that had happened to myself. I would say – I'll tell you one day.

We spent much of that summer holidays getting the harvest in at Crowood; this was before the days of combine harvesters (a year or two later my father was proudly one of the first possessors of one in Wiltshire); we would follow the cutter round the large fields and pile up stooks; throw them up later on to the cart for the thresher. It was a fine summer and we worked in trickling heat; we rested against dusty sheaves for picnics. All the children were there – myself and Vivien and Micky and Alexander and Max and Diana's two elder children Jonathan and Desmond. We were like Bacchanals and Cherubs: my father and Diana were Zeus and Demeter.

We would shoot the rabbits as they came out from the last circles of corn; we would later in the year embark on more formal shoots – my father must have been the only landowner in England at that time who had a black gamekeeper. I do not know how this occurred

– perhaps he had come with the estate. He was a West Indian: he organised pheasant and partridge shoots as if they were something like a carnival. He would say that my father was almost the only white Englishman he knew who did not seem to notice his colour. My father of course inevitably was still something of a taboo figure locally: not many people would come to shoot. There were one or two ex-military neighbours; and my friends, and friends of Diana who had not been involved in politics. There was a Swedish painter called Mogens who once wandered up on the wrong side of a hedge (the gamekeeper – 'Keep back dere on de right!') and was shot, somewhat harmlessly, in the thigh by one of my friends. Mogens went to the local doctor to have the pellets removed; he returned and announced, referring to the pellets (this was one of my father's favourite stories) – 'I still have one ball left!'

There would be the meals at which my father would hold forth as he loved to hold forth on his favourite themes – the world as a training-ground for spirits: the difficulties attendant on the vision that good can come out of evil. There was something so bright and assured about him that he held people entranced: the shooting-colonels and Swedish painters were entranced: my friends, who had expected – what? – stayed on and on to listen. He was like a dynamo switching lights on in people. Occasionally there was a brief fuse: a neighbour would ask a question about Hitler or Streicher perhaps: then what, in such circumstances, could be done? This was a time when the worst stories of German atrocities had not yet come out: there was not much news about the extermination camps, which were in territory overrun by Russia: the news was of Belsen and Dachau, the horrors of which could just conceivably and to some extent be explained by the disease and starvation resulting from the chaos and bombing of the last stages of war. There would be just a flash from my father's eyes; a guillotine look from Diana's bright blue ones. The people who came to dine at Crux Easton and Crowood during these months were mostly friends of Diana's and my father's from very old days – John Betjeman, Gerald Berners, Daisy Fellowes. With them the talk would go off into fireworks of laughter. Sometimes these friends would bring friends of theirs who did not know quite what to expect: there would then be some wariness again; people sat on the edges of chairs as if my father might swoop like Dracula.

From Crux Easton or Crowood I would go to London where parties were starting up after the war: I suddenly became aware – what on earth had I been aware of before? – of girls, of the ubiquitousness of

girls, of girls pink and white and massed like flamingoes. A year before
I had been writing to my sister – 'Can it be true that you and I are
really immune?': now it seemed not only that of course one fell in
love but how was it possible to fall in love with only one girl at once?
Love was a condition, surely, of either nothing or almost all. At these
parties I was like a donkey dashing between dozens of equidistant
bundles of hay: not like my father – the excitement was not in conquest; it was more like some stumbling egg-and-spoon race. But I began
most earnestly now to want to stay in England: there could be no
delights equivalent to this even in the Far East. But also what had
happened, what was to happen, to my determination to set up in some
alliance with my father? My feelings towards him had not changed:
it was just that these seemed to have moved into an area in which
there were no prospects.

One night in London in the ballroom of some enormous hotel
I met, at the bar, a man who looked and indeed behaved like someone
in an Evelyn Waugh novel: he was a Major in a fashionable Scottish
regiment: he asked me what I was doing nowadays. I said I was about
to be sent to the Far East. He said – What on earth do you want to
do that for? I said – I don't. He said – Then come and see me tomorrow
at the War Office. In the morning I did not know if he would
remember me – we had both of us been quite drunk – he was in a
not-very-grand office behind a desk. He said – I don't think I can get
you anything in the War Office, but would Eastern Command,
Hounslow, do? I said the Eastern Command, Hounslow, would do
very well. So some days later I got a notice saying I had been taken
off my draft for the Far East and I was to report to Hounslow where
I would become a Staff Officer. I could travel out each day like a
commuter on the underground.

In the Far East my friend Hugo Charteris was editing an English
newspaper and was trying out his short stories on the Javanese; my
friends Timmy and John were running a radio station and were filling
in time by reading their own poems to Sumatrans. At Hounslow of
course no one had expected me ('I suppose we can find you a desk')
and at first I had nothing to do so I thought I would try to write
about the war; but I found I could not write; there seemed to be no
traditional way to make sense about the war, people wrote about it
as if it were comedy or tragedy but it was neither (or was it both?);
some sort of style had to be found by which absurdity might yet howl;
horror might stop by being made ridiculous. After a time I was given
a job which was to do with officers' pay and courts-martial: what I

remember about this was the filing cabinet marked *Confidential* of which I sometimes had the key: in this were the files and the photographs (who on earth had taken them?) of officers who had been caught as transvestites. There were so many of these! I wondered – if there were more, might wars be fewer? people might thus work out their fantasies? But for the most part I sat and dreamed of girls: there was the terrible anarchy of these images: when let loose (or not let loose) what powers they had! did not victims end up bemused and dazzled somewhat like the transvestite officers? And what tenuous connections these images had with the forces of clarity and will that my father so rationally went on about: did he really think he had been immune personally from anarchy?

CHAPTER 29

'The Alternative'

The book that my father wrote after his apologia *My Answer* was called *The Alternative*: it was his statement about the future. He took care to emphasise that it was not a programme for a political party. 'This book is written by a man without a Party as an offering to the thought of a new Europe. Deliberately, I refrain from forming again a political movement in Great Britain in order to serve a new European idea ... All such ideas have originally been stated by individuals with nothing to sustain them except the power of the spirit.' This idea was to be 'beyond both Fascism and Democracy'. The book is written sometimes in the apocalyptic style my father had been using just before the war, but which had been in abeyance while he had been in prison.

At this time no other is in a position to state any real alternative to the present condition of Europe. The existing rulers of the earth are responsible for this darkness of humanity; they stand on the graves of their opponents to confront the Communist power of their own creation ... So I must give myself to this task. My life striving in the politics of Britain made known my name and character: my voice can now reach beyond the confines of one country because it has been heard before. The past has imposed the duty of the future. I must do this thing because no other can.

The idea was that Europe should be formed into one Nation and that this Nation should regard, and use, Africa as its 'estate'. Africa should provide the raw materials for a Euro–African closed economic system: 'trusteeship' of Africa should be 'on behalf of white civilisation and not on behalf of a nominal stability of Barbarism'. But in order to run this vast estate without the sort of barbarism which, it was admitted,

white men had been apt to practise before, a 'new' type of white man
was required; this was a concept similar to that of the 'new' man seen
previously as necessary for the proper working of the corporate state;
but in *The Alternative* the need for such a man is stressed even more
clearly. 'The mass of the people can only share in the benefits which
modern science can bring through the devoted service of those whom
they entrust with the task of government ... to secure that system
they must not only create a system of state, but must also produce
an altogether new and higher type of man who is dedicated in whole
life and purpose to the service of the people and the State. The latter
is by far the harder task'.

This higher type of man might be produced, my father suggested,
by a programme of 'breeding, selection and environment' such as can
be imposed on a species of animals: also – 'to these three factors a
voluntary movement to evolve a higher human species would add the
great fourth factor of training, or education, which, for all practical
purposes, is not present in the animal sphere'. No details of the sort
of training envisaged are given: in general – 'We require the union
of intellect and will ... we must give robustness to the intellect and
reflection to the will ... the genius of Greek civilisation consciously
sought that balance and harmony'. Then there might emerge 'a
Thought-Deed man who will be capable of high service to the people in
the conception and execution of great design ... The future is with the
Thought-Deed man because, without him, the future will not be. He is
the hope of the peoples of the world. His form already emerges from his
thought, in an idea which has been derived from theory and practice.'

My father saw the prototype of this Thought-Deed man as himself:

In the long years of prison and arrest opportunity was given to read
what the psychologists have to say ... In an earlier period I had
opportunity to study most leading statesmen of the world at first
hand which is an advantage lacking to most psychologists and men
of science ... In our system of ideas a Leader is appointed not by a
committee as in 'Democracy' but by the test of nature which is his
capacity to attract a following and to achieve ... My life is now dedicated to an Idea which transcends the diurnal politics of normality ...
I have very many friends in many places who will be ready to listen.

What had prevented the 'Thought-Deed man' coming to the front
before, he suggested, was 'the curse of the English' – a mixture of
Puritanism and the Oedipus Complex. Puritanism was 'that cold, dark

sickness of mind and soul' which had 'bent, twisted and deformed for generations the gay, vigorous and manly spirit of the English'. The Oedipus Complex of the English was exemplified by the desire of 'sons' to drag down anyone who might be a 'father' to them: Englishmen turned to leaders such as Lloyd George and Churchill in times of crisis, but afterwards 'the desire becomes overwhelming to destroy the strength to which they so recently looked for protection'. All this was due to the fact that the English, living on an island, had been protected by water from the necessity of choosing strong leadership: they had become tools in the hands of 'Mob' and 'Money' – 'Mob' being people such as communists who wish to drag down 'higher things' in order that in the resulting chaos they themselves might exercise power; 'Money' being those international financiers whose usury flourishes also in conditions of social disorder. Thus communism and capitalism, super-ficially at loggerheads, in fact go hand in hand to defeat the forces striving for a higher order.

In the last war the forces of order that Mob and Money defeated, my father suggested, were those of Nazi Germany. Nazi leadership had wanted an orderly Europe run by Germans and an orderly British Empire running world trade: if British leadership had wanted this too, then Mob and Money would not have been able to defeat them. Of course there had been roughnesses in the initial stages of the Nazi attempt to impose order; but these would not have come to such a head if there had not been a war in which the development of orderliness was lost. There was no evidence that Hitler had wanted world domination: how could anyone want this unless they were mad? And how could Hitler have been mad, when he had achieved so much in so short a time? For do not mad people destroy themselves?

The part of *The Alternative* where self-contradictions are most evident is where my father, having said all this, then describes graphically how Hitler did in fact seem to be mad; how there was something in him that seemed to set about destroying himself.

> The German leadership during the war ... appeared to violate every principle of realist policy ... History presents no more extraordinary phenomenon than the attitude of the German leadership towards the forcing of a quick decision with Great Britain ... All the evidence seems to suggest that the problem of invading Britain was never seriously faced and in requisite detail was vetoed by higher political direction ... The mystery deepens to the point of the inexplicable ... Did some extraordinary sentimental consideration traverse the

mind of German leadership to the destruction of every realistic consideration? ... It is one of the tear-laden paradoxes of history that
the man whom the mass of the English learnt to regard as their greatest
enemy cherished a sentimental feeling towards a 'sister nation' which,
in the eyes of historic realism, must border on the irrational and,
in the test of fact, was pregnant with the doom of all he loved. This
view seems too fantastic in such circumstances of life-or-death
decision to permit any credence; but it appears to be supported in
large measure by the sober testimony of diverse German General
Staff Officers.

But if my father saw that this sort of pattern was apt to be the case
– that forces dedicated to the promulgation of power by rationality
seemed almost blindly to fall prey to even stronger forces of irrationality
and self-destruction – what on earth was he himself doing in continuing
to advocate the need for power to be exercised just by such rationality?:
might this not be his own form of wilful self-destruction? He said that
he had made a study of psychoanalysis in prison and indeed he used
Freud's image of the Oedipus Complex to castigate others; but he
refused to admit that such insights could be turned towards himself,
and indeed for the most part he was dismissive of Freud as being
exaggeratedly materialistic. In *The Alternative* he was more appreciative
of Jung – 'the most outstanding and comprehensive intellect that the
new science has yet produced': but he was wary of Jung's more recent
work – 'the weight of years and pressure of current circumstances later
dimmed that great contribution'. Perhaps he had come across Jung's
lecture on Hitler and the Germans (quoted on p. 72) which had recently
(November 1946) been published in *The Listener*, in which Jung talks
of the probable appalling consequences of the inability of people to
learn how to deal with their own shadow.

I myself now could not make much of this: my father's apocalyptic
style was sometimes as evocative of strange stirrings as had been his
speeches: but it seemed to have less and less to do with what human
beings were actually like; it did not seem to have much indeed even
to do with the day-to-day manipulation of power. In *The Alternative*
my father said that he thought he and his ideas would win simply
because 'the power of God in nature is now with us'. (There is a lot
about God at the end of *The Alternative*.) But had my father not learned
from the war, and from everything that he and I had been talking
about for years, that the power of God in nature is not only to do
with order and rationality and light?

My father was of a generation that was perhaps instinctively dismissive of psychoanalysis. But one of the intellectual and imaginative interests he had in a heartfelt way at this time was concerning Greek literature. A favourite play of his was *The Bacchae* of Euripides: he would tell the story of the play in his best epic-narrator style. Pentheus, King of Thebes, and Agave, his mother, have denied the divinity of Dionysus the God of darkness and of passion and have insisted on the rule of order and light. As a result Agave becomes a wild and unconscious devotee of the dark god: Pentheus too is drawn to watch his mother in her savage and secret rites; she and her followers catch him, and tear him to pieces. There is a speech in the last scene in the play where the script has been lost: this is where Dionysus himself seems to be trying to bring reconciliation between darkness and light. My father loved to speculate on what this speech might have contained: he would say – Synthesis; eternal synthesis! But then – why was there no feel in *The Alternative* of a person's own darkness being faced; of the vital need for the bringing of this to light? It is as if my father felt the force and beauty of such terrors and efforts in literature: he imagined that politics could be swaddled in some sort of cocoon.

He continued to lead his life of a country gentleman farmer. The house at Crux Easton was given up; he moved to Crowood. He was proud, as his grandfather had been, of his herd of shorthorn cattle; he studied the latest techniques of undersowing corn for grass. There was an air of extraordinary elegance and benignity about surface life at Crowood: my father had spent £100,000 of his money on his fascist party in the thirties; he used to say he made up this amount by speculations on stock markets during and just after the war. The house at Crowood had an eighteenth-century front and a later drawing room with high windows at the back; here were Diana's pale blue wallpaper and French Empire furniture; a huge and very beautiful Aubusson carpet. There were a cook-and-housekeeper couple and a housemaid who did the chores of the house from a servants' wing; outside, were a gardener and the gamekeeper. I remember a ritual of going down with my father to the cellar to decant very old claret; we would carry candles and a bit of muslin; we were conspirators again, like Guy Fawkes. I could still talk with my father and Diana about literature more profitably than with others of their generation; Diana introduced me to Proust; she would tell the story of how she had tried to get my father to read Proust but had given up when, after he had dipped into the first volume, he said he didn't see much in a story about a young man having an affair with his servant Françoise. What I remember my father reading at this time was Karl Popper's *The Open Society and Its Enemies* which was just coming out: my father took delight in the fact that academic recognition seemed to be being given to what he had for so long proclaimed – that Plato's *Republic*, for instance, was some sort of blue-print for the fascist Corporate State.

But by force of circumstance there was something cut off, marooned, about my father and Diana: it was mainly friends of a somewhat bizarre sophistication who visited them; my father came across little serious intellectual challenge to his flights of oratory at the dinner table. Certainly I myself at this time was too tongue-tied and between two worlds. Such intellectuals as did meet him seemed not to know quite where to start; his mental defence works were so idiosyncratic, so powerfully self-contained. Also, perhaps it suited people to see him like this – not to have to take him on at the verbal sword-play at which he excelled.

Once two airmen from a local RAF station came and knocked on the door at Crowood; when Diana answered the knock she found the airmen backing away; they explained that they had done it as a dare – they had expected to find thugs in jackboots.

My father showed little bitterness about what had happened to him in the war: he sometimes became depressed about the future. Diana cherished him and protected him from both past and future: she created a garden with him in the present. They would seem very loving together: they had their rituals: when my father was disappointed he would sometimes put on a mock baby face and Diana would run to him and put her arms around him and he would pat her, laughing over her shoulder. This might have been in some sense babyish; it was also some recognition of what human beings were actually like.

But there had always been the mystery of how someone instinctively sophisticated in areas of personal life could become so unsubtle and unstable in those to do with oratory and politics. My father had said that he did not intend to return to everyday politics; that if he did, this might damage the promulgation of his idea. But then – he could find no publisher to print and distribute his books; he decided he would have to publish them himself. And so – it was natural that he should turn for help to some of his old and trusted political followers; and it was natural that they, in spite of (or rather because of) their years in gaol, should wish to work for him. When his plans to publish his own books received publicity he had offers of help from all over the country: 'I have been reading of your new venture in the *Sunday Pictorial*; my own sympathies have always been with National

Socialism'; 'I have always admired you and what you stood for, it has always been an ambition of mine to belong to your Society'. At the same time others of his old followers had started up again on their own; they were holding meetings on street corners in London; headlines appeared in the press – 'Fascists Crawl Out': 'Our Impudent Fascists': 'Anti-Jew Chant Alleged'. Jeffrey Hamm, a member of the pre-war British Union, started a 'British League of Ex-Servicemen' (Jeffrey Hamm had been interned during the war first in the Falkland Islands where he had been a school teacher and then in South Africa); members of the League told the press that they were hoping that Oswald Mosley would come back as their political leader once he had finished his book – 'The Leader is a fast worker, and the book will be finished within the next two months.' There was a story headlined 'Mosley Records at Garden Fete' which told of complaints by local residents in a village in Essex about a recording of a 1934 Albert Hall speech which had boomed out from loudspeakers and had been heard 'over a quarter of a mile away'. When questioned about all this my father would repeat: 'I am not interested in active politics: my only interests are in books and farming.'

When I talked to my father about politics at this time and would try to encourage him to delve deeper into some of the ideas raised by *The Alternative* he would say, with a half frown – But I am a speaker, not a writer. But then, since so many of the things he said he was interested in were complex, could he not learn to be a writer? Speakers had to be so simplistic by the nature of their trade; and had he not recognised that involvement in practical politics would be harmful? But he seemed to see complexity as a matter for wit at the dinner table; it was difficult for him for long to imagine seriousness apart from politics. He wrote to his friend Henry Williamson who had made some criticisms of a proof copy my father had sent him of *The Alternative* – 'The ultimate life of my book will not be determined by any question of style, but by its thought-content. To me, only two things matter in style – clarity and power.' He was in fact to get a good deal of admiration for the style and content of *The Alternative* from members of a younger generation of writers: Desmond Stewart wrote to him – 'Without doubt it is the most important book on the future of Europe since – but it is hard to think of a parallel!'

Before long there were disturbances at the meetings in London of the British League of Ex-Servicemen. Rebecca West reported in the *Evening Standard* that the content of the speeches was 'anti-semitism and economic nationalism': however – 'contrary to popular belief' the speakers devoted 'far more time to their economic doctrine than to their anti-Jewish campaign. Their attacks on the Jews consist usually of vague references to international finance, abstract malignity about Palestine, and the disclosure of such weighty scandals as that Mr Litvinoff was born a Finkelstein and Mr Zinoviev an Apfelbaum'. Rebecca West observed that it was not, also as might have been expected, Jews who were causing the disturbances at the League's meetings but the communists who 'heartlessly exploited the grievances of the Jews against the Fascists in order to create disorder under the Labour government and to capture the Jewish vote in the forthcoming municipal and parliamentary elections'; and it was as if in reply to this that the 'fascists' were joined by the 'curious mob which attaches itself to them at such moments, though they never seem to listen to a speech'. The mob consisted of 'boys and girls between 16 and 20, adolescents who were children during the war and spent every night in the under-ground and now miss the excitement. These, singing and shouting about a Mosley whom none of them has ever seen, marched on a communist meeting and tried to break it up.'

Rebecca West saw that the aim of the 'fascists' in these meetings was to act as bait to lure my father back into politics. But she found it hard to believe (as he said he did) that he would fall for this: it would be 'indeed as if the proposition that Queen Anne is dead were disputed by Queen Anne herself'.

I went down to one of these East End meetings in 1946 or 1947: there was a man on top of a van shouting and waiting for the responses of the crowd: it was like some revivalist prayer-meeting. I remember one small man in a raincoat who put his head down at the edge of the crowd and dashed into the restraining arms of policemen; he bounced back as if from the ropes of a boxing ring; he seemed satisfied. After the meeting a paper-seller was set upon by a crowd and he crouched by a wall with his arms over his head and was kicked and pummelled. It was all, once more, quite like a crowd at a present-day football match.

My father was now publishing a monthly pamphlet called the *Mosley Newsletter* which was largely subscribed to by his old followers. It consisted of articles by him on current topics. Its tone became more overtly political.

One day I was driving my father up from Crowood to London – I had a small car in which I now commuted to and from Hounslow – and my father said that he was going that evening to some re-union of the old BU members in an East End pub and would I like to take

him there, and join them. He said he did not think there would be
many people. So I drove him and Diana to a street-corner rendezvous
– they had arranged to be picked up by a guide – and then suddenly
there were two motor bikes in front of us and we were being escorted
through streets like VIPs. We arrived outside some enormous East End
pub; there were men on the pavement in two lines as if at a wedding,
with their arms raised. My father had been the joking family father
in the back of the car; now he became urgent, with his chin up, striding.
What else could he be? As he entered the pub people clapped and
cheered; there were hundreds of them; as he walked between them
from the door to the bar they touched him, just touched the hem of
his garment, they wanted to get some magic from him. I could see
this because I was walking just behind him. And he was acknowledging
them, slightly lifted, glowing; his hand moving up no higher than his
shoulder, perhaps, in some not quite fascist salute. And then when he
reached the bar and we were being stood pints of beer he was called
on to make a speech of course – but no, he had given up speeches.
But he was called on again – and he was so modest, and wise, and
flashing. I suppose he was some sort of life to these people: they had
many of them been five years in jail; they had given up their lives
for him. So in the end he did make a speech: he did not say much
– just how glad he was to be amongst them again. And they were
all getting a glow from him. This was what he was so good at after
all – making people adore him – even if it might be the ruination
of his ideas. At the end of his short speech there were the hands coming
out again to clap him on the back, to shake his hand, just to come
to rest on him; and it was as if he were King Pentheus of *The Bacchae*
being fêted or about to be torn to pieces.

CHAPTER 30

Where Do We Go From Here?

For the two years after the war I remained close to my father: I would go to him on leave, for holidays, at weekends: I would bring my friends to stay. My sister and brother and their entourage had moved to a cottage near Wantage some fifteen miles away: I alternated between this 'nursery world' as I had called it and my father and Diana's home as I had done when I was a child. I had a girl friend at this time who got on well with my father; she said in later years that life at Crowood had given her a first glimpse, after war-time austerity, of what peace-time elegance might be. When her family saw that there might be some seriousness in her relationship with me her father said to her – 'But I would rather shake hands with Oscar Wilde than with Oswald Mosley!' I told my father this story: I imagined, somewhat naively, that he would laugh, as he laughed about so many of the attitudes struck against him by a crazy world. But he said – 'Does her father think I'm a bugger?' I tried to explain – 'No, Dad, it's not that he thinks you're a bugger'. But my father sometimes did not seem to see the sort of feelings there were against him.

One day there was a burglary at Crowood and six beautiful pistols I had brought back from the war as loot were stolen (my one other item of loot was a concertina): the thief, when caught, tried to ingratiate himself with the authorities by claiming to have discovered an 'arms cache' in Oswald Mosley's house. There were questions asked in Parliament about this: ones of the expected kind from Labour; then a Conservative – 'Can we have an assurance that these revolvers were not issued to Sir Oswald Mosley when he was Chancellor of the Duchy in the Socialist Government?' (cheers and laughter). Although I was still a serving officer I was charged in the civil courts with the illegal possession of firearms; my father was good about this: he hired a lawyer to make a passionate and embarrassing speech in my defence – 'Is this the gratitude society shows to a young man just back from war?' and so on. I was acquitted.

I went out to my staff job each day: I stayed up much of the night, talking and dancing. I chatted with my father about my party-going activities: he seemed anxious lest what seemed to be my lack of a steady physical relationship might be injurious to health. I half agreed with him about this; but then, were there not other and possibly worse dangers in being either a conqueror, or trapped?

From Hounslow I went two or three times a week to a stammer-man who worked under the auspices of the army authorities: he was the best stammer-man I ever went to. He spoke not of elocutionary techniques but of states of mind: stammering was some failure of relationship with oneself. One was too close: if one could stand back from one's words as it were, then words might be freed but watching them one might deal with them. He would say – But perhaps you don't want to get rid of your stammer. I thought – Me not want to get rid of my stammer? But then, when I was with him, I was some-times so tired I fell asleep. It was true there were simply too many impressions coming in: and I did not want to stop these.

My father wrote to me: 'I had probably not realised adequately your feelings on the matter, for the reason that your stammer never bothers me when we are talking and never seems to worry you. In fact psycho-logically it occurred to me that, by the strange law of compensations, it might in part account for your great gift for writing.'

There was a day when my father, Vivien and myself went down to pack up what remained at Savehay Farm; we had not lived there for five years; the civil servants and scientists had moved out; my father wanted to be rid of the place. There were my mother's glass walking sticks on the walls; the locked chest in my father's bedroom where I had imagined he kept her letters. My father told me that I could pick out any books from the shelves I liked; I found there were surprisingly few of these, and most of them had been given to her by her literary friends. There were no Proust, Joyce, Lawrence, Henry James. In the huge barns where my sister and I had climbed as children there were stored the old fascist 'armoured cars' from the 1930s. In the wood by the river there was my mother's marble tomb; it had a tarpaulin over it, as if someone had been trying to snuff it out.

At the house near Wantage my sister and I, with Nanny and Andrée, carried on with our friends playing the games we had played years ago. My brother Micky, aged fourteen, was in some state of rebellion at this time: from Eton he took to making anonymous telephone calls to my father: this was discovered when my father got in touch with the police. I remember admiring my brother's dash and courage. My father wrote a memorandum:

It is difficult for me to be helpful in this matter because I have never succeeded in establishing any real contact with the boy ... my experience with him has been as difficult as my relationship with my eldest son has been ideal ... I have never had occasion to speak to him any word of reproof, or to experience with him any occasion ever approaching the unpleasant.

There were other manifestations of tension amongst the children – some probably arising from the separations enforced by war. When Alexander was young he had a fantasy in which he was called 'Mr Russian' and he would say – 'I have my home there: I have been dragged away.' Now, aged seven or eight, he would argue cogently the case for there being no good reason to stay alive.

I myself became invaded by feelings of futility. In war one had been told what to do and one's identity had been shaped by the style in which one either did or did not do it. Now, in the mornings, there did not indeed seem much reason to get out of bed. This nothingness – was it not a reason why people liked wars? but was not this realisation in turn a cause of nothingness?

My girl friend had a job in the Foreign Office. She worked for an official involved in the setting up of the United Nations. I would visit her in offices in Westminster and would lurk behind filing cabinets containing plans for re-ordering the world. But even concerning this effort people seemed best able to pass the time by threatening to fight one another. My girl friend wrote to me, 'Perhaps you can rescue me from this ghastly void; and perhaps I, at intervals, can rescue you from madness.'

I had earlier tried to get out of the army on the grounds of being needed as a farm worker on my father's estate; this had failed. Then there was a ruling that people would be demobilised early if they had a place assured them at a university. The scholarship exam I had taken at Balliol five years previously made me eligible for this: I got out of the army and was given a grey pin-stripe suit and a brown felt hat. I went up to Oxford in the autumn of 1946.

I did not expect much from Oxford: I had not liked Balliol when I had been there for the few days in 1941; now there were the people

of the usual age-group of eighteen to twenty-one but also the older
people such as myself (I was twenty-three) who had come back from
the war. Balliol was crowded: rooms had to be shared: it was a cold
winter. I remember writing my essays at one end of the room with
a paraffin pressure-stove on the table beside me; at the other end my
room-mate worked in a balaclava helmet and gloves. I was reading
Philosophy, Politics and Economics – specialising in Philosophy. I
would try to keep myself as it were like Odysseus strapped to my
mast, while down the road in coffee-bars were the girls like sirens
combing their hair.

Descartes, in his search for a certainty of which he could be sure
beyond his doubt, had come across the statement 'I think therefore
I am'. From this he attempted to create a whole system of philosophy.
But this statement is indubitably valid only if it is taken to mean
exactly what it says and no more.

Hume denied that the Self had any existence as a substance
possessing endurance and identity. To him the self was no more than
a collection of mental facts, experiences and ideas – we find ourselves
thinking, hoping, desiring, fearing: but we never have an impression,
either immediate or continued, of the Self that thinks, hopes, desires
or fears. In fact there is no impression that is constant and invariable.

These arguments, however, fail to take into account one very important consideration. Hume talks about the 'I' – that is, the Self
that is able to look into itself in order to take note of its impressions.
He says – When I enter most intimately into what I call myself,
I always stumble upon some particular perception. But what is this
'I' that possesses the faculty of entering into itself? It must be something, because Hume treats it as if it were; and moreover it is evident
from experience that we do possess the faculty, in some way or other,
of observing ourselves. And yet this cannot itself be one of the
perceptions that it is endeavouring to perceive. What then is this
primary Self?

The first time I read out an essay to my tutor the person who was
sharing the tutorial with me asked – 'But is this the sort of stuff you
want us to write?'

When I talked to my father about these things he seemed to have
moved away from the interest in speculation that he had shown in
the war: he would now talk about philosophy more in catch-phrases
such as might be used by a politician. He would say – 'Descartes said,

"I think therefore I am"; then along came Bertie Russell and said, "How do you know it's you thinking?"' And then my father would laugh, as if the scoring of such a point had ended the discussion.

I did not quite agree with my father about this: of course philosophy was absurd; but by knowing this, might there not still be good philosophy?

I continued to write my not-good poems in imitation of T. S. Eliot –

> ... And so to tea.
> The cups reflect
> The images of you and me
> Reserved, correct.
> I pass you silence on a plate
> And wonder if my feelings show;
> You mention that it's getting late
> And rise to go ...

And so on. My girl friend went to America to continue with the business of disputing how to bring peace to the world. I thought – This is all very well, but what people are drawn back to are the sounds of cheering; the crowds coming out with their hands up.

It began to seem essential that I should get away and try to write my first novel. My relationship with my father had got as far as it could; now there seemed to be nothing happening, and he seemed set on going back to the battlegrounds of his old wars. If words were ever to mean anything, there had to be some effort by which victories could be held in my head.

There was a morning at Oxford when I knocked off work and went down for elevenses at the Playhouse Bar. Here there was the usual chatter like bullets, like fireflies; but there was one girl, a blonde, who did not seem part of this at all. When I spoke to her she did not appear to register what I was saying – Da da di dum dum, da da di da – we both seemed to be listening for something quite different. Later that day, in a pub, she said, 'Do you play darts?' and she threw a dart so wildly that it went into the next compartment right out of the gravitational orbit as it were of the bar. When I took her to lunch at Crowood with my father it was as if she did not hear him talking either; his words seemed to be contained within some sphere like that of a homunculus.

After some time Rosemary (that was her name) and I became engaged (we did not use the word engaged: we had some agreement, I think,

to go to Hemel Hempstead). I wanted to get out from my past; Rosemary wanted to get out from hers: we planned, after our honeymoon,
to buy a mountain farm in North Wales. Our parents met rather
formally for lunch. Rosemary's mother told a funny story about how
Lady So-and-so had gone to a seance to try to get through to
her dead husband and all she got through to was her chauffeur who
told her her car was at the door. Everybody laughed. Rosemary wrote
to me: 'It seems to me that you and I are like your dream of standing
on the world and everything whirling around in chaos. You do promise
you will always tell me the truth, which is always less hard in the
end.'

I wrote a poem to Rosemary which was the only good poem I
ever wrote:

> You pause upon a sofa where
> A trembling shadow lends your hair
> The urgency of sunlight; there
> A sudden attitude betrays
> The cautious reticence of days
> And fracturing confusion lays
> Its finger on your meaning. Now
> A formal tension turns your brow
> And murmurs to the moment how
> Its policy has been decreed.
> The knowledge formulates the need
> Presenting each intended deed
> In glittering precision dipped
> And silhouetting that and this
> Like silver limbs of statues gripped
> Beneath a sunset's emphasis.

Rosemary and I were married on 14th November 1947.

The next day my father attended a conference of Mosley Book Club
fans at the Memorial Hall in Farringdon Street – the site of the New
Party's inaugural meeting eighteen years before and the site of the early
meeting of the BUF at which my father had referred to 'three warriors
of the class war all from Jerusalem'. Here, just a month after the
publication of *The Alternative* in which he had said it was not his
intention to found a new political party because this would not be
helpful to his ideas, he announced it was his intention to found a new
political party.

Rosemary and I did not, I think, want to get away from our pasts because we felt they had been bad, but because we had learned from them all we could: it is if things have gone to some purpose that children feel free to move on. I had had a dream of being with my father after the war but it had been this that had got me through the war; it had not much to do with what came after. What I had learned from my father was how to be passionate and serious and amused in circumstances that seemed daft: there was still the question of what proper circumstances one might make for oneself. I wanted to be a writer: Rosemary wanted to be a painter: we were lucky enough to be able to try to make of these desires what we could. It seemed to me that novels might be a way of using words by which one could not only set out what one saw of life but by this see the way in which one saw; and through this, because it was to do with not being trapped by life, something might change. What usually happened with words was that people argued in a straight line; and then it was as if after all the curve of space brought them back to the beginning, and nothing changed.

My father stepped back on to some wheel of repetitions: he never lost, within himself, his capacity for seriousness or laughter. He continued to say when I encouraged him to write books – But I'm not a writer, I'm a speaker. A writer sets out words to look at them as if they were the plumes of ridiculous armies: a speaker gets carried away by the crowds with their arms up cheering.

Rosemary and I had obtained two rare seats on an aeroplane going to the West Indies. There was a new type of plane doing this trip, and one had just disappeared in the mysterious area known as the Bermuda Triangle. Here ships and planes became lost and no wreckage was found: there were fantasies about their reappearing in some quite different dimension.

I had become confronted by a present nothingness: I had learned from my past that it was possible to move on. One thing we could always agree on, my father and I, was that there were the virtues of a possible freedom in being beyond the pale.

Epilogue

Oswald Mosley officially launched his post-war political party, which he called Union Movement, in February 1948. It was composed largely of pre-war members of British Union. In policy, it expanded the area of patriotism from Great Britain to Europe-with-Africa.

In 1951 my father gave up his farm at Crowood and went to live in Ireland and at Orsay on the outskirts of Paris. In answer to questions about how he thought he could lead a British political party from abroad he replied that he was now dedicated to achieving a united Europe. He made political contacts with right-wing forces in Germany, Italy, Spain and South Africa: he made only social contacts in France because, he said, he did not want to abuse the hospitality of the country in which he lived. He was the British representative at a congress of extremist right-wing groups in Venice in 1962; he made speeches (in German) to enthusiastic admirers in Germany where the translation of *The Alternative* had been a success; but nothing much came of his efforts at European organisation.

In South Africa he formed a relationship with Oswald Pirow, a pro-Nazi Afrikaner ex-cabinet minister. They produced a plan by which Africa would be clearly divided between whites and blacks – whites would take South Africa and the 'high central plateau'; blacks would have autonomy in the rest. This, it was claimed, would be a more reasonable form of apartheid than the present system in which blacks were kept in white areas as second class citizens. My father argued in his usual style that it would be possible to uproot millions of people and to transport them to new areas without there being too much fuss once the advantages of the scheme had been rationally and clearly explained.

From 1953 to 1959 he and Diana edited and published a monthly

magazine called *The European* which contained literary articles as well
as my father's political commentary and Diana's *Diary*. I myself sometimes contributed: I was warned by literary friends – did I not realise
that if one wrote anti-fascist articles for a fascist magazine this made
one a fascist? My father produced his best non-political essays for *The
European*. There was one in particular called *Wagner and Shaw: A
Synthesis* in which he argued against Shaw's interpretation in *The Perfect
Wagnerite* of Wagner's *The Ring*. Shaw had claimed that *Götterdämmerung* was a superfluous addition to an otherwise admirable mytho-
logical construction: the fall of Siegfried as a victim to the temptations
of ordinary human passion was senseless after all the hopes of super-
human achievement offered by the earlier operas. My father suggested
that in this respect Wagner had seen further than Shaw: it was inevitable
that Siegfried who sought 'adventures' as a conqueror rather than
'supreme creation' as someone dedicated to the task in hand should
fall a victim to humdrum passion; what was required before there could
be super-human achievement was the emergence of the being 'who
weeps because he has killed a swan rather than exults because he can
kill a dragon; who holds the all-powerful spear on condition that he
does not use it'. And my father claimed that Wagner had in fact outlined
such a being in *Parsifal*. Parsifal was not only Wagner's vision of
a Christian knight who was superior to Siegfried; he was also a prototype
of Nietzsche's third metamorphosis of the Child – though neither Shaw
nor indeed Nietzsche saw this.

In 1958 my father published a book *Europe: Faith and Plan* in which
there are elaborated many of the ideals, and reiterated many of the
begged questions, that had characterised most of his political life. The
ideals were – a united Europe running a large part of Africa and
governed by a democratically elected parliament and executive; this
Euro-African power-block would be independent of, and indeed
stronger than, the blocks of America on one side and Russia, to whom
control of Asia would be left, on the other. The begged questions were
– the assumption that all this could be done if Europeans just had 'will'
to 'greatness'; that it would even be possible to come to reasonable
agreements with leaders of the other power-blocks because they, having
got to such positions of power, must be rational men themselves –
and would not want to destroy the world by conflict. This left out
of account what my father had learned so painfully of the irrationality
and even will-to-destruction of someone like Hitler and indeed of other
politicians; it ignored what he himself had experienced of the absurdities
of political leadership during the one year when he had had govern-

mental power. He still had the conviction, against all the evidence, that human beings liked things to be neat and orderly.

During the early years of Union Movement my father held meetings at Ridley Road in North London and at Kensington Town Hall: later he spent much of the time in his houses in France and in Ireland promulgating his ideas in *The European*. Life at Clonfert, in County Galway, was something like pre-war Wootton; there was fishing and rough shooting; the house was a fine old Protestant bishop's palace at the end of a long avenue of yew trees. Then in 1955 my father was writing to me – 'I have a feeling that before long the rush may begin again, though I am as usual premature. But when it does, all charm of life flies, as well as all sense, for a long season!'

What brought him back to London to local day-to-day politics was, as it had been twenty years earlier, a particular issue – that to do with 'alien' immigration. In 1936 the issue had been that concerning Jews in the East End: in 1956 it was the coloured immigration into the area of Kensington north of Notting Hill. At this time there was no restriction on immigration from the Commonwealth: there was unemployment in the West Indies owing to the pact which the English Labour Government had made to buy sugar from Cuba; workers came from the West Indies to Britain where there was still the promise of jobs. In North Kensington after a time there began to be street fights between blacks and gangs of white youths who were at that time known as Teddy Boys: these fights came to a head in the summer of 1958 when there were what the press referred to as race riots in Notting Hill. Union Movement announced it would launch its largest campaign in the area; it professed to aim at trying to bring order to a troubled situation. Its stated policy was reasonable; a pamphlet was distributed which proclaimed, 'Most coloured immigrants are decent folk: they are victims of a vicious system which they do not understand.' My father wrote articles advocating forcible repatriation for recent immigrants but 'with fares paid ... and to good jobs with good wages'. What was required was capital investment in the West Indies: 'I say – Let the Jamaicans have their country back, and let us have ours.'

This was the policy: but – as had happened so many years ago – some quite different picture became lodged in people's minds. For the most part the Union Movement's weekly newspaper (at first called *Union* and then as in the old days *Action*) maintained a disciplined tone with little of the racialist jargon that had bedevilled the old *Action*: occasional lapses were noted: Diana wrote a memo to my father pointing out, a bad example of *Action*'s fussy, indignant style, 'so repugnant to intelligent people who might otherwise heed our economic argument: "Fuzzie Wuzzies" "Hottentots" ... do not play into the hands of those who imagine our policy is based on hatred of the blacks'. But more important than any of this were the questions people asked about what was Union Movement doing in the area anyway: why had they chosen this area rather than any other to concentrate their attention on? what did they think would be the effect of a statement such as 'blacks should be sent home' on a volatile population? In September 1958 the Trades Unions' Council put out a statement that Union Movement was 'fanning the flames of racial violence' in Notting Hill. Union Movement replied with reiterations of its policy which it said was aimed at being helpful to blacks; it also claimed that it was serving the community by providing a means of keeping so-called Teddy Boys under control. In September 1958 *The Times* sent a reporter to the area to try to find out what was in fact happening:

The Movement is exploiting rather than creating the disturbances. It will not condemn the violence, but is rather pointing to a target behind the one that is now being attacked. At least a part of those responsible for the clashes hold a certain sympathy for the Movement. 'We both want the same thing; we're just going about it in different ways,' one demonstrator commented.

A clear distinction must be drawn between official Union Movement policy which has been formulated by Sir Oswald Mosley and the reasons most members have had for joining. Those immediately below the Leader look to him for political guidance and seem to have a genuine desire to see his policies instituted ...

All this is incomprehensible to the majority of his followers, who understand the clichés in which the ideas are expressed rather than the ideas themselves. They have joined the movement for a variety of reasons; some, because they are anti-semitic, but the largest number, it seems, because they like fighting Communists and painting slogans on railway bridges. They fight because they have an instinctive desire to do so.

It is admitted by the leaders that these elements are out of the control of the party, and probably would not have joined if it was not for the sinister evocation of the word 'movement', the dramatic salute, the hero-worship implied in the word 'leader' and the fanatical hatred of the word 'Communism'. This element would riot whatever organisation they belonged to, or if they belonged to none at all.

The problem for someone close to my father was – how was it that he did not see (or did he?) the dangers inherent in becoming involved politically in such an area and in such a predicament no matter what the virtues of his policy and his stated insistence on discipline? Did he not remember the thirties? I myself had been too young to be an outspoken witness of events then: but over the years (as I had listened to my father's so rational explanations) I had wondered about what seemed to be the two sides to his character – the reasonable, and that which nevertheless seemed to go headlong looking for trouble: how much had his left hand known what his right hand was doing?

There was an incident from the early days of Union Movement just after the war that stuck in my memory. My father had summoned to him one of his lieutenants who had disobeyed orders that members should not become involved in the breaking-up of opponents' meetings: my father reprimanded the man in a room next door to where Rosemary and Diana and I were having dinner. My father shouted at him for a time; the man was saying, 'Yes sir, sorry sir'; then my father said quietly, 'Well don't do it again'. And as he showed the man out into the passage some sort of wink seemed to pass between the man and my father – some touch on the arm perhaps – a recognition of comradeship or complicity beyond the demands of discipline. And it was as if we all knew that the man of course would do whatever he had done again; my father knew this; the man knew that my father knew this – it was as if the reprimand was just some ritual by which my father might effectively not quite let his left hand know what his right hand was doing. And it must have been something like this, I supposed, that had happened in the thirties – both with my father, and with other national socialist leaders.

When I talked to my father about such incidents he would say – with his half-self-mocking half-smile-half-frown – 'It's a rough game' – or – 'One must keep the boys happy'.

During the fifties I had become involved in increasingly passionate arguments with my father about the kind of style that I now felt was characteristic of his politics. Rosemary and I in the early years of our marriage had spent summer holidays with him and Diana: we had come down from our Welsh mountain and had dallied happily in old haunts in the south of France: he and Diana moved from time to time into the powerful vacuum of social life in Antibes and Monte Carlo and Rosemary and I had not been much part of this; but when we were on our own with him and Diana there was, as there could always be, the gentleness, the funniness, his way of making quite ordinary things seem luminous. But as time went on I became involved in my own struggles to deal with or get beyond, areas and threats of double-think and nothingness. I had long since become convinced of the justness of the second world war; I had become something of a Christian, and an anti-racialist; I was a friend of Father Raynes and Father Huddleston who had been deeply involved in political and missionary work on behalf of blacks in South Africa. My father more and more professed himself scathingly anti-christian. As he entered into the politics of Notting Hill so I tried to take him on in argument head on, in a way I had not felt able or inclined to do before; I wrote him letters; discussions became less of a game and more belligerent at the end of dinner. The argument which I came to see with increasing passion as an area for battle was on the grounds not only that I thought his apartheid racialism ethically wrong (it seemed to me that simplification by separation was to do with death: evolution of life depended on the acceptance of ever greater connections and complexities) but that I thought his present attitudes and activities were evidence of his, and perhaps all fascists', tendencies to self-destruction. Whatever good ideas he had had in the 1930s had been destroyed by his laying himself open to charges of anti-semitism; now, any reasonable ideas of his were being treated with contempt because of his deliberately exposing himself to the charge of anti-black racialism; and if he had not learned how such exposure could defeat even the best ideas, what on earth had he learned? Of course he had the answers to this: there were real problems about the unlimited immigration from the Commonwealth; local people had asked him to come to Notting Hill as their champion; there was a chance at least in theory that he might be able to harness and discipline the gangs of white toughs. I would say – But did he not see that the point at issue was not so much what he himself said or did, but what people made of what he said and did, and especially his opponents? He would say – But were not all movements advocating new ideas at first unpopular? And should he yield to misrepresentation by the press?

It was difficult to make headway in arguments with my father because as always there was the deployment of words as if they were inexhaustible armies. I tried, as other people had done, to go into the attack. In October 1958 I wrote to him:

Your policy regarding black men is to provide jobs for them in their own homelands by providing capital for backward areas. This is admirable. Your intention in general is to have a movement which is 'manly, disciplined, restrained and self-controlled, which never begins trouble and never exults in it: just is prepared to meet it if others absolutely insist'. Again, this is unexceptionable. But what in practice happens is that your movement holds a meeting in Notting Hill, which is followed by violence.

To say that the speakers never wanted nor intended violence is meaningless. To believe this would be an opinion of such astonishing political naivety that it were surely better to be hushed up – it must still be better for a politician to be thought something of a villain rather than an idiot. If anyone does believe this then you've handed the game to your opponents without a struggle: for the explanation can only be pathological. It must always be remembered that this is what the struggle is – not one of policy versus policy, because no one is fighting you on this level; but one of your opponents accusing you of madness through the evidence of your actions and you, presumably, concerned with producing evidence that they are wrong. If you hand this game to your opponents so easily, you cannot blame them for not bothering to take you on in the further battle about policy ...

I've written at length because I care about it all perhaps more than you think ... I cannot bear to see the whole structure of thought and prophecy seeming to be led towards the ditch by exactly the same blind forces that ruined and destroyed it before the war. I sometimes complain that history repeats itself; yet I am bewildered that it can do so in this immediate and despairing way.

To sum up – Fascism, and therefore Union Movement, has got the general reputation, whether fairly or unfairly, of having to depend upon racial hatred in order to maintain its appeal and impetus. It was this reputation that made fascism so hated years ago.

Now you and your followers say that this reputation is unfair: but it is still in people's minds. Your obvious intention therefore, since it is so harming your cause, would be to take steps to eradicate it.

One would have thought these steps would have included instructions to avoid, in speech and writing and action, all controversial racial issues like the plague: there would be orders, surely, to hold meetings anywhere in London rather than Notting Hill: to keep all sneering references to colour out of *Action*: and when any unfortunate incidents did occur through the stupidity or indiscipline of subordinates, then immediately to take disciplinary steps against the subordinate and to publicise these steps fully, and with apologies to those concerned, in the national press.

Failure to take this sort of action seems only to mean that in spite of your words on paper, your intention is not seriously to eradicate from people's minds the impression of your need for racial hatred.

Your reasons for not wanting to do this are beyond my competence to guess. But the results of it are that your words seem destined only to bluff yourselves, and not to influence responsible people who will go only by your actions.

To this my father replied briefly that in fact no Union Movement meeting in Notting Hill had resulted in violence; and he challenged anyone to produce concrete evidence that it had.

In 1959 he stood as the Union Movement candidate for North Kensington in the general election. I went up to hear him speak: I stood on the edge of the crowd without his knowing I was there. There was Dad on top of a van again and bellowing; so much older now with his grey hair and grey suit; it was true that the crowd around him was large and quiet and respectful. I had expected that he at least would be putting over the aspect of his case that was reasonable; but instead – I still find it difficult to believe this but other witnesses have confirmed it – there he was roaring on about such things as black men being able to live on tins of cat food, and teenage girls being kept by gangs of blacks in attics. And there were all the clean-faced young men round his van guarding him; and somewhere, I suppose, the fingers of the devotees of the dark god tearing at him.

Shortly before the election I said that I must see him and talk to him; he said he was too busy to see me; I said I would come to his office and sit outside it and wait. At this time in addition to my feelings about his politics I was involved in a passionate struggle with him about the welfare of my half-brother Alexander. At the time of the race riots the year before, Alexander and Max, aged nineteen and eighteen, had been photographed in Notting Hill: they had said they were there to help Union Movement. Since this time Alexander had tried to get out: he was a brilliant boy; my father was refusing to let him go to a university. He had become (so Diana informed me) somewhat ill. In the waiting room outside my father's office I suddenly realised that I was frightened in a way that I had not been since the battle of Casa Spinello. When I finally got into my father's tiny office he and Diana and his lawyer were in a row behind a desk; I stood as if to attention like some private soldier; then I spewed it all out, in some frail rage, both the politics and the personal stuff – my father was not only a racialist but was using racialism to destroy himself;

what he was doing was not only wrong it was squalid; he had done this before, he was doing it again, was he so crazy as not to know what he was doing? And he was a lousy father – I might as well tell him everything now – he had never cared a damn about any of his children, he got rid of responsibility for them as soon as he could; when they tried to go their own way, when anything went against him, he was just contemptuous of them. I carried on like this for some time; then I stopped. I had thought perhaps some great thunderbolt would come down on me. But instead he said very quietly – 'I will never speak to you again!' He turned to Diana as if haunted. I had not expected this. I said something like – Well, I'll always speak to you. Then I left.

A day or two later I wrote to him saying that I took back just the thing about his having been a lousy father to me because I did not think he had been. He did not answer this letter. When I talked about this to my brother Alexander he said – 'Well, he wouldn't, would he?' Alexander did get away – eventually to a university in America.

In the election of 1959 at North Kensington my father got 2,821 votes out of a total of 34,912: he came bottom of the poll, and lost his deposit. This had never happened to him before. He had been confident almost of winning. His canvassers had taken unofficial polls just before and just after the voting and they had told him they had been assured of such support as to justify this confidence. When the result was known they would not believe it: they said that the ballot boxes must have been tampered with. My father went so far as to bring a court action about some irregularities that had been observed in the procedures; he planned to call witnesses to give evidence about how they had told his canvassers that they had voted for Mosley and now it seemed that they had not: how could this be explained? But when it came to the matter of appearance in court witnesses could not be found, or said they had changed their minds, or had forgotten. Nothing came of the case. What seemed to have happened was what had happened so often before to my father – he had charmed people with words; he had charmed himself into confidence by his ability to charm others with words; then when it came to a vote, to assurances being made effective, people behaved quite differently.

After 1959 there were renewed outbreaks of organised communist hostility against him: meetings were broken up; for a time he held meetings in Trafalgar Square, but then these were banned. In 1962 he was knocked down on his way to address a meeting in Ridley Road and was rescued from possible serious injury by the brave intervention of my half-brother Max. Max was acting as one of his right-hand men at this time. When I saw photographs of my father on the ground with demonstrators putting the boot in I had atavistic feelings – should not I, his eldest son, have been there to defend him? But then – what on earth were the people around him doing wheeling him out like an old Aunt Sally?

Max assisted my father loyally for a time; then moved on, with great success, into the motor-racing business.

The last time my father stood for parliament was for Shoreditch in 1966; he polled 1,600 or 4.6% of the votes. After this he gave up the leadership of Union Movement, and retired from active politics.

During this time I had been fighting the battles to do with myself: the problems were, as always – what happens when you realise that orderliness cannot be imposed by will? how do you get out of nothing-ness without finding yourself in a commitment which part of you knows is not to do with truth? The novels I had written soon after the war had been to do with doom and damnation: this had been a way of expressing perhaps something I had felt about the war: but in fact what I had also learned was that there was something in war's absurdity that was not a lie – though this, I had realised, could perhaps not quite be put into words. So what was I doing writing novels? Into this impasse there had emanated the hollowed-out, piercing figure of Father Raynes CR – a monk. Through the door that opened to Christianity there seemed to be a hope of impossibilities being made possible. But hope still seemed to lead if not to damnation still through doom – you did what you had to do, but the world crucified you: it was through this there was redemption. I gave up writing novels for a time; there seemed to be more obvious immolation in good works. But then if one read the Bible, as one was told to do, did it not in fact say some-thing quite different from what people seemed to think it said? Had I not found this so many years ago? People thought it was talking about salvation-through-sacrifice but in fact it suggested that this sort of thing had been done; and now there was in operation some chance to trust life that indeed could not quite simply be put into words but which was to do with the Holy Ghost. And so – might it not be about this that one could write novels?

After a few years my two older sons, aged twelve and thirteen, said to me – Why do you never take us to see our grandfather? Is it that you are afraid he might influence us? I thought about this: I said – Perhaps it is. So it had to be arranged that Rosemary and I should take our two older sons to stay with my father and Diana in their house at Orsay. There had already been one or two moves towards reconciliation: there had also been jokes relayed to me from my father that indeed, yes, it would be some fitting recompense to him in our dispute if he could now influence my older sons away from the shadowy world of Christians. And so we went over and sat in my father's and Diana's elegant dining room with its Empire furniture and marvellous food and I was at one end of the table and my two sons were on either side of my father at the other and he poured out his lava-flow of words – was not the present political predicament like that of people in an aeroplane who suddenly find themselves without a pilot; they are about to crash; is it not the first essential to give authority to a competent pilot and then later the debates concerning methods of selection and safeguards can continue. My sons listened to him gravely. I thought – Is not twelve or thirteen the sort of age at which it is proper to be fascists? to believe that life should be rational? Then – Ah yes, but I trust, do I not, that enough caring has been built up for them to know that these words go round and round like tigers trapped in cages.

For the last thirteen years of his life my father became more as he had been in prison; in his seventies and eighties he liked to talk about ideas; he went for walks and ruminated on his own; he entertained his and Diana's old friends; he liked things to be funny. Occasionally he would roar off on one of his runaway slides with words – about the folly of war, the ruination of Europe, the hypocrisies of democratic politicians. He never ceased to be amazed that the communist world had fallen out within itself – Russia and China, for instance, had become enemies when just by being rational what power together they might have wielded! He did come more to accept the horror of things that had been done under the Nazis: when Hitler's name was mentioned his eyes would cloud over and he would sometimes murmur – Terrible little man! In certain moods he seemed to be waiting for the crisis in Britain and in Europe to materialise which he had for so long expected and which, he still believed, might cause people to turn to him as the one man who had foreseen it and which might be a means at least of his at last being called to power; but then with part of him he seemed to accept that this was a fantasy. For the most part when one was staying with my father during these years there was an air of celebration: the celebration was just for having come through.

The house outside Paris where he and Diana lived was called, of all things, Le Temple de la Gloire – it had been built for one of Napoleon's generals to celebrate his victory at Hohenlinden in 1800. There was a central block of just a dining room on the ground floor and a drawing room on the first floor and, on either side of these, two small wings containing my father's bedroom and sitting room and bathroom and Diana's bedroom and sitting room and bathroom; underneath these were the kitchen and servants' rooms, and two guest rooms and a bathroom. There was a portico like that of a Roman temple at the front; a lawn led down from this to a lake on which there floated one or two swans. There was a suburban road to one side of the lake and the municipal sports stadium on the other. The whole scene was like one of those microcosms of a grand world you look at through a peep-hole in a box: it was immensely elegant, yet almost on the edge of a parody. My father liked to see it like this; he called it 'our funny little house'. It seemed a perfect setting for him and Diana; they grew old there happily; they gave happiness to people around them.

The last time I saw my father was in November 1980, ten days before he died. I had gone over with my second wife to spend a weekend with him and Diana; now more than ever he seemed anxious to talk. He would be up in the mornings long before his usual time, and when I appeared in the drawing room he would say – Have some pink champagne! I would say – Now Dad? and then – Yes! It was quite like, after all, the times I had visited him in Holloway. Then we would talk for most of the day – of the past, of life before the war, of my mother, of her sisters. He wanted, I think, to make something clear about the past: he told me – as he had used to tell me so many years ago – how good his first marriage had been; how now of course his second marriage was very good, but what he wanted now, with and for everyone, was reconciliation. He said – Throughout the thirties, you know, it was as if I had two wives: do you think that was immoral? I said – Ah, Dad, immoral! He was this very old man who had Parkinson's disease; he took pills to make himself stop shaking. Sometimes when standing he would lose his balance and topple over like an enormous tree; from the floor he would explain, laughingly – 'It's these pills, you know; it's a wonder what can be done by modern science!' I told him that I wanted to write something about his life; that I wanted to try to write the truth; that no one of course ever quite caught the truth, but if one made efforts then these could stand for it. I said that I thought however peculiar his life had been – or just because of this – the story of it would be best served by truth; there had had to be prevarications in the past perhaps, but his life had been passionate enough and a struggle enough and concerned with real things enough for it to be proper that there should now be efforts at truth: and anyway, what other forms of reconciliation were there? And he watched me with the small rather distant eyes that I suppose had never trusted anyone very much – he had felt he had such reason to trust himself! – and there had always been people round him, as indeed there were now, to encourage him in this; who were not much interested in ways of reconciliation. And then my father said in a loud voice – my stepmother Diana was getting rather deaf – that he wanted me to have all his papers.

Notes on Sources and Acknowledgements

Material for this book was for the most part provided by my father's papers which, after his death, were put at my disposal by my stepmother, Diana Mosley. She has asked that it should be made clear that she is not associated in any way with these memoirs, and that she strongly disapproves of many of my interpretations and of the publication of private letters.

Of published works I owe most to my father's autobiography *MY LIFE* (Nelson, 1968) and my stepmother's autobiography *A LIFE OF CONTRASTS* (Hamish Hamilton, 1977) from both of which I quote. My other chief debt is to Robert Skidelsky's admirable biography, *OSWALD MOSLEY* (Macmillan, 1975). I have quoted also from *THE FASCISTS IN BRITAIN* by Colin Cross (Barrie & Rockliff, 1961), from the *POR-TRAIT OF A LEADER* by A. K. Chesterton (Action Press, 1936) and from *THE COLLECTED WORKS OF C. G. JUNG* (Routledge & Kegan Paul, 1978). Other helpful books about fascism in Britain in the thirties have been *POLITICAL VIOLENCE AND PUBLIC ORDER* by Robert Benewick (Allen Lane, 1969) and *ANTI-SEMITISM AND THE BRITISH UNION OF FASCISTS* by W. F. Mandle (Longmans, 1968).

Other works by Oswald Mosley that I have quoted from in addition to *MY LIFE*, are *THE GREATER BRITAIN* (BUF Publications, 1932); *TOMORROW WE LIVE* (Greater Britain Publications, 1938); *MY ANSWER* (Mosley Publications, 1946); *THE ALTERNATIVE* (Mosley Publications, 1947); and *EUROPE: FAITH AND PLAN* (Euphorion Books, 1958).

I have quoted from Albert Speer's *INSIDE THE THIRD REICH* (Weidenfeld & Nicolson, 1970). I have quoted extensively from the unpublished diaries of my aunt, Irene Ravensdale, which are in my possession.

My thanks are due to Mr David Irving for most generously allowing me to see the documents relating to the Mussolini payments and for allowing me to quote from them and to reproduce one in this book. I am grateful to Mr Dennis Mack Smith for his advice about the chapter on Mussolini.

My thanks are due to the Rt. Hon. Sir Frederick Lawton for giving me valuable help with Chapter 14 regarding Air Time Ltd.

My thanks are due to Mr Richard Bellamy, who most generously made available to me his unpublished typescript of his years with the BUF.

My thanks are due to Sir Mervyn Davies for checking the wartime chapters.

Index